Family Relationships in Shakespeare and the Restoration Comedy of Manners

FAMILY RELATIONSHIPS IN SHAKESPEARE AND THE RESTORATION COMEDY OF MANNERS

Sarup Singh

DELHI

OXFORD UNIVERSITY PRESS

BOMBAY CALCUTTA MADRAS

1983

Oxford University Press, Walton Street, Oxford OX2 6DP

LONDON GLASGOW NEW YORK TORONTO
DELHI BOMBAY CALCUTTA MADRAS KARACHI
KUALA LUMPUR SINGAPORE HONG KONG TOKYO
NAIROBI DAR ES SALAAM CAPE TOWN
MELBOURNE AUCKLAND
and associates in
BEIRUT BERLIN IBADAN MEXICO CITY NICOSIA

© Oxford University Press 1983

Filmset by Model Press Pvt. Ltd., New Delhi 110055
Printed by Rajbandhu Industrial Co., New Delhi 110064
and published by R. Dayal, Oxford University Press
2/11 Ansari Road, Daryaganj, New Delhi 110002

For my granddaughter
YAMINI DEEPIKA
and my grandson
AJAY

Preface

A new book on Shakespeare is a hazardous undertaking. So also perhaps is one on Restoration comedy. Bringing Shakespeare and Restoration comedy together within the scope of a single book may seem arbitrary and to some purists, to use the seventeenth century jargon, even 'barbarous'. Somehow nothing seems to dispel the feeling that Shakespeare and the Restoration comedy of manners have nothing in common. The only concession that John Wain is willing to make is that it is only when they write the dialogues for their 'grotesques' that the Restoration comic playwrights are Shakespeare's 'heirs'. Anne Barton adds insult to injury when she declares that in the marriages that we see at the end of the comedies, the Restoration comic hero and heroine 'confront this solution with a dubiety which, in Elizabethan comedy, had been reserved only for clowns and fools'.

Perhaps the time has come when we should start focussing on the continuities rather than the discontinuities between Shakespeare and his late seventeenth century successors. Dryden may have been exaggerating, but surely he must have had something more than a mere compliment in mind when he declared in his commendatory verses prefixed to Congreve's *The Double-Dealer* (1694):

> Heaven, that but once was prodigal before,
> To *Shakespeare* gave as much: she cou'd not give him more.

The mere fact that while eulogizing the greatest comic playwright of the period he should have thought of Shakespeare seems to suggest that he saw Congreve as a genuine inheritor of Shakespeare's tradition.

In one area — his handling of the man–woman relationship— Congreve clearly seems to follow in Shakespeare's footsteps. Society has, of course, considerably changed between 1600 and 1700 and so have people's attitudes, particularly their attitude to marriage. But there is enough evidence in Congreve and in other Restoration playwrights to show that the questions raised by Shakespearean comedy and the answers provided by it are still valid. Indeed, they have become much more valid now precisely because the Restoration permissive society challenges their validity. We may take the case of Rosalind and Millamant. Millamant appears on the scene about a hundred years later than Rosalind and it is quite instructive to see how she uses the same feminine technique as her predecessor. Rosalind had said to Orlando: 'Come, woo me, woo me: for now I am in a holiday humour, and like enough to consent' (*As You Like It*, IV.i.61-62). Millamant makes a similar offer to Mirabel in *The Way of the World*: 'Well, Mirabel, if ever you will win me woo me now. Nay, if you are so tedious, fare you well' (II.ii). There is no 'holiday humour' in Millamant's offer. She clearly lacks Rosalind's spontaneity, sense of youthful abandon and confident vitality. Her tone is tentative and even anxious and she immediately shies away from an offer which she had made in a state of excessive exuberance but which she now suddenly recognizes as a violation of 'decorum'. Millamant's anxiety can be removed only if she can be assured of the same kind of stable and satisfying relationship with Mirabel that Rosalind had established with Orlando. Irrespective of who takes the initiative in which play, whether man or woman, it is clear that *The Way of the World* is moving in the direction of *As You Like It* in its search for values stabler than those that the Restoration age provides.

It is the realization of these basic continuities in the handling of the human relationships by Shakespeare and the Restoration comic playwrights that has prompted the present study. It was felt that perhaps these continuities could be brought out more sharply if they were studied in the context of family relationships. Shakespeare's characters — whether parents and children or husbands and wives — operate within the limitations imposed on them by the moral and social code of a patriarchal family. Shakespeare shows both the benefits of a cohesive family system and its cruelties. Without being too dogmatic — indeed without seeming to take sides — he is able to show how individuals with tact, intelligence and patience can achieve genuine companionship in an environment in which such relationships were rare. In almost all his plays, including the tragedies, the family bonds remain intact even when individuals transcend them, whether successfully or otherwise. Shakespeare does not launch a frontal attack on the repressive social system but he does permit his characters to undermine this system and show us glimpses of an ideal world. Often this ideal world becomes his main theme and this world, by implication, exposes the deficiencies and the tyranny of that which exists in the England of his times.

The cultural context in the Restoration period has its own compulsions. To expose the real by presenting the ideal will not serve the purpose of the Restoration comic playwrights. The real has now become too oppressive and the moral sanctions of a patriarchal family have lost their sustaining power. So the playwrights have no option but to expose the immediate social reality and in the process often launch a frontal attack on some of its uglier features. Their common theme is the total indifference of parents to the needs of their children, on whom they try to impose mercenary marriages. This leads to protest and revolt on the part of children. This revolt, it is true, sometimes assumes extreme forms which a conventional moralist would find highly immoral, but it is only fair to say that behind this revolt — whether of children against their parents or of wives against their husbands — there is an urge for a more civilized and humane social order. It could also be claimed that but for this revolt the companionate family may not have easily emerged in England. The conflicts and tensions in Restoration comedy, then, should be seen as performing a positive function in so far as they made society conscious of the need to change its attitude to children and to women.

I would also like to mention here, something which will be obvious to any one who reads this book even cursorily. With the dramaturgy of the playwrights discussed, with the finer points of their art and craft — the subject of several excellent recent studies — I am not directly concerned. My subject is the 'life' that the playwrights treat of — certain basic human relationships as determined or influenced by the problems of larger social relations. I see the situations in these plays more or less as I would see similar situations in life. Whether it is a legitimate critical approach or not, I find it very rewarding.

I naturally owe a great debt to a large number of scholars in the field. I have tried to acknowledge it wherever possible in the body of the text. But one person to whom my debt is greatest — who in a sense is the 'onlie begetter' of this study — is Mythili Kaul, my colleague in the Department of English in the University of Delhi. She read the whole manuscript carefully and removed many errors of fact and language. The judgments and the prejudices are, of course, mine. Her husband, Professor A.N. Kaul, read Chapter V and made many valuable suggestions. So did Professor Yudhishtar, specially in the initial stages, which are often the most difficult. Dr Amrik Singh, my old friend and colleague, read the complete manuscript and I greatly benefited from his advice. Professor Carol Thomas Neely of the University of Southern Illinois sent me to some very perceptive articles on Shakespeare published in recent years. I am most grateful to her for the help. My daughter Kalpana Deepak, two of my old students, Dr Vashisht Malhotra of the University of Southern California, Los Angeles, and Dr Shivaji Sengupta of New York, have sent me material from the United States which would otherwise have been inaccessible for me. Dr Malhotra, particularly, has overwhelmed me by his kindness, for which hardly any thanks are adequate.

I should also like to express my sense of appreciation to the library staff of the University of Delhi, the British Council Library, New Delhi, and the Parliament Library, New Delhi. Mr H.C. Jain of the South Campus Library of the University of Delhi and Miss Geeta Balasubramaniam of the Reference Section of the British Council Library have been specially helpful. They have often gone out of their way to procure books and other material for me and I am most grateful to them.

Sarup Singh
New Delhi, 1983

Note — wherever page references are given after quotations from Restoration plays, the text referred to is the first edition.

Contents

CHAPTER I
THE CHANGING PATTERN OF THE FAMILY

I

Any discussion of family relationships in Shakespeare and Restoration comedy must take into account the generally accepted view that family and religion were the two governing principles of the inner life of most people in England in the sixteenth and seventeenth centuries. In Puritan thinking, the family took precedence over religion as it was 'the very *First Society* that by the Direction and Providence of God, is produced among the Children of Men.'[1] It is from this 'First Society' that all other social organizations have grown. The Puritans believed that God laid 'the foundation both of State and Church, in a family, making that the Mother Hive, out of which both these swarms of State and Church, issued forth.'[2] These 'swarms of State and Church', it may be noted, were not needed in the Garden of Eden where the first family of Adam and Eve lived innocently and happily without the need of any social or political organization. This first family, however, was patriarchal in character and, as Milton said, Adam was 'for God only' whereas Eve was 'for God in him'. (*Paradise Lost*, IV. 299). Eve herself thus defined her relationship with Adam:

> O thou for whom
> And from whom I was formed flesh of thy flesh,
> And without whom am to no end, my guide
> And head. (Ibid., IV.440-443)

We hardly need to say that Milton's definition of the relationship between husband and wife was wholly acceptable to sixteenth and seventeenth century Englishmen and women. In the sixteenth century, however, the need for the reinforcement of the patriarchal principle was specially urgent as loyalty had to be forged for the new nation state now emerging. England had just

1

come out of 'troublesome' times and it was widely felt that the Tudor dynasty offered a real chance to the nation to settle down. It was, therefore, vital to create a general climate in which the King could be respected and obeyed. The surest way to create such a climate was to inculcate respect for authority and a sense of obedience to one's superiors in the family itself. It is not surprising that the flood of official propaganda deliberately fostered an increase in the power of the husband and the father within the family, and thus strengthened patriarchy. Wilhelm Reich has rightly pointed out that 'in the figure of the father, the authoritarian state has its representative in every family so that the family becomes the most important instrument of power.'³

It is notable that almost all political and religious writers in the period used the father of the patriarchal family for their argument in favour of absolute royal authority. Such thinking was a natural consequence of the view that 'all kings ruled as sucessors to the power God had given Adam at the Creation' and hence 'Disobedience to one's ruler was contrary to God's law.'⁴ The church's position clearly was that the fifth commandment ('Honour thy father and thy mother') placed upon the individual the obligation to obey all persons in authority whether they were parents or magistrates or masters or priests. John Poynet's interpretation of this commandment in *A Short Catechism* (1553) is perhaps the most memorable. In addition to obliging men to 'love, feare, and reverence' their natural parents, the fifth commandment, he said, 'byndeth us also most humbly, and with most natural affection to obei the magistrate, to reverence the Minysters of the Church, oure Scholemasters, with all oure elders, and betters.'⁵ An anonymous catechism entitled *Short Questions and Answers* (1614) defined the father and mother of the fifth commandment as 'Our naturall Parentes, the fathers of our Countrie, or of our houses, the aged, and our fathers in Christ.'⁶ Several others also described political rulers as fathers. In Robert Ram's *The Countrymens Catechisme* (1655), we have perhaps the best description of those to whom obedience was due as '1. Our naturall Parents, Fathers and Mothers in the flesh. 2. Our Civil Parents, Magistrates, Governours, and all in Authority. 3. Our spiritual Parents, Pastors, Ministers, and Teachers.'⁷

These ideas were so commonplace in the age that King James in *The Trew Law of Free Monarchies* (1598) compared political obligation with filial duty and insisted that as children could not rise against their fathers even when their fathers' acts were wicked or foolish, so subjects could not rebel against their rulers:

> . . . if the children may upon any pretext that can be imagined, lawfully rise up against their Father, cut him off, & choose any other whom they please in his roome; and if the body for the weale of it, may for any infirmitie that can be in the head, strike it off, then I cannot deny that the people may rebell, controll, and displace, or cut off their king at their owne pleasure, and upon respects moving them.[8]

In 1615, an author went so far as to say that the political meaning of the fifth commandment was in fact even more important than the filial one. Richard Mocket, in his popular tract called *God and the King* has the following dialogue between two friends:

THEODIDACTUS: You are well met friend Philalethes; your countenance and gesture import that your thoughts are much busied: what may be the occasion of these Meditations?

PHILALETHES: Somewhat I heard this Evening-Prayer from our Pastor in his Catechistical Expositions upon the Fifth Commandment, Honor thy Father, and thy Mother: who taught that under these pious and reverent appellations of Father and Mother are comprised not only our natural Parents, but likewise all higher Powers; and especially such as have Soveraign Authority, as the Kings and Princes of the Earth.

THEODIDACTUS: Is this Doctrine so strange unto you as to make you muse thereat?

PHILALETHES: God forbid; for I am well assured of the truth thereof, both out of the Word of God, and from the Light of Reason. The sacred Scriptures do stile Kings and Princes the nursing Fathers of the Church (Isa. 49:23), and therefore the nursing Fathers also of the Common-weal: these two Societies having so mutual a dependance, that the welfare of the one is the prosperity of the other.

And the Evidence of Reason teacheth, that there is a *stronger and higher bond of Duty between Children and the Father of their Country, than the Fathers of private Families.* These [latter] procure the good onely of a few, and not without the assistance and protection of the other, who are the common Foster-fathers of thousands of Families, of whole Nations and Kingdoms, that they may live under them an honest and peaceable life.[9]

(Italics mine)

How strong the identification of the King and the father was in the contemporary mind is seen in a somewhat dramatic manner

in the sentiments expressed by Arthur Lord Capel, Baron of Had-
ham, before he went under the executioner's blade in 1649. He
justified his obedience to Charles I on the basis of God's command to obey parents. It was because he kept the fifth commandment, Capel said, that he was going to his death:

> I die, I take it for maintaining the Fifth Commandment, enjoin'd by God
> himself, which enjoins all hands, tho' they contradict one another in
> many several Opinions, yet most Divines do acknowledge that here is
> intended Magistracy and Order; and certainly I have obeyed that Magis-
> tracy and that Order under which I have liv'd, which I was bound to
> obey; and truly, I do say very confidently, that I do die here for keeping,
> for obeying that Fifth Commandment given by God himself, and written
> by his own Finger.[10]

II

The propagation of loyalty to the king in the name of one's duty
to one's parents may have served a definite political need in
Tudor times, but the political happenings of the seventeenth century were bound to make the analogy between political obligation and filial duty utterly meaningless. Indeed, in the later
seventeenth century, this analogy was turned upside down and
instead of patriarchal authoritarianism serving the cause of absolute monarchy, the theory of a mutual contract between the king
and his people resulting in a limited monarchy led people to
search for a new basis of family relationships themselves. Some
radicals even used the analogy of the overthrow of the king to
recommend rebellion against the authority of the father or the
husband in the family. Mary Astell is not, of course, recommending rebellion, as she claims, in *Some Reflections Upon Marriage*,
but her statement is clearly most militant:

> . . . if absolute Sovereignty be not necessary in a State, how comes it to be
> so in a Family? Or if in a Family why not in a State since no Reason can
> be alleged for the one that will not hold more strongly for the other? The
> Domestick Sovereign is without Dispute elected, and the Stipulations
> and Contracts are mutual; is it not then partial in Men to the last degree,
> to contend for, and practice that Arbitrary Dominion in their Families,
> which they abhor and exclaim against in the State? . . . *If all Men are
> born Free*, how is it that all Women are born slaves?[11]

(Italics Mary Astell's)

Much before Mary Astell made this memorable statement, the

two most important political thinkers of the seventeenth century, Thomas Hobbes and John Locke, had challenged the analogy between the king and the head of the family and described the power of a sovereign over his subjects as totally different from the power of a father over his children. Thomas Hobbes explained that there existed a clear distinction between these two kinds of 'Sovereigne Power': 'One, by natural force, as when a man maketh his children, to submit themselves, and their children to his government', and the other 'when men agree amongst themselves, to submit to some man, or assembly of men, voluntarily, on confidence to be protected by him against all others.' These two kinds of power he called 'a common-wealth by *acquisition*' and 'a political common-wealth'.[12] John Locke also made a distinction between 'the Power of a *Magistrate* over a Subject' and 'that of a *Father* over his Children, a *Master* over his Servant, a Husband over his Wife, and a Lord over his Slave.' Indeed, he added: 'All which distinct Powers happening sometimes together in the same Man, if he be considered under these different Relations, it may help us to distinguish these Powers one from another, and shew the difference betwixt a Ruler of a Commonwealth, a Father of a Family, and a Captain of a Galley.'[13]

The clear distinction made by Hobbes and Locke between the power of a sovereign over his subjects and the power of a father over his children was destined to have a powerful impact on political ideas in the age. Its effect on people's thinking about domestic relations was also to be considerable. For our purposes, it is enough to indicate that some of the Restoration playwrights reacted to the overthrow of the king more or less on the same lines as Mary Astell. An excellent example is provided by Otway in *The Atheist* (1683). When asked by her cousin Sylvia why she is so 'transported', Otway's widowed heroine gives the following revealing answer: 'With hopes of Liberty . . . it is an English woman's natural Right. Do not our Fathers, Brothers and Kinsmen often, upon pretence of it, bid fair for Rebellion against their Sovereign: And why ought not we, by their Example, to rebel as plausibly against them?' (V). However conservative Dryden may have been in his ideas about the monarchy, he also felt that if parents became as tyrannical as kings, children had a plausible reason to rebel against them. Here is the outburst of a son against his father in *Love Triumphant* (1694):

When Kings and Fathers, on their Sons and Subjects
Exact intollerable things to bear,
Nature and Self-defence dispense with Duty.   (III)

Vanbrugh's Lady Brute in *The Provoked Wife* (1697) is almost as
sharp in her tone as Mary Astell: 'The argument's good between
the king and the people, why not between the husband and wife?'
(I.i).

The Elizabethan age, of course, is obsessed with the analogy
between the head of the family and the head of the state. It is not
an accident that Shakespeare's Katherine in *The Taming of the
Shrew* uses precisely this analogy in eulogizing the role of the
husband in the family in her famous speech at the end of the play.
It was not necessary for a woman in that age to do so. The Christian scriptures themselves provided enough material to establish
the superiority of the husband over the wife, who was enjoined to
obey him in all respects. This is in fact what Katherine of *The
Taming of A Shrew* had done:

Then to his image he did make a man,
Olde *Adam* and from his side asleepe,
A rib was taken, of which the Lord did make,
The woe of man so termed by *Adam* then,
Woman for that, by her came sinne to us,
And for her sin was *Adam* doom'd to die,
As Sara to her husband, so should we,
Obey them, love them, keepe, and nourish them.

But, as Juliet Dusinberre says, 'Shakespeare's Kate is political':[14]

Such duty as the subject owes the prince,
Even such a woman oweth to her husband;
And when she is froward, peevish, sullen, sour,
And not obedient to his honest will,
What is she but a foul contending rebel
And graceless traitor to her loving lord?
I am asham'd that women are so simple
To offer war where they should kneel for peace;
Or seek for rule, supremacy, and sway,
When they are bound to serve, love, and obey.
(V.ii.155–164)[15]

III

Apart from the political considerations which tended to streng-
then the patriarchal family, there are other factors in Elizabethan

times which reinforce the authority of the head of the family. We may mention the Puritan emphasis on the family prayer in the period. Even though they often preached a more liberal view regarding the position of women and children, the preachings of the Puritans specially emphasized the role of the head of the family in 'Educating, Instructing and Charging our Children and our households, to keepe the ways of the lord.'[16] They believed that 'Without Family Care the labour of Magistrates and Ministers for Reformation and Propagating Religion, is likely to be in a great measure unsuccessful. It's much to be fear'd, Young Persons wont much mind what's said by Ministers in Publick, if they are not Instructed at home: nor will they much regard good Laws made by Civil Authority, if they are not well counsel'd and govern'd at home.'[17]

Family prayers became such a cardinal principle with Puritan preachers that they put full responsibility on the father for the moral well-being of all members of his family. This moral supervision of one's dependants was treated as part of man's 'Covenant' with God, and as John Cotton put it, 'when we undertake to be obedient to [God]', we undertake not only 'in our owne names, and for our owne parts, but in the behalfe of every soule that belongs to us . . . our wives, and children, and servants, and kindred, and acquaintance, and all that are under our reach, either by way of subordination, or co-ordination.'[18] 'Fatherhood', thus, as Michael Walzer has said, 'was transformed into a religious office, with its duties and its obligations prescribed in the Word.'[19] This meant that fathers began to be looked upon 'as intermediaries between the Central Government and their own servants and dependants, no less than between the latter and God.'[20] It is no wonder that fathers ruled over their families and dependants with absolute authority.

After the Restoration, however, it was inevitable that the restored aristocracy which dominated English culture and politics should have spurned religious prayers in general and family prayers in particular. Indeed decline in religious enthusiasm was bound to cause decline in family prayers. Lawrence Stone sees an intimate relationship between the decline of family prayers and that of patriarchalism:

It is no coincidence that this formal ritual of regular, daily, collective

family prayers developed in the sixteenth century, along with patriarchalism; declined in the eighteenth century as a more egalitarian, indi-
vidualistic and companionate family type developed; revived again in the
nineteenth century along with the Victorian patriarchal family; and died
out once again in the twentieth century with the revival of the more
egalitarian and permissive family type. The rise and fall of family prayers coincided not only with the rise and fall of religious enthusiasm, but
also with the rise and fall of patriarchy in the family.[21]

IV

Tudor political theory and the family prayers introduced by the
Puritans must have, of course, strengthened Elizabethan patriarchalism, but the origins of patriarchalism are to be traced to
Christianity itself. In Elizabethan England, patriarchalism is in
fact merely a reflection in domestic relationships of the larger
'Elizabethan World Picture' according to which the universe is a
divinely planned hierarchical structure where man has to accept
the place assigned to him. The Elizabethan view clearly was that
'the Almighty as a God of order formed his earthly kingdom in a
pattern of subordination.'[22] Order in society, therefore, was
entirely dependent on the recognition that all human relationships, including relationships in the family, are hierarchical. As
William Hubbard said in *The Happiness of a People in the Wis-
dome of their Rulers* (1676), 'whoever is for parity in any society,
will in the issue reduce things into an heap of confusion.'[23]

All this, however, need not make us conclude that the Elizabethan family was necessarily repressive and tyrannical. Such a conclusion would be too simplistic a view of the situation. It is
important to recognize that official doctrines and religious
injunctions can never wholly determine human relationships.
Moreover, a patriacrchal society is very complex in its nature and
structure, and often quite deceptive on the surface. Even though
most 'conduct books' in the sixteenth century proclaimed that
woman 'by nature and by divine ordinance' was inferior to man,
it would be quite wrong to assume that women in Shakespeare's
time were chattels. As Keith Thomas has said, 'Theoretical patriarchalism was consistent in practice with almost every kind of
conjugal equality.' In the upper classes, 'the actual independence
of the wives and daughters' was 'always greater than theory
allowed' as is proved by 'the very frequency with which that
independence was denounced.'[24] Other scholars have shown, on

the basis of contemporary evidence, that even in the middle classes the position of women was not necessarily all that inferior. The thrifty Elizabethan tradesman, it has been pointed out, was:

. . . aware of the positive service rendered by so important a functional unit as the home to the organization of that society which made his goods safe and gave his accumulated possessions continuity. Hence, he was seriously concerned to maintain a code fostering ideals useful in the efficient conduct of the household, so that the home might make the greatest possible contribution to the happiness of its component parts, without friction and waste, either material or emotional. In this middle-class code of domestic relations, the husband was recognized as the primary earner of wealth, while upon the wife devolved the duty of the thrifty utilization of the income for the comfort of her household. Therefore the wife became, acknowledged or unacknowledged, the factor determining the success of the individual home.[25]

This concern for harmonious domestic relationships may also explain why Protestant reformers came to regard the chastity of a wife as a superior virtue to the virginity of a nun. In the sixteenth century, the whole monastic way of life itself came under attack. It was claimed that this way of life was not meant for ordinary people, and among other things, that it engendered hypocrisy. The critic of the nunneries in one of Erasmus' *Colloquies* said: 'They are not all Virgins that wear Vails, believe me.'[26] Freed from the theological chains of Catholicism, English preachers were busy evolving a more honest and realistic approach to the whole question of virginity. This they did by attaching to married life a definite spiritual significance, and by declaring that marriage was 'a state in it selfe, far more excellent, than the condition of single life.'[27]

Such thinking naturally improved the position of the married woman in society. She was no more either the goddess of the medieval poet or the temptress of the medieval priest. She was man's mate and companion, his sexual partner and his sharer of joy and grief. Louis Wright has shown how contemporary manuals on domestic life 'continually insist that woman must be treated as the lieutenant of her husband, sharing his confidence and trust, and not as his chattel and slave.'[28] He cites the view of the well-known minister of London, Reverend William Gouge, who declared in 1622 that although the wife must acknowledge the husband as titular head, in reality the family is a joint-stock company and ' he [i.e. the husband] ought to make her a joynt-

Governour of the family with himselfe.'[29] Almost all contemporary conduct-books have in fact only one theme: how to mould 'the sort of wife who would have just the proper amount of obedience and humility and yet would possess the spirit and capacity to be a real helpmeet of her husband.'[30]

It is clear, then, that Elizabethan patriarchalism should not be treated as a static phenomenon. We should also hesitate to interpret family relationships in Shakespeare wholly and rigidly in terms of a patriarchal family. Indeed, Shakespearean society is so clearly in a process of change that not to notice this change can lead to a grave misunderstanding of his plays. It is important to recognize that Shakespeare operates within two somewhat conflicting world views. One, of course, is the traditional view according to which the father is to the family, or the husband to the wife, what God is to man, or the King to his subjects. There is also another view, fostered largely by the new social and economic forces, which demanded the freedom of the individual and asserted the possibility of change and evolution. Shakespeare has to take note both of the hierarchical and patriarchal structure of contemporary society as well as of the forces which subtly or otherwise tend to undermine this structure. Alvin Kernan believes that 'a conflict between the two views' lies at 'the centre of the drama of the age.'[31] The conflict, of course, exists, but there is also a consistent attempt on the part of Shakespeare to seek a reconciliation between the two views – between what has been hallowed by tradition and custom and what is possible and practicable in actual life.

Katherine in *The Taming of the Shrew* expresses the official doctrine regarding the position of the wife in an Elizabethan family when she says to women:

> Thy husband is thy lord, thy life, thy keeper,
> Thy head, thy sovereign. . .   (V.ii.146–7)

Petruchio also expresses the same doctrine in language which is deliberately coarse and crude:

> I will be master of what is mine own—
> She is my goods, my chattels, she is my house,
> My houshold stuff, my field, my barn,
> My horse, my ox, my ass, my anything.

>   (III.ii.225-28)

And yet all this does not really mean that Katherine is Petruchio's slave. She is in fact one of Shakespeare's most spirited young women, and at one stage tells Petruchio;

> Why, Sir, I trust I may have leave to speak;
> And speak I will. I am no child, no babe,
> Your betters have endur'd me say my mind,
> And if you cannot, best you stop your ears.

(IV.iii.73–76)

Such a girl is not easy to handle, far less to win. Indeed Germaine Greer has made her classification of Shakespeare's women into those 'who are people' and those 'who are something less'[32] largely on the basis of Katherine's character. Katherine is clearly an individual who cannot be treated as property. But once her love is won, she will make an ideal wife. It need not surprise us that even modern feminists have chosen her for special praise. Germaine Greer's own estimate of her character is worth quoting:

He [Petruchio] wants her spirit and her energy because he wants a wife worth keeping. He tames her . . . and she rewards him with strong sexual love and fierce loyalty. . . . Kate's speech at the close of the play is the greatest defence of Christian monogamy ever written. It rests upon the role of a husband as protector and friend, and it is valid because Kate has a man who is capable of both, for Petruchio is both gentle and strong (it is a vile distortion of the play to have him strike her ever). The message is probably two-fold: only Kates make good wives, and then only to Petruchios; for the rest their cake is dough.[33]

Portia's case in *The Merchant of Venice* is even more revealing. It is conceded by everyone that Bassanio is quite colourless and insipid compared to Portia. No one can imagine even for a moment that she is likely to be anyone's chattel. And yet the moment Bassanio chooses the right casket, to Portia's utter delight and relief, she opens her heart to him:

> You see me, Lord Bassanio, where I stand,
> Such as I am. Though for myself alone
> I would not be ambitious in my wish
> To wish myself much better, yet for you
> I would be trebled twenty times myself,
> A thousand times more fair, ten thousand
>   times more rich,
> That only to stand high in your account
> I might in virtues, beauties, livings, friends,
> Exceed account. But the full sum of me

Is sum of something which, to term in gross,
Is an unlesson'd girl, unschool'd, unpractis'd;
Happy in this, she is not yet so old
But she may learn; happier than this,
She is not bred so dull but she can learn;
Happiest of all in that her gentle spirit
Commits itself to yours to be directed,
As from her lord, her governor, her king.
Myself and what is mine to you and yours
Is now converted. But now I was the lord
Of this fair mansion, master of my servants,
Queen o'er myself; and even now, but now,
This house, these servants, and this same myself,
Are yours – my lord's.   (III.ii.149–72)

                                              (Italics mine)

The Elizabethans would have regarded Portia's attitude to her
husband not only as normal but indeed as the surest basis for a
happy conjugal life. It is curious, however, that even such a perceptive critic as Alvin Kernan finds this 'surprising'. After stating
that 'women always occupy a special place in the Shakespearean
world' and that Portia, Beatrice and Rosalind 'dominate their
plays', he adds: 'Only in their love for men, who are so much
inferior to them, are these women at all surprising, and they
submit to this love as some curious but functional part of their
beings.'[34] It is, of course, a functional part of their beings, but to
see in this the surrender of a superior being to an inferior one is
clearly to misunderstand the nature of a genuine man–woman
relationship.

V

It is by and large true that the picture of family life that the
Restoration Comedy of Manners presents is not a pleasant one. It
is also clear that, generally speaking, the patriarchal concept of
the family declined quite considerably after the Restoration. We
may not, of course, claim that the Restoration age had come to
believe that in society – as in Hobbes' state of nature – there is
'war of everyman against everyman'[35] and that men must become
one another's 'enemies, and in the way to their end, which is
principally their own conservation, and sometimes their delectation only, endeavour to destroy, or subdue one another.'[36] But we
cannot ignore altogether the influence of Hobbes' ideas on the

age, more particularly on the court circles and the Comedy of Manners which reflects their life–style. The temper of the Comedy of Manners certainly owes quite a lot to the aggressive individualism and naturalism of Hobbes. It is not an accident that some of its most memorable characters – both male and female – treat life as a ruthless and self–seeking battle either for survival or for conquest or for sheer glory. The new economic forces in society may also have made their own contribution to the evolution of the competitive spirit in man to the detriment of his moral and human qualities. The 'Elizabethan World Picture' had come under attack and a new philosophy seemed to have become popular 'calling all in doubt'. St Evremond expressed this new scepticism: 'We have other notions of Nature, than the Ancients had. . . . In short, every thing is changed, Gods, Nature, Politicks, Manners, Humours, and Customs.'[37] Evremond is clearly exaggerating, but the England of the Restoration period was obviously different from that of the first Queen Elizabeth.

The Puritan Revolution, however, had not been in vain, and even though it had failed, it had left behind a legacy which could not be wished away. While talking of the country as a whole it would be utterly wrong to claim that Restoration England had suddenly lost the older moral values or that it had come to treat a cohesive and harmonious family life as irrelevant to human beings. England, in this age, was not less moral than Tudor England or the England of Charles I and Cromwell. Trevelyan has, in fact, claimed that in this age 'conscience meant more, not less, than of old.'[38] He mentions that 'two thousand Puritan ministers had just given up their livings and gone out to endure persecution for conscience's sake [in 1662], following the example of their enemies of Anglican clergy, who had suffered like things for twenty years past rather than desert the Church in her extremity.'[39] Even the sexual morality of the age has been found by social historians to be distinctly superior to that of the Elizabethans. Peter Laslett has found the problem of illegitimacy much less acute in the Restoration period than in the later part of the sixteenth century:

Perhaps everyone would have expected the dramatic drop coming with the Puritan ascendancy in the 1650's. But who would have guessed that after this the rate of bastardy would fail to go up again in the supposedly dissolute society of Restoration England, and remain at a low point for the whole period up to the 1720's.'[40]

Thus England, in Trevelyan's words, was 'sound enough'

but the king himself and the younger generation of the aristocracy had been demoralized by the break-up of their education and family life, by exile and confiscation leading to the mean shifts of sudden poverty, by the endurance of injustice done to them in the name of religion, by the constant spectacle of oaths and covenants lightly taken and lightly broken, and all the base underside of revolution and counter-revolution of which they had been the victims.

'For these reasons', Trevelyan concludes, 'a hard disbelief in virtue of any kind was characteristic of the restored leaders of politics and fashion, and was reflected in the early Restoration drama which depended on their patronage.'[41]

It is the attitudes of these 'restored leaders of politics and fashion,' then, that students of Restoration comedy have to contend with, and not the attitudes prevalent in Restoration England as such. It is clear that 'a hard disbelief in virtue of any kind' is destructive not only of the patriarchal family but of all kinds of human relationships. Since these leaders of politics and fashion dominated – at least for some time – the moral tone of the articulate sections of society, they were seen as a threat to all healthy institutions, including the family. It is not surprising that some prominent contemporaries did see the crisis that the country was facing. Clarendon bewailed that times had changed to such an extent that 'Parents had no Manner of Authority over their children, nor children any Obedience or Submission to their Parents.' This 'unnatural Antipathy' he attributed to 'the Beginning of the Rebellion; when the Fathers and Sons engaged themselves in the contrary Parties, the one choosing to serve the King, the other the Parliament.' Clarendon links this decline of the family directly to a general moral decline in society and sees it in the replacement of the older human values by greed. 'In the place of Generosity, a vile and sordid Love of Money', he said, had come to be 'entertained as the truest Wisdom' and anything is regarded as 'lawful that would contribute to being rich.'[42]

It is, of course, true that this 'vile and sordid Love of Money' was not a new thing in English society. But with economic individualism having become the only slogan of progress, things had become desperate indeed. Lord Keynes has described the Elizabethan and Jacobean era as the 'golden years of modern capitalism'. He has also said that 'never in the annals of the modern world has there existed so prolonged and so rich an opportunity for the businessman, the speculator and the profiteer.'[43] One effect of this capitalism on the seventeenth century was the dislocation of the class structure of society. As J. P. Kenyon says, 'A man who acquired money and land entered the upper classes; a man who lost his land left it. Any other distinction was meaningless.' This naturally meant that 'Men with any common sense and practical ability could improve their fortune; conversely, in a period of stiff competition, when abstract class status provided no buffer, the penalties for failure were absolute.'[44] In this ruthless world, money had come to be identified with all the virtues that man can possess. An anonymous author in 1647 wrote what, according to L. C. Knights, had become a commonplace by the middle of the seventeenth century:

Whosoever wanteth money is ever subject to contempt and scorn in the world, let him be furnished with never so good gifts, either of body or of mind. . . . In these times we may say with the wise man: My son, better it is to die than to be poor, for now money is the world's god, and the card which the devil turns up trump to win the set with all. . . . *Pecuniae omnia obediunt*: hence it is so admired that millions venture both souls and bodies for the possession of it.[45]

These new economic forces and pressures must have made a powerful impact on the family system in the period. According to L. C. Knights, England's 'transition from a subsistence economy to the early stages of an economy of plenty' in the early seventeenth century caused 'a corresponding change in man's habits, attitudes and general outlook.'[46] By the time of the Restoration, in any case, the effects of this economy of plenty were becoming visible in many fields of national life.[47] Perhaps the greatest victim of these new economic forces in the upper-class was the patriarchal family.

VI

Before we examine the effects of the economy of plenty on women in the Restoration age, it is worth emphasizing that an important factor which made the patriarchal family a meaningful and often fulfilling institution for the Elizabethan wife was her active participation in its economic life. Irrespective of whether she belonged to the aristocracy, the landed gentry, the middle-classes or the lower-classes, she had a definite productive role in the family. This gave her an importance which theoretical patriarchalism might not have accorded her. Of course each class had its own social conventions, but broadly speaking, it is safe to agree with Eileen Power that 'the position occupied by women was one neither of inferiority nor of superiority but of a certain rough and ready equality.'[48]

In the hierarchical Elizabethan society, the aristocracy naturally played the most important part in the life of the nation. Women of this class had many roles to play, and we have contemporary evidence to show that they often played them well. Eileen Power's comment on the life of women in aristocratic families in medieval Europe is almost wholly applicable to similarly placed Elizabethan women:

While her lord was away on military expeditions, on pilgrimages, at court or on business, it was she who became the natural guardian of the fief, or manager of the manor, and Europe was full of competent ladies not spending all their time in hawking and flirting, spinning and playing chess, but running estates, fighting law suits and even standing sieges for their absent lords.[49]

The age clearly did not expect from its women the same qualities as from its men, but there is no doubt that women were expected to possess diverse talents. The famous maxim 'That sexes as well as souls are equal in capacity' comes from Sir Anthony Cooke, the tutor to Edward VI. Sir Anthony's 'fondest hope' was that 'his daughters might have for their husbands *complete* and perfect men, and that their husbands might be happy in *complete* women.'[50] (Italics mine). This completeness demanded from aristocratic women not only the qualities of courtiers, scholars and soldiers, but also of managers of homes and families.

In middle-class families the demands made on women must have been different, but by no means less exacting. In his *The necessarie fit and convenient Education of a Young Gentlewoman* (1598), Giovanni Michele Bruto has given a picture of the extent of a woman's knowledge in this station of life:

our gentlewoman shall learne not only all manner of fine needle-work. . . but whatsoever belongeth to the distaffe, spindle, and weaving: which must not be thought unfit for the honour and estate wherein she was borne. . . . And which is more, to the end that being become a mistress, she shall looke into the duties and offices of domesticall servants, and see how they sweepe and make cleane the chambers, hall, and other places:

make ready dinner, dressing up the cellar and buttery: and that she be not so proud that she should disdaine to be present when they lay their bucks ['laying bucks' refers to a detail of washing clothes], and when they bake, but to be present at all household workes.[51]

Ben Jonson's Otter in *Epicoene* scoffed at the daily chores performed by women: 'Wife! . . . There is no such thing in nature. I confess, gentlemen, I have a cook, a laundress, a house-drudge, that serves my necessary turns, and goes under that title (IV.i.),' Otter's statement exposes his own distorted image of a wife rather than the position of the Elizabethan woman, who did not think it was below her dignity to perform the domestic duties that Otter mentions. Indeed, even women in higher circles firmly believed that no duty in the house was to be shunned by them. It was a common saying in the age: 'Let nobody loathe the name of the Kitchen'[52] and we have the example of Shakespeare's Lady Capulet whose interest in her kitchen is obvious when she tells the nurse: 'Hold, take these keys, and fetch me spices, nurse.'[53] Talking of domestic work and skill in housewifery, Vives says: 'I would in no wise that a woman shoulde be ignoraunt in these feates, that must be done by hand, no, not though shee be a Princesse or a Queene.'[54] In the middle classes, thrift and industry were treated as the most important qualities of a good wife. Industry was indeed regarded as 'a preventive of sin', as is seen in Richard Whiteford's *A Werke for householders* (1530) and several other conduct books of the period. Women of these classes participated so fully in the economic life of their households that in many cases most of the needs of the family were met by the products of women's own labour.

The situation in the Restoration age seems to have radically changed. Social historians have noticed that Restoration upper-class women led very circumscribed lives compared to women of the Elizabethan period. Alice Clark believes that the comradeship that existed between the husband and the wife in the earlier period was 'stimulating and inspiring to both' and consequently helped Elizabethan women to develop 'courage, initiative, resourcefulness and wit in a high degree.' She adds: 'Society expected them to play a great part in the national life and they rose to the occasion; perhaps it was partly the comradeship with their husbands in the struggle for existence which developed in them qualities which had otherwise atrophied.' She sees a 'marked contrast in this respect' between Elizabethan and Restoration upper-class women. The latter, according to her, declined rapidly in 'physique', 'efficiency and morale'. This decline she largely attributes to 'the spread of the capitalistic organization of industry which. . . made possible the idleness of growing numbers of women.'[55]

VII

L. C. Knights has shown how 'housekeeping' as an institution started declining with the rise of merchant lords. 'Housekeeping' was essentially a patriarchal institution sustained by noblemen and gentlemen who stayed in their country-houses 'from age to age and from ancestor to ancestor.' Through hospitality they not only won the love of their neighbours but also 'relieved many poor wretches, and wrought also diverse other good effects.'[56] This institution, it must be admitted, had started declining during the Elizabethan age itself. When we find a reference to it in a late Restoration play it is already being treated as somewhat exceptional, and indeed as belonging to Elizabethan times. In Shadwell's comedy, *The Lancashire Witches* (1682), Sir Edward Hartford is described in the list of characters as 'a worthy Hospitable true English Gentleman'. This conversation takes place between him and his two guests:

DOUBT : You have extremely delighted us this Morning, by your House, Gardens, Your Accommodation, and your way of Living; you put us in mind of the renowned *Sidney*'s Admirable description of *Kalandar*.
SIR EDW : Sir you Complement me too much.
BELL : Methinks you represent to us the Golden days of *Queen Elizabeth*, such sure were our Gentry then; now they are grown servile Apes to foreign customs, they leave off Hospitality, for which we were famous all over *Europe*, and turn Servants to Board-wages.
SIR EDW : For my part, I love to have my servants part of my Family, the other were, to hire day Labourers to wait upon me; I had rather my Friends, Kindred, Tenants, and Servants should live well out of me, than Coach-makers, Taylors, Embroiders, and Lacemen should: To be pointed at in the Streets, and have Fools stare at my Equipage, is a vanity I have always scorn'd.   (III.i)

The scene also shows how the character of the English gentry was changing. This was inevitable when land was changing hands at a rapid pace and the old gentry was being supplanted by a newly rich commercial class which was buying land to exploit it for profit. The values of this class were very different from those of the older aristocracy. This class was the founder of the new 'acquisitive society', and it was to find its real spokesman in Adam Smith. Adam Smith's comment on 'housekeeping' is most revealing: 'A man grows rich by employing a multitude of manufacturers; he grows poor by maintaining a multitude of menial servants.'[57] Dr Johnson's comment, four years before the publication of *The Wealth of Nations*, is more practical still:

That ancient hospitality, of which we hear so much, was in an uncommercial country, where men, being idle, were glad to be entertained at rich men's tables. But in a commercial country, a busy country, time becomes precious, and therefore hospitality is not so much valued. . . . Promiscuous hospitality is not the way to gain real influence. . . . No, Sir, the way to make sure of power and interest is by lending money confidentially to your neighbours at a small interest, or perhaps at no interest at all, and having their bonds in your possession.[58]

This is language that members of the older aristocracy might not have understood at all. Indeed they might even have felt offended by its tone. They would, in any case, have found the suggestion of acquiring influence in this way thoroughly dishonourable. They – and others in the earlier period – regarded their households as 'very notable social institutions and schools of manners if not of learning.'[59] They were specially excellent training grounds for ladies who were destined to preside over such households. What John Smyth, the steward of the Berkeley estates, has to tell us about Anne, second wife of Thomas, Lord Berkeley (d. 1534), throws a significant light on this training:

Country huswifry seemed to be an essential part of this lady's constitution; a lady that. . . would betimes in winter and summer mornings make her walks to visit her stable, barns, day-house, poultry, swinetroughs and the like; which huswifry her daughter-in-law. . . seeming to decline, and to betake herself to the delights of youth and greatness, she would sometimes to those about her swear, by God's blessed sacrament, this gay girl will beggar my son Henry.[60]

In the Restoration period, more than a century after the age of this distinguished lady, it would not have been altogether the fault of the daughter-in-law if she took no interest in household affairs. With the rise of new means of producing wealth in which a woman played no part, she had nothing else to do but 'to betake herself to the delights of youth and greatness' and to go 'gay'. One result of this 'Economy of plenty', clearly, was that it tended to give a woman only a decorative role.

Whatever the disability imposed by a patriarchal family on a woman, she does come to acquire a sense of belonging and a sense of sharing wherever she is a partner in the economic life of the family. But once she comes to have only a decorative role, she tends to lose this sense of belonging and sharing. Juliet Dusinberre has this to say on the decorative role of women in Restoration comedy:

One difference between the position of wives in Caroline drama – a difference which was to dominate Restoration comedy – and of wives in the earlier plays, is that women cease to work. Written for people of leisure, Caroline plays project characters without a working context. There are no business relationships, only social ones. Women have already become part of the luxury of life, behaving in ways which enhance their desirability rather than their usefulness. In *The Way of the World* pleasure is the purpose of a woman's life: there is no longer any distinction between the function of a wife and the function of a whore.[61]

The statement is clearly misleading in its emphasis – more particularly with regard to *The Way of the World* – but there is no doubt that most women in the Restoration Comedy of Manners do come to be treated by men merely as objects of sexual satisfaction. We may also add that at least some women in Restoration comedy, like some women in modern times, do become victims of the boredom of ever-increasing leisure. Such boredom alone can explain the activities of women like Lady Fidget in Wycherley's *The Country Wife.*

VIII

At this stage we may notice that another phenomenon which considerably undermined the patriarchal family in the Restoration period was the urbanized life-style of the new aristocracy. Peter Malekin has said: 'The traditional, settled country world, which survived into the Restoration among the small gentleman farmers of Kent, may have had some similarity in feeling to the world of Shakespeare's romantic comedies.'[62] But this world was now coming increasingly under the threat of both commercialization and urbanization. The important fact to notice is the development of a new culture, specially in London, which is the real habitat of most of the denizens of Restoration comedy. As noticed

by Peter Malekin, the population of London had risen 'from
about 200,000 in 1600 to well over 500,000 by 1700.'[63] Moreover,
after the Great Fire, new and fashionable areas had sprung up in
the western parts of the city and London now provided theatres,
coffee-houses, pleasure-gardens and fashionable drawing-rooms
for select dances and pleasant conversation between men and
women. For those men and women from the countryside who
visited London during the 'season', it was an altogether new
world, wholly different from the 'small, immobile, close-knit,
face-to-face, status-bound community,'[64] that they had known.
Here they felt free to indulge in many of the forbidden pleasures.

This new urban culture naturally weakened family ties and we
are not surprised to learn from Witwoud that 'tis not modish to
know relations in town' (*The Way of the World*, III.iii). Witwoud
tells his half-brother, Sir Wilful Witwoud, that things in town
are wholly different from those in the country 'where great lub-
berly brothers, slabber and kiss one another when they meet, like
a call of serjeants – 'tis not the fashion here; 'tis not indeed, dear
brother' (III.iii). Sir Wilful is naturally outraged: 'The fashion's a
fool; and you're a fop, dear brother' (III.iii). Witwoud, of course,
is not a suitable spokesman for the new London culture, and Sir
Wilful is distinctly superior to him as a human being. It is, however, a fact that Sir Wilful does not fit in at all in Lady Wishfort's
circle. Millamant calls him 'rustic, ruder than Gothic' (IV.i), and
Lady Wishfort herself is 'ashamed of [him]' (IV.ii) and tells him
that he is fit only to live with the 'Saracens, or the Tartars, or the
Turks' and 'not fit to live in a Christian Commonwealth' (IV.ii).
It is a curious Christian Commonwealth indeed where all traditional values have been subverted and where, as Valentine says in
Congreve's *Love for Love,* 'Husbands and wives will drive distinct
trades, and care and pleasure separately occupy the family.
Coffee-houses will be full of smoke and stratagem. And the croft
prentice, that sweeps his master's shop in the morning, may, ten
to one, dirty his sheets before night' (IV.iii).

The effect of this culture on women is electrifying. Their
attempt is to somehow persuade their guardians or husbands to
take them to London, and once they are there, they breathe a
different air. Young Bellair in *The Man of Mode* asks Harriet if
she is in love and she replies: 'Yes, with this dear town, to that
degree, I can scarce indure the country in landscapes and in hang-

ings.' (III.i). Wycherley's Hippolita in *The Gentleman Dancing Master*, too, cannot endure the country and tells Gerard that she would prefer to be a 'prisoner in London' to being taken to 'Yorkshire, Wales, or Cornwall, which is as bad as to Barbadoes' (II). Millamant declares: 'I loathe the country, and everything that relates to it' (IV.i). One reason for the women's love for London is stated by Miss Betty in Vanbrugh's *A Journey to London*: 'We have bought a new coach, and an ocean of new clothes, and we are to go to the play to-night, and tomorrow we go to the opera, and next night we go to the assembly, and then the next night after, we–.' The girl is so full of the pleasures of London that she could have gone on if Lady Headpiece had not stopped her (III.i.). But Miss Betty is clearly too young to understand the full cultural significance of London for women. For that we have to hear a mature woman like Mrs Sullen in Farquhar's *The Beaux-Stratagem*. She tells her sister-in-law, Dorinda, that the only way to reform her husband (Mr Sullen) is to take him to London, for 'London, dear London, is the Place for managing and breaking a Husband' (II.i). She declares that it is—

a standing Maxim in conjugal Discipline, that when a Man wou'd enslave his wife, he hurries her into the Country; and when a Lady would be arbitrary with her Husband, she wheedles her Booby up to Town – A Man dare not play the Tyrant in London, because there are so many Examples to encourage the Subject to rebel. O Dorinda, Dorinda! a fine Woman may do anything in London: O' my Conscience, she may raise a Army of forty thousand Men.   (II.i)

Mrs Sullen is obviously too optimistic about London and she clearly knows nothing about the fate of some wives in that city, as we shall have occasion to see later. But her main point is very clear, namely, that the city stands for women's emancipation, for equality between the sexes, and consequently for a juster and more humane basis of domestic relationship.

IX

There may, however, be a real danger for women who are too naive to realize that raising an 'Army of forty thousand Men' has its own implications. Indeed only those women who have acquired sufficient intellectual self-sufficiency and social poise to compel men to treat them as equals can survive in the free atmosphere of London. This needs proper education, which, unfortunately, had been denied to most women in England before the Restoration. This was as true of upper-class women as of others. Many upper-class women had spent the earlier years of their lives in conditions of real hardship. They suffered as much of a break – up of family life and education as men. They too had become victims of 'the mean shifts of sudden poverty' during the civil war and the commonwealth, when men had gone to war, leaving their homes and lands in the care of women.

Even if their lives had not been disrupted by the Civil War, it is very doubtful that most of them would have received any worthwhile education. It is a painful fact that during the seventeenth century the education of women in England was almost *deliberately* neglected. The Humanists of the sixteenth century had made no distinction between men and women in the field of education. Indeed, Sir Thomas More had categorically stated that he saw no reason why 'learning . . . may not *equally* agree with both sexes.'[65] (Italics mine). But this movement towards equal opportunities for men and women did not last longer than forty years – from about 1520 to 1560. Lawrence Stone blames Castiglione's *The Courtier* – its translation appeared in England in 1561 – for setting the clock back. This book advocated a different ideal of womanhood, a courtly ideal which could be easily sustained by skill in music, painting, drawing and dancing, along with a sprinkling of letters. The Puritans added their own requirement – needlework and other household duties – so that a young woman would become a docile wife.[66] Either way, women were denied any real education, and this trend continued till almost the beginning of the eighteenth century.

We have enough evidence of such discrimination against women in contemporary writing. In a pamphlet entitled *The Women's Sharpe Revenge* (1640), the writers – presumably two middle-class women – hold this discrimination responsible for the low position that women occupy in society. In a well-known passage they describe at some length the social disabilities which society imposes on women:

But it hath beene the policy of all parents, even from the beginning, to curbe us of that benefit, by striving to keep us under, and to make us mens meere Vassails: even unto posterity. How else comes it to passe, that when a Father hath a numerous issue of Sonnes and Daughters, the sonnes forsooth they must bee first put to the Grammar Schools, and after perchance to the University, and trained up in the Liberall Arts and Sciences, and these (if they prove not Block-heads) they may in time be book-learned . . . [Daughters, on the contrary] are set onely to the Needle, to pricke our fingers: or else to the Wheele to spinne a faire thread for our owne undoings, or perchance to some more durty and debayst drudgry: if wee be taught to read, they then confine us within the compasse of our Mothers Tongue, and that limit wee are not suffered to passe, or if (which cometimes happeneth) wee be brought up to Musick, to singing, and dancing, it is not for any benefit that thereby we can ingrosse unto our selves, but for their own particular ends, the better to please and content their licentious appetites, when we come to our maturity and ripeness . . . if we be weake by Nature, they strive to makes (sic) us more weake by our Nurture. And if in degree of place low, they strive by their policy to keepe us more under . . . lest we should bee made to vindicate our own injuries.[67]

Mary Astell's complaint in *Some Reflections Upon Marriage*, more than half a century later, is even sharper. Boys, of course, have all the facilities to be 'initiated in the Sciences . . . made acquainted with ancient and modern Discoveries' and great 'Care and Cost bestow'd on their Education.' With girls the situation is altogether different – and it seems there is a *deliberate* attempt to keep them ignorant: 'The latter [girls] are restrain'd, frown'd upon, and beat, not *for*, but *from* the Muses; Laughter and Ridicule, that never–failing Scare-Crow, is set up to drive them from the Tree of Knowledge.'[68] Earlier in the period, we have Sir Ralph Verney who tried to dissuade his god-daughter, in a letter of 1652, from learning classical languages. When this lady announced her intention to learn Hebrew, Greek and Latin, this is what Sir Ralph wrote to her:

Good sweet hart bee not too covitous; beleeve me a Bible (with the common prayer) and a good plaine cattachisme in your Mother Tongue being well read and practised, is well worth all the rest and much more suitable to your sex.[69]

The situation did not change very appreciably even in the eighteenth century. Indeed, Lady Mary Wortley Montagu's complaint in that century is no different from that of Mary Astell. 'We are educated', she said, 'in the grossest ignorance, and *no art omitted to stifle our natural reason.*' (Italics mine). The age's real attitude to female education is perhaps best seen in her caution to her daughter to conceal whatever learning she [the grand-daughter] attains with as much solicitude as she would hide crookedness or lameness; the parade of it can only serve to draw on her the envy and consequently the most inveterate hatred, of all he – and she – fools, which will certainly be at least three parts in four of all her acquaintance.[70]

Damaris Lady Masham perhaps understood the difficulties of an educated woman much better than Lady Mary. She could sense that most men distrust, and even perhaps fear, women with cultivated minds. She herself did want women to 'read English perfectly, to understand ordinary Latin and arithmetic, with some general knowledge of chronology and history but she feared that women with a good education 'might be in danger of not finding husbands, so few men, as do, relishing these accomplishments in a lady.'[71] It is difficult to explain this attitude unless we conclude that it is caused by the feeling that education would 'liberate' women's minds, and women would then refuse to suffer some of the indignities to which they were subjected.

In the Restoration period itself there is Aphra Behn who lamented, in lines addressed 'To Mr. Creech on his Translation of Lucretius', her lack of proper classical education:

> Till now, I curst my Birth, my Education,
> And more the scanted Customes of the Nation;
> Permitting not the Female Sex to tread,
> The mighty Paths of Learned Heroes dead.
> The God-like Virgil, and great Homers Verse,
> Like Divine Mysteries are conceal'd from us.
> > We are forbid all grateful Theams,
> > No ravishing thoughts approach our Ear,
> > The Fulsom Gingle of the times,
> Is all we are allow'd to understand or hear.

This lack of proper education became a real handicap for the Restoration upper-class woman, more especially when she was confronted with a much more licentious appetite in men than the anonymous writers of *The Womens Sharpe Revenge* could have anticipated. In her circle, she was face to face with a new breed of Englishmen who were fed on and steeped in the culture of France. It is not surprising that some women became easy victims of these licentious men and strengthened the contemporary masculine belief that the sole aim of a woman's life was to be 'toused' and 'moused' by men. It is not without significance that Etherege and

Congreve make Harriet and Millamant quote Waller, a real sign of culture in the period, and thus indicate that they are to be treated differently from other women. Kenneth Muir writes, 'The fact that while Harriet also quotes from Cowley's *Davideis*, we cannot imagine Belinda or Mrs Loveit being familiar with poetry, is an indication that Dorimant's relationship with Harriet has more chance of becoming permanent.'[72]

Harriet, of course, is an exceptional character. But surely what Restoration comedy clearly brings out is the need for proper education if women are to survive in their society. As we shall see, the Restoration comic heroine does not accept a situation in which the man she loves makes no distinction between a wife and a whore. Indeed, she demands an equality with men which Shakespeare's heroines had not done – though, of course, many of Shakespeare's women achieve such equality owing to their outstanding intellectual and moral qualitites. The Restoration comic heroines face a much more difficult world than their predecessors in Shakespeare, and they are clearly much more conscious of the need to acquire some of the qualities of their predecessors.

X

Some developments in this period, of course, improve the position of comic heroines considerably. Perhaps the most important of these is their acquisition of some measure of economic independence. Lawrence Stone has specially mentioned the 'new property arrangements among wealthy landowners' in the Restoration period which may have reduced the authority of the father and thus weakened the patriarchal family. He finds that 'between 1500 and 1660, the current owner was relatively free to dispose of his estates as he wished, which gave him a formidable weapon to help impose his will upon his children.' During this period, 'the threat of partial or even complete disinheritance as a penalty for disobedience was a very real one.' After 1660, however, owing to certain developments in the early seventeenth century, the powers of the current owner were reduced to those of a life trustee and he could 'neither alienate the property nor deprive any of his children of their arranged inheritance.'[73]

It is difficult to establish whether in contemporary drama these new arrangements play any very important role. Quite a few characters in Restoration comedy are clearly afraid of disobeying their parents lest they should be disinherited. In Etherege's *The Man of Mode* Young Bellair has been 'commanded' by his father to marry the girl he has selected for him 'or expect to be disinherited.' (I.i). But as against this, there is Harriet. When her mother asks her never to see Dorimant again, it emerges that she has no control over Harriet's 'fortune'. Clearly the contemporary property arrangements are in operation here. The situation of Valentine in Congreve's *Love for Love* is perhaps similar. Valentine's father is extremely keen to disinherit him, but it is clear that he cannot do so without Valentine's consent in *writing*. It seems, on the whole, that the situation of children during this period has improved considerably compared to that of their counterparts in the Elizabethan age. It is very likely, therefore, that this affected their attitude towards their parents. We have Defoe's evidence to the effect that the new property arrangements had adversely affected the hold of parents over their children. In *The Family Instructor* (1715), he describes 'the mischievous consequence of leaving estates to children entirely independent of their parents' as 'a fatal obstruction to parental authority.'[74]

Another development which must have reduced the authority of the husband over his wife was the far greater care taken in this period to protect the property rights of the wife. Marriage settlements specified the pocket-money – 'pin money' – that the wife was to receive, and what is more, she could keep more of her own money under her personal control. Stone's reference to the precaution taken by many women, especially widows, 'of vesting their property in separate trustees before marriage, so that their husbands could not touch it'[75] is of special interest to us as it is this precaution which saves Mrs Fainall, and indeed all the other characters (including Mirabel himself), from disaster in Congreve's *The Way of the World* (1700). Miranda and Clarinda in Shadwell's *The Virtuoso* (1676) also use this precaution when they decide to make Bruce and Longvil – the young men they are going to marry – their guardians to protect their fortune from Sir Nicholas Gimcrack, their uncle.

XI

Some people may have felt that the new property arrangements weakened family discipline, but surely they have a positive role to play in the evolution of the nuclear family and the companionate marriage. The same positive role cannot be ascribed to the contemporary political climate. We have already noted how 'the restored leaders of politics and fashion' had come to acquire 'a hard disbelief in virtue of any kind.' Such an attitude was hardly conducive to moral health and the growth of a stable family life. But such an attitude cannot sustain even an individual for long, and so it was natural that soon enough, often very imperceptibly, newer attitudes to life and its problems – including marriage and family life – started asserting themselves. After the glorious revolution of 1688 these attitudes come to dominate both life and literature. This is also the time when the English as a people start feeling politically settled.

The Restoration, people had hoped, would help England to settle down after a stormy period, but it failed to achieve any reconcilation between the warring ideologies. The nation had been so badly split that it was not easy to resolve either the political or the social tensions. However loudly the new ruling class might yell – 'We are back, and the King's back, and we'll see you don't forget it',[76] it was not a yell of triumph as much as of fear. Indeed, as Christopher Hill says, 'The wits of Charles II's court, insecurely restored to the highest positions in a society increasingly alien to them because increasingly commercial, were in a sense themselves outsiders, social misfits. Hence their desire at all costs to *"epater"* the triumphant bourgeoisie.'[77] It is this sense of political and social insecurity which may have made them search for satisfaction in physical pleasure. L. C. Knights' view that these people were 'fundamentally bored' and 'badly . . . *needed* to be entertained',[78] does contain a substantial part of the truth when applied to certain members of the court circle. John Wain's claim that the comedy of this period is 'one of the symptoms of a sick society'[79] is, of course, misleading in its emphasis, but there is no doubt that some of the leaders of fashion in this period did behave like Milton's 'Sons of Belial' who 'when Night Darkens the Streets . . . wander forth . . . flown with insolence and wine.' These men recognize no family or other relationships, except as a means of personal aggrandisement. Their lives centre on lust – 'lust after other people's bodies and cash.'[80] They seem to have lost their roots and they float through life feeding on others. They are certainly 'free' compared to the men in Shakespeare – free from parental tyranny, filial gratitude, marital fidelity and indeed from all social responsibility. There are some women too, who are as 'free' as these men and who are also predators of society. These men and women do influence the ethos of Restoration comedy quite considerably, but to believe that this comedy is content merely with exhibiting the life–style of these 'liberated' men and women would be to ignore the very important point that this comedy makes — that even in a fallen state men and women search for and often find, reasonably stable moral values and satisfying human relationships.

XII

If any one individual in England could provide an adequate ideology for the evolution of a stable nuclear family in the new society emerging after 1688, it was John Locke. Other writers merely protested against the erosion of discipline and proper family feeling, but never went deep into its causes. The protests did come in large numbers, though largely from clergymen. The Puritan Divine Richard Baxter said that 'most of the mischiefs that now infest or seize upon mankind through the earth, consist in, or are caused by the disorders and ill-governedness of families.'[81] Cotton Mather's statement is more emphatic still: '*Well-Ordered families* naturally produce a Good Order in other *Societies*. When *Families* are under an *Ill Discipline*, all other *Societies* being therefore *Ill Disciplined*, will feel that Error in the *First* Concoction.'[82] James Fitch simply stated: 'Such as Families are, such at last the Church and Common-wealth must be.'[83] All this is well enough, but none of these people suggested how families should learn to govern themselves. To suggest, as it had been for centuries, that the father or the husband should be treated as a god served no purpose when a son could decide to challenge his father, as Leonides did in Dryden's *Marriage A-La-Mode* (1672):

POLYDAMAS [the father] : You shall dispute no more; I am a king, And I
    will be obey'd.
LEONIDES : You are a king, sir, but you are no God; Or, if you were, you
    could not force my will.

(II.i)

Daughters and wives may have hesitated to use such strong language, but there is no doubt that the climate had changed and a new basis for family relationships had to be evolved if conflicts were to be avoided.

John Locke provided this new basis. He was acutely conscious of the conflict between parents and children in the age, and so he advised parents not to alienate the affection of their children by harsh behaviour. He argues that though children are born dependent upon their parents, temporary dependence is not the same thing as life-long subordination. Children cast off this subordination as they grow into adults: 'The Bonds of this Subjection are like the Swadling Cloths they are wrapt up in, and supported by, in the weakness of their Infancy. Age and Reason as they grow up, loosen them till at length they drop quite off, and leave a Man at his own free Disposal.'[84] In this context Locke's advice to Clarke is most revealing: 'as [your son] approaches more to a Man, admit him nearer your Familiarity: So shall you have him your obedient Subject (as is fit) whilst he is a Child, and your affectionate Friend, when he is a man.'[85] He also said that children should come to regard their parents as 'their best, as their only sure Friends; and as such, love and reverence them.'[86] He did not like the attitude of parents who discouraged such a relationship. 'Many Fathers', he said:

though they proportion to their Sons liberal Allowances, according to their Age and Condition; yet they keep the knowledge of their Estates, and Concerns from them, with as much reservedness, as if they were guarding a secret of State from a Spy, or an Enemy. . . . And I cannot but often wonder to see Fathers, who love their Sons very well, yet so order the matter by a constant Stiffness and a mien of Authority and distance to them all their Lives, as if they were never to enjoy, or have any comfort from those they love best in the World.[87]

Stone has described the late sixteenth and early seventeenth centuries as 'the great flogging age' in England. Between 1450 and 1660, he says, 'colleges freely used physical punishments on their younger students . . . either by public whippings in the hall or over a barrel in the battery, or else by putting them in the stocks in the hall.' Deans and even tutors had been given powers of physical punishment, and Aubrey, who entered Oxford in 1642, noted that there 'the rod was frequently used by the tutors and deans on his pupils, till Bachelor of Arts.[sic]'[88] In the Restoration period, the situation was not as bad, but beating children was still a common feature of the educational system. Locke condemned this in the sharpest language. 'Frequent *Beating* or *Chiding*', he said, 'is therefore carefully *to be avoided*' as it 'lessens the

Authority of the Parents and Respect of the Child.' Beating, he emphasized, looks 'more like the Fury of an enraged Enemy, than the good will of a compassionate Friend.' The only way to teach children, he said, is through example. His main advice to parents is most radical in its period: 'The sooner you *treat him as a Man*, the sooner he will begin to be one.'[89] This approach could certainly provide a healthier basis for a stable and companionate family.

What Locke said about the husband–wife relationship sounds even more radical considering the times when he wrote. Building on Hobbes's concept of the social contract, he made an important departure when he claimed that the contract between a husband and a wife was not irrevocable. Treating marriage as a civil contract, he stated: '*conjugal Society* is made by a voluntary compact between Man and Woman.'[90] He explicity rejected the notion that marriage requires the absolute sovereignty of the husband over the wife: 'the ends of Matrimony requiring no such Power in the Husband, the Condition of *Conjugal Society* put it not in him, it being not at all necessary to that State.'[91] What he regarded as necessary was 'such a Communion and Right in one anothers Bodies, as is necessary to its Chief-End, Procreation', along with 'mutual Support, and Assistance, and a Communion of Interest too, as necessary not only to unite their Care, and Affection, but also necessary to their Common Off-spring, who have a Right to be nourished and maintained by them, till they are able to provide for themselves.'[92] He also stated that once these conditions of the contract were fulfilled, the contract might even be terminated. He asked: 'Why this Compact where Procreation and Education are secured, and Inheritance taken care for, may not be made determinable, either by consent, or at a certain time, or upon certain Conditions, as well as any other voluntary compacts, there being no necessity in the nature of the thing, nor to the ends of it, that it should always be for Life.'[93]

From these arguments we should not conclude that Locke rejects the basic assumptions of a patriarchal family. His aim clearly is not to reject, but to soften the rigours of this type of family. He does this in the interest of harmonious relationships between parents and children on the one hand, and between husbands and wives on the other. He does mention the possibility of the marriage contract being terminated, but this is merely to stress the *voluntary* aspect of the contract. Moreover, the values of the new society now emerging in England were clearly dominated by the rising forces of capitalism and the needs of an expanding economy, and demanded continuity in families for the preservation of property. Easy dissolution of marriage would hardly have been acceptable to this society. Marriage, in these circumstances, cannot be treated too lightly. Consequently, whatever the professions of Locke, women could not have thought that they had acquired equality with men or were equal partners in the contract. Indeed, as Mary Lyndon Shanley has said, marriage for Locke 'could not be a completely egalitarian relationship', and whenever 'husband and wife disagreed on anything concerning the management of the family',[94] the final decision had to be left to the husband. Locke gives a reason for this: 'But Husband and Wife, though they have but one common Concern, yet having different understanding, will unavoidably sometimes have different wills, too; it therefore being necessary, that the last Determination i.e. the Rule, should be placed somewhere, it naturally falls to the Man's share, as the *abler and the stronger*.'[95] (Italics mine). With children, too, the final authority lies with parents, though both parents and husbands are advised by Locke to show understanding and avoid conflicts. It is such avoidance of conflict that Locke recommends in the interest of domestic peace, happiness and prosperity.

We in modern times might not consider Locke sufficiently radical, but then we have travelled far from Tudor times when a wife was 'to set down this conclusion in her soule: Mine husband is my superior, my better, he hath authority and rule over me, nature hath given it him. . . . God hath given it him',[96] or where a daughter was the father's property so that he could confidently say, 'As she is mine, I may dispose of her.' (*MSND*, I.i.42). Shakespeare may soften the cruelties of a patriarchal family in his plays, but most of his contemporaries would certainly have found Locke's ideas an encroachment on their rights as parents and husbands. Almost a century had to pass before these ideas could become generally acceptable.

CHAPTER II
PARENTS AND CHILDREN

I

Daughters are perhaps the greatest victims of a patriarchal family and Elizabethan daughters were no exception. Nor, for that matter, were sons, though in their case there was greater latitude. The view of contemporary preachers in Elizabethan times was that parents were not strict enough in exercising authority over their children and were often far too affectionate to be good Christian parents. The effect of this, according to these preachers, was that children became too familiar, and as Thomas Cobbett complained, there were too many children 'who carry it proudly, disdainfully and scornfully towards parents.'[1] It was, therefore, strongly recommended that 'Doctrine and Example alone are insufficient; Discipline is an essential part of the nurture of the Lord.'[2] Doctrine, example and discipline all served to make children understand that 'Parents in regard to their children, doe beare a singular image of God, as he is the Creatour, Sustainer, and Governour.'[3] In his advice to children, Thomas Cobbett categorically stated: 'Present your Parents so to your minds, as bearing the Image of Gods Father-hood, and that also will help on your filiall awe and Reverence to them.'[4]

This 'filiall awe' is best tested when children decide to get married. Chilton Powell has told us that contemporary 'family books all contain a discussion of whether or not children should marry without their parents' consent, and are pretty well agreed that they should not, even though they were of age.'[5] The reason was not that the parents' choice was better, but that God had ordained it so. John Stockwood in his book *A Bartholmew Fairing for Parentes . . . . Shewing that Children are not to marie, without the consent of their Parentes, in whose power and choise it lieth to provide wives and husbands for their sonnes and daughters* (1589), claimed on Biblical authority that children should submit entirely to their parents' dictates:

The question here [he says] is not, what children in regards either of age or wit are able for to do but what God hath thought meet & expedient. . . . For there are many children found sometimes far to exceede their fathers in wit and in wisedome, yea and in all other giftes both of mind & body, yet is this no good reason that they should take upon them their fathers authoritie.[6]

In his *Catechism* (1560), Becon is not talking in terms of 'what God hath thought meet and expedient' but of what is in the *interest* of children. He warns maidens that when they come to marry, they should—

presume not to take in hand so graue, weighty and earnest matter, nor entangle them selues with the loue of anye person, before they haue made their parents, tutors, frendes, or suche as haue gouernaunce of them priuye of their entent, yea and also require their both councel and consent in the matter.[7]

The views of Becon and Stockwood are traditional, and by and large acceptable to most people in the age. But Shakespeare's age is in a process of change, and in such periods of history traditional ideas have a tendency of being quietly ignored. Moreover, the two ideas spread by contemporary preachers, namely, that children should obey their parents in all matters without question (this being the spirit of the fifth commandment) and that an ideal Christian marriage is one 'wherein one man and woman are coupled and knit together . . . by the *free . . . consente* of them both',[8] (Italics mine), are clearly contradictory. The position seems to be that while religious scriptures are the normal diet on which Elizabethans are fed, there are occasions when social realities or the needs of human beings dictate a different course of action. In the ultimate analysis it all depends on the individuals. It should, however, be admitted that by and large Elizabethan children obey their parents and are indeed willing to sacrifice their personal urges and aspirations at the altar of parental obedience. Only rarely do we come across individuals who disobey their parents and act in defiance of accepted norms of conduct.

It would, of course, be wrong to claim that all contemporary conduct-books *dogmatically* insist on the absolute right of parents to impose their will on their children in the matter of marriage. Some of them do recommend a more flexible approach to social questions in the interest of social harmony. Charles Gibbon's book entitled *A Work Worth the Reading* (1591) is clearly one of them. It presents both traditional and advanced views on the question of parent-child relationship for the consideration of its readers. In the form of a dialogue between 'two lovers of learning', Tychichus and Philogus, Gibbon specifically discusses the question 'whether the election of the parents is to be preferred before the affection of their children in marriage.' It is significant that Tychicus, who defends the 'right of parents in marriage', supports 'his arguments more from the Scriptures', whereas Philogus, who speaks for the children, does so 'rather from common experience'. Tychicus' argument is simple: 'if a man may bestow his goods to whom he will, he may as well bestow his children where he thinkest best, for children are the goods of parents.' Philogus' answer to this is 'that if parents impose upon their children a match more to content their desire for more than their children's goodly choice for love then they should not be obeyed, for what greater occasion of incontinency could be given than to match a young and lusty maid against her own mind with an infirm and decrepit person to satisfy another's pleasure?' Even Tychicus has to admit 'that to match a young maid and an old man is indeed most miserable.'⁹ Tychicus cannot help recognizing that the imposition of parents' will on children can degenerate into a serious social evil, leading not only to domestic unhappiness but also to immorality and family disruption.

G. B. Harrison, in his note on Gibbon's work, tells us that 'the question of the rights of parents to enforce a marriage on their children was much discussed at this time, especially after the sensational murder of old Mr Page of Plymouth by his girl-wife Ulalia in 1590, recorded in ballads, a pamphlet, and afterwards in a play (now lost) by Jonson and Dekker.'¹⁰ For our purposes, some lines from Thomas Deloney's broadside ballad on the incident, entitled 'The Lamentation of Mr Pages Wife of Plimouth, who, being forc'd to wed him, consented to his Murder, for the love of G. Strangwidge: for which they suffered at Barnstable in Deuonshire', are most relevant:

> On knees I prayde they would not me constrain;
> With teares I cryde their purpose to refrain;
> With sighes and sobbes I did them often move,
> I might not wed whereas I could not loue. (11.17–20)
>
> You parents fond, that greedy-minded bee,
> And seeke to grafte upon the golden tree,

Consider well and rightful judges bee,
And give your doome betwixt parents' loue and mee.
I was their childe, and bound for to obey,
Yet not to loue where I no loue could laye.
I married was to much and endless strife;
But faith before had made me Strangwide wife.   (11.57–64)

You Denshire dames, and courteous Cornwall knights,
That here are come to visit wofull wights,
Regard my griefe, and marke my wofull end,
But to your children be a better friend.   (11.69–72)[11]

It is clear that traditional views regarding the right of parents to impose their will on their children are not being accepted by all, and there are several writers in the period who are offering advanced views on the subject. There was indeed a general ferment in the air, and all kinds of writers – both churchmen and others – were jumping into the fray. Books on domestic relations were in fact so popular that there are instances in this period when, under different names, the same writer wrote on both sides of the question.

We have already seen Thomas Becon advising maidens not to 'entangle themselves with the love of any person' without their parents' *consent*, and at the same time saying that an ideal Christian marriage is based on a *free consent* of both the partners. It is also significant that Becon attacks enforced marriages involving dowry and child marriages. 'We see daily by experience', he says in his *The Book of Matrimony* (1564), 'that they [the nobility] for the most part marry their children at their pleasure when they are very young, even to such as will give them most money for them, as men use to sell their horses, oxen, sheep, or any other cattle.'[12] In another passage he talks of the 'abuse' of 'authority' by some parents who 'sell' their children 'to be married for worldly gain.' There is also a passage in Shakespeare which mentions people bargaining in marriage as they bargain for 'oxen, sheep, or horse.' The burden of the passage, however, is that it is dishonourable for a prince or a noble man to marry for money. Suffolk in *King Henry VI Part I* has, of course, a personal motive in arranging the marriage of Henry VI with Margaret, the daughter of Reigner, Duke of Anjou and titular King of Naples, but Exeter objects to this marriage on the ground that she will bring no dowry as 'Reigner sooner will receive than give' (V.v. 47). Suffolk's reply to this must surely reflect the sentiments of at least some of Shakespeare's contemporaries:

> A dow'r, my lords: Disgrace not so your king,
> That he should be so abject, base and poor,
> To choose for wealth and not for perfect love.
> Henry is able to enrich his queen,
> And not seek a queen to make him rich.
> So worthless peasants bargain for their wives,
> As market-men for oxen, sheep, or horse.
> Marriage is a matter of more worth
> Than to be dealt in by attorneyship;
> ....
> For what is wedlock forced but a hell,
> An age of discord and continual strife?
> Whereas the contrary bringeth bliss,
> And is a pattern of celestial peace.   (V.v.48–56, 62–65)

Suffolk is clearly unfair to the 'peasants' as the upper classes were more to blame than the lower or the lower-middle classes, for they had more to bestow on their daughters. But his general point that forced marriages can cause great unhappiness is very true. Wright cites a passage from an anonymous journalistic pamphlet entitled *Tell-Trothes New-Yeares Gift* which appeared in 1593 – more or less at the time when Shakespeare was emerging as a playwright – which describes compulsion by parents as the chief cause of unhappiness in marriage:

The first cause (quoth he) is a constrained loue, when as parentes do by compulsion coople two bodies, neither respectinge the joyninge of their heartes, nor havinge any care for the continuance of their wellfare, but more regardinge the linkinge of wealth and money together, then of loue with honesty: will force affection without liking, and cause love with jelousy. For either they marry their children in their infancy, when they are not able to know what love is, or else matche them with inequality, joyning burning summer with kea-cold winter, their daughters of twentye yeares olde or vnder, to rich cormorants of threescore or vpwards.[13]

Amongst secular writers there is Francis Bacon in whose *The New Atlantis* one of the merchants says: 'They say that ye have put marriage out of office. . . . And when they do marry, what is marriage to them but a very bargain; wherein is sought alliance, or portion, or reputation, with some desire (almost indifferent) of issue; and not the faithful nuptial union of man and wife that was first instituted.'[14]

Most of the attacks on marriages of convenience were, of course, prompted by the new spirit of individualism which was sweeping across the country. Though many of the Puritans may never have intended it, the emphasis on the individual in their thinking inevitably led to marriage being treated as an affair between two individuals. To demand the assertion of individual rights in religious, political and economic spheres and yet to deny these rights in the domestic sphere would have been grossly dishonest. Such ideas could not, however, easily change traditional modes of thought, more particularly when obedience to parents was a fundamental tenet of all sermons. Moreover, since 'The Tudor family was an institution for the passing on of life, name and property', 'obedience to parental orders was . . . held not only to be a moral duty, but also in the child's best interests.'[15] Often children had no option but to obey when their fathers made their bequests conditional upon strict obedience. Stone mentions the case of the second Earl of Southampton who stipulated in his will that both portion and maintenance were to be cut off entirely if his daughter disobeyed the executors.[16] 'Such clauses', says Stone, 'were common in the sixteenth and continued to appear in the early seventeenth century, though with diminishing frequency and with diminishing effect.'[17] From this Stone concludes that 'on the basis of surviving evidence, the doctrine of the absolute right of parents over the disposal of their children was weakening in the late sixteenth and early seventeenth centuries.'[18] This may explain why King James put a limitation on the absolute authority of parents in his well-known declaration that 'parents may forbid their children an unfit marriage, but they may not force their consciences to a fit.'[19]

II

King James' declaration, unfortunately, is too vague to be helpful to children. For instance, who is to decide whether a match is a fit or an unfit one? Desdemona's father clearly regards her marriage to Othello an unfit one, though his reasons for thinking so are not very laudable. Hermia's father, in *A Midsummer Night's Dream*, who regards her marriage to Lysander equally unfit gives reasons that are altogether incomprehensible. So how can anyone judge a fit from an unfit marriage? And yet society would not normally challenge the right of these fathers to take a final deci-

sion in the matter. It is curious, however, that neither of the
fathers succeeds in preventing the marriage. What is still more
curious is the fact that even though both the daughters disobey
their fathers they never lose our sympathy. Indeed, our sympathies are so much on their side that we resent the utterly irrational
and vindictive conduct of the fathers. From this – and also from
the general tone of Shakespeare's plays – we may conclude that
Shakespeare is sympathetic to the children's point of view. His
view seems to coincide with that of Philogus in Gibbon's *A Work
Worth the Reading* and this may be the reason why nowhere in
Shakespeare is there a typical 'morality' situation showing the
evils of marriages made against the wishes of parents. It would be
absurd to believe that Desdemona suffered because she disobeyed
her father. Her father's warning to Othello may have strengthened Iago's case against Desdemona:

> Look to her, Moor, if thou hast eyes to see:
> She has deceiv'd her father, and may thee.

(I.iii.292–3)

But the real tragedy of Desdemona has nothing to do with her
father. Nothing proves it more conclusively than Shakespeare's
treatment of his sources in this play. He wholly rejects Cinthio's
contention that Desdemona's case can serve as 'an example to
young women not to marry against the will of their families.'
Cinthio made Desdemona herself confess: 'Italian ladies may
learn from me not to link themselves to a man whom nature,
climate, and manner of life separate from us.'[20] All these factors,
including the colour difference, may have led to Desdemona's
tragedy. And yet at no stage does Shakespeare permit such
thoughts to enter Desdemona's mind. Indeed, such thoughts
come naturally only to Iago. It seems clear that Shakespeare
rejects the moralistic approach altogether and looks at the question of the parent–child relationship in the light of his understanding of human nature.

This rejection of the moralistic approach does not, however,
mean that Shakespeare ignores the compulsions and constraints
of a patriarchal family. These compulsions and constraints are
indeed the very stuff of which his plays are made. But it is notable
that almost nowhere does he present the parent–child conflict in
terms of simple parental tyranny. The case of *Romeo and Juliet*,

where this may seem to be true, is very instructive. To claim, as is
sometimes done, that this play shows the cruelty of parents in a
patriarchal family is not altogether fair. Unlike his sources,[21]
Shakespeare shows Capulet, whom we tend to regard as unreasonable and even irrational, as possessing some affection or at least
regard for his only daughter Juliet. He tells Paris in the second
scene of the play:

> But woo her, gentle Paris, get her heart;
> My will to her consent is but a part.
> And, she agreed, within her scope of choice
> Lies my consent and fair according voice.
>
> (I.ii.16–19)

Even Lady Capulet, who is often regarded by critics as a somewhat unsympathetic character, asks Juliet: 'What say you? Can
you love the gentleman?' (I.iii. 80). Juliet's reply shows that she is
a perfectly dutiful daughter:

> I'll look to like, if looking liking move;
> But no more deep will I endart mine eye
> Than your *consent* gives strength to make it fly.
>
> (I.iii.98–100)
> (Italics mine)

Thus, before the tragedy overtakes them, Shakespeare presents a
family in which the relationship between parents and daughter is
a conventional one. He even reflects the enlightened views of the
period in the scene where the parents ask their daughter's opinion
of the proposed match and the daughter in turn acquiesces in
their choice. But this, of course, is before Juliet sees Romeo who is
a Montague, and between whose family and hers there is a deadly
feud. Indeed, as soon as Juliet learns Romeo's identity, she is
filled with a sense of foreboding – 'My only love sprung from my
only hate! Too early seen unknown, and known too late'
(I.v.136–7) – for she realizes that their families, conditioned as they
are by their feudal outlook, are the real enemies of their love:

> O Romeo, Romeo! – wherefore art thou Romeo?
> Deny thy father and refuse thy name;
> Or, if thou wilt not, be but sworn my love
> And I'll no longer be a Capulet.   (II.ii.33–36)

For a patriarchal society, in which people are identified first by

their names and only then as individuals, Juliet propounds a
radical doctrine:

> 'Tis but thy name that is my enemy;
> Thou art thyself, though not a Montague.
> What's Montague? ....
> ....
> What's in a name? That which we call a rose
> By any other name would smell as sweet.
>
> (II.ii.37–40, 43–44)

'Thou art thyself, though not a Montague' makes no sense in a
patriarchal society. The name Montague by itself gives Romeo an
identity in such a society. Romeo is also conscious of this and
after Tybalt's death asks the Friar:

> O, tell me, friar, tell me,
> In what vile part of this anatomy
> Doth my name lodge?   (III.iii.106–108)

The play does begin with that 'freeing of sexuality from the ties of
family' which C. L. Barber finds a recurrent theme in Shakespeare's 'regular comedy'.[22] Here that process is not to be allowed to
operate without impediments. However, to believe that the sole
impediments are the parents would not do justice to the complex
pattern of the play. The parents certainly make their own contribution to the tragedy, as does the patriarchal system of the society
of which they are a product.[23] But there are other factors which
complicate the situation. As the Friar explains at the end of the
play, the lovers could still have been saved and the two families
brought together if some of the misadventures had not taken
place. The lovers were indeed 'star-crossed'.

There is no doubt that whatever Capulet does is, according to
him, in the best interests of his daughter. Lady Capulet proudly
calls him 'a careful father' (III.v.107), and it is beyond her comprehension and Capulet's that Juliet should not be happy with
the match that they are making. Count Paris has all the qualities
of an ideal husband, and when Juliet objects to him her mother
can only feel exasperated. Only a few minutes before, the father
had told Paris that they had 'had no time to move our daughter'
because of the death of Tybalt. But before Paris leaves, he adds:

> Sir Paris, I will make a desparate tender
> Of my child's love. I think she will be rul'd

In all respects by me; nay, more, I doubt it not.
                                              (III.iv.12–14)

And then comes the resistance of his daughter. It is in this context that we should take Capulet's outburst. He now talks of his 'decree' and threatens that if she does not go to church on the day appointed, he will 'drag [her] on a hurdle thither.' (III.v.155). Her mother is perturbed and intervenes, but Capulet is blinded by anger and completely loses his sense of proportion:

> Hang thee, young baggage! Disobedient wretch!
> I tell thee what – get thee to church a Thursday
> Or never after look me in the face.   (III.v.160–162)

This man will, of course, repent, but the repentance will come too late. It is noteworthy, however, that he is the first to extend his hand of friendship towards Montague:

> O brother Montague, give me thy hand.
> This is my daughter's jointure, for no more
> Can I demand.   (V.iii.296–298)

He is also the man who describes Romeo and Juliet as 'Poor sacrifices of our enmity.' (V.iii.304).

We may now ask whether the fault was that of the parents *alone*. We may also ask whether the parents were given a chance to show the depth of their affection. Capulet functioned all along in ignorance. His outbursts may be condemned – as they deserve to be – but would we be fair in saying that in this play Shakespeare is exposing the cruelty and tyranny of the patriarchal family? Surely he is presenting a complex picture in which many factors contribute to the tragedy – including parents and children. The real test of Capulet would have come if he had known the truth. The test never came and he bungled. But Shakespeare has not painted him as a monster.[24] His society would have regarded Capulet as an affectionate though unfortunate father.

III

The play does, however, expose one special feature of the patriarchal family. On the whole such a family is, in Stone's words, a 'low-keyed' and 'unemotional, authoritarian institution.'[25] Its chief shortcoming is not the tyranny of parents – though that is there – but the lack of communication between parents and children. Maynard Mack has summarized the usual attitude of parents as embodied in contemporary domestic advice books: 'Keep your distance from your children, never make companions of them, set them a good example.'[26] He cites Thomas Becon's advice to parents contained in his *Catechism* written in 1560. 'Laugh not with thy son', Becon says, 'lest thou weep with him also, and lest thy teeth be set on edge at the last. Give him no liberty in his youth and excuse not his folly. Bow down his neck while he is young: hit him on the sides while he is yet but a child, lest he wax stubborn and give no force of thee, and so thou shalt have heaviness of soul.' For comparison, Mack mentions the experience of Lady Jane Grey who confided to Roger Ascham when she was fifteen:

When I am in the presence either of father or mother, whether I speake, kepe silence, sit, stand, or go, eate, drinke, be merie or sad, be sowying, plaiying, dauncing, or doing anie thing els, I must do it, as it were, in such weight, measure, and number, even so perfitelie, as God made the world, or els I am so sharplie taunted, so cruellie threatened yea presentlie some tymes, with pinches, nippes, and bobbes, and other waies which I will not name, for the honour I beare them, so without measure misordered, that I thinke my selfe in hell. [27]

The plays of Shakespeare do not, of course, paint such a harsh picture, but there is no doubt that in them the lack of intimacy between parents and children persists. It is, after all, not an accident that Lady Capulet does not even remember the age of Juliet. Nor is it surprising that in a moment of crisis Juliet turns to her nurse and not to her mother. The father and the mother – however concerned they might otherwise be about her welfare – have never cared to understand her as a person. She is their only heir and it is their duty to find a suitable husband for her. But beyond this they seem to have no other interest in her. In such a situation a daughter cannot have sufficient courage to speak her mind. So she becomes secretive and feels that it is safer to deceive them. She is the product of a culture where, however courageous daughters may otherwise be, the presence of parents is intimidating, or at least inhibiting.

This does not happen to Juliet alone. She is, after all, only a girl of fourteen, but even Desdemona, who is a maturer person, deceives her father. Indeed, the father in this case is so shocked by her elopement that he can think only that Othello has used 'charms / By which the property of youth and maidhood / May be abus'd' (I.i.172–174). He tells Othello:

> Damn'd as thou art, thou hast enchanted her;
> For I'll refer me to all things of sense,
> If she in chains of magic were not bound,
> Whether a maid, so tender, fair, and happy,
> So opposite to marriage that she shunn'd
> The wealthy curled darlings of our nation,
> Would ever have – to incur a general mock,
> Run from her guardage to the sooty bosom
> Of such a thing as thou.   (I.ii.63–71)

'So tender, fair, and happy' – but how does he know whether she is happy or not? In traditional societies it is the mothers who try to understand the needs and urges of their daughters. Desdemona has no mother and Brabantio, an important senator, has hardly the time or the capacity to know Desdemona's mind. Even mothers like Juliet's are of no help. In aristocratic families, the care of children was left to servants and only very exceptional parents would care to spend time with them, especially if they were daughters. Desdemona is the typical shy daughter of a patriarchal family who instinctively knows that any show of independence would be resisted. So she quietly slips away to marry Othello. In every society women have to evolve their own strategies for self-expression and survival, and in this kind of a society deceit is perhaps the only strategy available.

In the comedies the daughters are more forthcoming – but not necessarily in their dealings with their parents. The father of Hermia in *A Midsummer Night's Dream*, for example, finds his daughter's conduct almost as incomprehensible as Desdemona's father does hers. He is completely puzzled that his daughter should prefer Lysander to Demetrius. He does not talk of 'drugs and minerals' but he, too, claims that his daughter's adolescence has been abused by charms. The charms in this case are, however, the normal modes of wooing in his society. He tells Lysander:

> Thou hast by moonlight at her window sung,
> With feigning voice, verses of feigning love,
> And stol'n the impression of her fantasy
> With bracelets of thy hair, rings, gauds, conceits,
> Knacks, trifles, nosegays, sweatmeats – messengers
> Of strong prevailment in unhardened youth.   (I.i.30–35)

In this play, however, the disagreement between father and daughter is not allowed to take an ugly turn even though it begins with a much more serious confrontation than the one in *Romeo and Juliet*. The stand taken by Hermia's father in the first scene makes him look not only much more irrational than Juliet's father but also much more inhuman. Capulet may have said harsh things to his daughter but surely he never wished her dead. Hermia's father, on the other hand, proposes in cold blood that if Hermia does not obey him, she should be put to death. It is perhaps best to hear his plea to Theseus, the Duke of Athens:

> And, my gracious Duke,
> Be it so she shall not here before your Grace
> Consent to marry with Demetrius,
> I beg the ancient privilege of Athens;
> As she is mine I may dispose of her;
> Which shall be either to this gentleman
> Or to her death, according to our law
> Immediately provided in that case. (I.i.38–45)

To give one's child the choice between the man the father has chosen as her spouse, and death – and to do it in the name of the law – is something that happens nowhere else in Shakespeare. This father is almost a monster compared to Capulet.

We should also notice that for all his sympathy for Hermia, the Duke accepts the father's right to dispose of her as he likes. He advises Hermia: 'To you your father should be as a god' (I.i.47). When Hermia pleads that when it comes to the choice of a husband her father should look 'but with my eyes' (I.i.57), the Duke replies with the wisdom of a whole tradition behind him: 'Rather your eyes must with his judgment look' (I.i.58). She pleads that she cannot marry Demetrius because she does not love him. When she makes bold to ask 'the worst that may befall me in this case, / If I refuse to wed Demstrius' (I.i.63–64), the Duke gives her only two options: either to die or to deny her sex and 'abjure / For ever the society of man' (I.i.65–66), and grow, live and die as a nun. Hermia gives perhaps the boldest reply that any daughter in Shakespeare's times could give:

> So will I grow, so live, so die, my lord,
> Ere I will yield my virgin patent up
> Unto his lordship, whose unwished yoke
> My soul consents not to give sovereignty. (I.i.79–82)

Neither her father nor the Duke relents. The Duke, in fact, advises her again 'To fit your fancies to your father's will.' (I.i.118). The situation is saved through the intervention of supernatural powers (embodied in Puck) and the play ends with the Duke administering a rebuff to Hermia's father: 'Egeus, I will overbear your will' (IV.i.176). He presides over the marriage of Hermia and Lysander and somehow the passion of youth and the judgment of age are reconciled in the play.

The same reconciliation is presented in *The Merchant of Venice*, and Portia is able to marry the man of her choice. But here again the daughter is confronted with an awkward situation. Her very first sentence in the play is not without significance: 'By my troth, Nerissa, my little body is aweary of this great world' (I.ii.1–2). When Nerissa tells her that she has no genuine reason to feel so, Portia starts a general discussion on the futility of sound advice and then adds: 'But this reasoning is not in the fashion to choose me a husband' (I.ii.16–17). It is this word 'choose' which makes her say what is perhaps constantly in her mind: 'O me, the word "choose"! I may neither choose who I would nor refuse who I dislike; so is the will of a living daughter curb'd by the will of a dead father. Is it not hard, Nerissa, that I cannot choose one, nor refuse none?' (I.ii.18–23). Nerissa's reply that Portia's father 'was ever virtuous, and holy men at their death have good inspirations' (I.ii.24–5) may be well enough, but there is no doubt that Portia is faced with 'the lott'ry of my destiny' (II.i.15) — which could go either way. Portia, therefore, has to manipulate this lottery and yet do so in such a way that no one gets the impression that she had not been 'obtained by the manner of my father's will' (I.ii.95). So at the critical moment, she subtly sways Bassanio's mind in the right direction. If this were not so, why introduce the song, 'Tell me where is Fancy bred?' Bullough says that this song 'cannot be intended as a clue laid by Portia' but he also concedes that 'it may be said to assist Bassanio by suggesting a distinction between outward appearances, the shortlived Fancy bred by them, and Truth.'[28]

Anne Page, in *The Merry Wives of Windsor*, also faces the threat of an arranged marriage. Both her parents have their own preferences but she loves Fenton, a young gentleman. Anne's father suspects that Fenton wants to marry Anne for her money. He is, therefore, determined that he will not give his consent to this marriage: ' if he take her, let him take her simply; the wealth I have waits on my consent, and my consent goes not that way.' (III.ii.65–67). He completely misunderstands Fenton, who, like the King of France in *King Lear*, believes that 'Love's not love / When it is mingled with regards that stands / Aloof from th' entire point.' (*King Lear*, I.i.238–240). He informs Anne that according to her father

> . . . 'tis a thing impossible
> I should love thee but as a property.   (III.iv.9–10)

He tells her in very candid terms:

> . . . I will confess thy father's wealth
> Was the first motive that I woo'd thee, Anne:
> Yet, wooing thee, I found thee of more value
> Than stamps in gold, or sums in sealed bags;
> And 'tis the very riches of thyself
> That I now aim at.   (III.iv.19–21)

Anne, however, is keen not to disobey her father, and so she tells Fenton:

> Yet seek my father's love; still seek it, sir.
> If opportunity and humblest suit
> Cannot attain it, why then – hark you hither. (III.iv.19–21)

At this stage, they converse apart. It is obvious that they will get married someday, but it is typical of the daughter that she will not disobey her father if she can help it. In this play she cannot help it, and so at last quickly slips away to marry Fenton. What Fenton says to her parents after the marriage is the best comment that we have in Shakespeare on contemporary 'forced' marriages:

> You would have married her most shamefully,
> Where there was no proportion held in love.
> The truth is, she and I, long since contracted,
> Are now so sure that nothing can dissolve us.
> Th' offence is holy that she hath committed;
> And this deceit loses the name of craft,
> Of disobedience, or unduteous title,
> Since therein she doth evitate and shun
> A thousand irreligious cursed hours,
> Which forced marriage would have brought upon her.
>   (V.v.208–217)

The girl's parents recognize the truth of what Fenton says and bless him.

It is characteristic of Shakespeare that even though he consistently rejects arranged marriages, he nowhere (except in 'this speech by Fenton) exposes the evils of such marriages. Unlike some of his contemporaries, he rejects the 'moralistic' approach either to evils caused by the defiance of parents by children or the imposition of unwanted suitors by parents on their children. In this play itself, there is a hilarious exposure of the whole institution of arranged marriages and yet there is not the slightest hint of a moral judgment. This exposure takes place in the scene where Master Slender – Anne's father's choice – is shown wooing Anne. Master Slender is a shy young man who needs the assistance and encouragement of his uncle, Master Shallow:

SHALLOW: She's coming; to her, coz. O boy, thou hadst a father!
SLENDER: I had a father, Mistress Anne; my uncle can tell you good jests of him. Pray you, uncle, tell Mistress Anne the jest how my father stole two geese out of a pen, good uncle.
SHALLOW: Mistress Anne, my cousin loves you.
SLENDER: Ay, that I do; as well as I love any woman in Gloucestershire.
SHALLOW: He will maintain you like a gentlewoman.
SLENDER: Ay, that I will come cut and long-tail, under the degree of a squire.
SHALLOW: He will make you a hundred and fifty pounds jointure.
ANNE: Good Master Shallow, let him woo for himself.
SHALLOW: Marry, I thank you for it; I thank you for that good comfort. She calls you, coz; I'll leave you.
ANNE: Now, Master Slender —
SLENDER: Now, good Mistress Anne —
ANNE: What is you will?
SLENDER: My will? 'Od's heartlings, that's a pretty jest indeed! I ne'er made my will yet, I thank heaven; I am not such a sickly creature, I give heaven praise.
ANNE: I mean, Master Slender, what would you with me?
SLENDER: Truly, for mine own part, I would little or nothing with you. Your father and my uncle hath made motions; if it be my luck, so; if not, happy man be his dole. They can tell you how things go better than I can. You may ask your father; here he comes.

(III.iv.36–65)

Nothing could have better established the absurdity of yoking Anne and Slender together than this scene. Shakespeare does not have to moralise, it is enough for him to show them together. Master Slender says elsewhere:

I will marry her, sir, at your request, but if there be no great love in the beginning, yet heaven may decrease it upon better acquaintance, when we are married and have more occasion to know one another. I hope upon familiarity will grow more contempt. But if you say 'marry her', I will marry her – that I am freely dissolved, and dissolutely.

(I.i.224–229)

If we forgive his slips of language – even the Welsh parson, Evans, catches one slip when he says the word should be 'resolutely' and not 'dissolutely' – what Slender says was happening in Shakespeare's age on a large scale.[29] In Shakespeare's plays, however, such marriages are consistently rejected.

V

The distinguishing feature of Shakespeare's plays is that even when the daughter rejects the arranged marriage, she never gives us the impression of *open rebellion* against her father or of violating the sacred bond that exists between parents and children. It is the fathers who are not willing to tolerate even the slightest disobedience from their daughters. In a patriarchal society, family honour or interest is so important that the happiness of children is of no consequence. Shakespeare does, of course, try to soften the harshness of a patriarchal society, but the fact remains that fathers in his plays do not find it easy to treat their children as individuals with minds of their own.

The daughter's constant attempt in Shakespeare is to reconcile love and respect for her father with duty towards her husband. Whenever she fails to do so, the fault is clearly that of the father. This is best seen in the case of Cordelia, the most affectionate daughter in all of Shakespeare. Cordelia describes her duty to her father and to the man she is going to marry:

> Good my lord,
> You have begot me, bred me, lov'd me; I
> Return those duties back as are right fit,
> Obey you, love you, and most honour you.
> Why have my sisters husbands, if they say
> They love you all? Haply, when I shall wed,
> That lord whose hand must take my plight shall carry
> Half my love with him, half my care and duty.
> Sure I shall never marry like my sisters,
> To love my father all.
> (I.i.95–103)

Her language sounds somewhat blunt in the circumstances – 'Let

pride, which she calls plainness, marry her' (I.i.128), retorts the
father – but the position regarding the relationship between
children and parents is deliberately softened by Cordelia so as not
to hurt her father. Cordelia cannot state the correct position in
view of what Goneril and Regan have said. King Lear clearly is
one of those possessive fathers who want their daughters 'to love
[their] father all.' Goneril and Regan know how to exploit this
weakness of his character, whereas Cordelia, in the context of
their fawning lies, has no option but to talk of 'half' of her love
for her father and 'half' for the man she is going to marry.

The correct position is stated by Desdemona in *Othello* when
she claims that the girl owes a greater duty to her husband than to
her father:

> My noble father,
> I do perceive here a divided duty:
> To you I am bound for life and education;
> My life and education both do learn me
> How to respect you; you are the lord of duty —
> I am hitherto your daughter; but here's my husband,
> And so much duty as my mother show'd
> To you, preferring you before her father,
> So much I challenge that I may profess
> Due to the Moor, my lord.   (I.iii.180–187)

Erasmus, Dod and Cleaver had written about the love that a husband owed his wife in comparison with the love that he owed his
parents, but obviously what they have to say is applicable both to
husband and wife. Erasmus had said as early as 1526 that God had
prescribed the laws of marriage saying: 'And they [husband and
wife] shall be two in one flesh. And for this shall a man leave his
father and mother, and cleave to his wife.'[30] It was taken for
granted by the age that a daughter owed greater loyalty to her
husband than to her parents. The preachers, therefore, emphasized that the husband too owed greater loyalty to his wife than to
his parents. Dod and Cleaver in *A Godlie Forme of Household
Government* (1612) said:

Matrimony then, being an indissoluble bond and knot, whereby the
husband and wife are fastened together by the ordinance of God, is farre
straighter than any other coiunction in the society of mankind. Inso-
much that it is lesse offence for a man to foresake father and mother, and
to leave them succourlesse, (who nothwithstanding ought, by Gods com-

mandment to be honoured) than it is for him to doe the like towards his lawful married wife.[31]

Desdemona is really saying the obvious but Brabantio – another possessive father – is shattered by her reply. All that he can say is:

> For your sake, jewel,
> I am glad at soul I have no other child;
> For thy escape would teach me tyranny,
> To hang clogs on them.　　　　　　　(I.iii.195–197)

The fact, however, is that fathers like Brabantio always try to 'hang clogs' on their children and do harm both to the children and to themselves.

VI

Perhaps the ideal father in Shakespeare is Prospero. He has brought up his daughter since she was three years of age, and in his banishment she has been his only comfort. At one stage, she says:

> Alack, what trouble
> Was I then to you!　　　　　　　(I.ii.151–152)

What Prospero says in reply at once indicates not only the depth of his affection for her but also the nature and sustaining quality of this affection:

> O, a cherubin
> Thou wast that did preserve me! Thou didst smile,
> Infused with a fortitude from heaven.
> 　　　　　　　(I.ii.152–154)

There is another daughter in Shakespeare who preserves the life of her father, and the father (Pericles) says to the daughter (Marina):

> O, come hither.
> Thou that beget'st him that did thee beget　(V.i.193–194)

But Pericles finds sustaining power in Marina precisely because she reminds him of his wife:

> My dearest wife
> Was like this maid, and such a one
> My daughter might have been: my queen's
> 　　　　　square brows;

> Her stature to an inch; as wand-like straight;
> As silver-voic'd; her eyes as jewel-like,
> And cas'd as richly; in face another Juno
>
> (V.i.106–110)

The daughter, it is true, restores him to life, but, as D. W. Harding says, his restoration is 'as lover of his wife'.[32] This is evident in Thaisa's 'sexual response' to him in her very first words:

> O, let me look!
> If he be none of mine, my sanctity
> Will to my sense bend no licentious ear,
> But curb it, spite of seeing.   (V.iii.29–32)

Pericles' response, too, is that of a lover:

> O, come, be buried
> A second time within these arms.   (V.iii.44–45)

The relationship between Prospero and Miranda, however, is a special one. She has known no mother, nor any man apart from Prospero. Prospero is both a father and a mother to her and all his actions are motivated by only one desire: to secure a happy future for her. When he raises the storm with the help of his magic powers, he tells her:

> I have done nothing but in care of thee,
> Of thee, my dear one.   (I.ii.16–17)

He has also given her whatever education he was in a position to give:

> and here
> Have I, thy school master, made thee more profit
> Than other princess' can, that have more time
> For vainer hours, and tutors not so careful.
>
> (I.ii.171–174)

One may not necessarily agree with Prospero's high notion of himself as a tutor[33] but the fact remains that Miranda embodies in her character the highest feminine virtues, according to the best ideas of the age. Her father's role, however, does not end with her education: he has also to arrange her marriage. Indeed the entire action initiated by the storm moves in that direction. When Prospero sees that Ferdinand and Miranda are charmed by each other, he is delighted. He sees that 'At the first sight / They have chang'd eyes' (I.ii.440–441), but as a man of the world he decides that 'this swift business / I must uneasy make, lest too light winning / Make the prize light.' (I.ii.450–52). His daughter is too innocent for the world outside and her happiness can be blasted by a false step. He therefore does something that his age, unlike the present one, would have regarded a normal part of parental duty: he watches over the wooing between Ferdinand and Miranda. Miranda does not know, what Shakespeare and his age regarded as the most important part of contemporary sex education, that premarital sex can destroy the very possibility of a happy married life. To save this kind of a relationship from contamination, he has no option but to warn Ferdinand:

> If thou dost break her virgin-knot before
> All the sanctimonious ceremonies may
> With full and holy rite be minister'd,
> No sweet aspersion shall the heavens let fall
> To make this contract grow; but barren hate,
> Sour–ey'd disdain, and discord, shall bestrew
> The union of your bed with weeds so loathly
> That you shall hate it both: therefore take heed,
> As Hymen's lamps shall light you.   (IV.i.15–23)

Ferdinand's reply (IV.i.24–28) is not only reassuring, but it is clear from it that he understands the full implication of what Prospero has said.

The way Prospero watches over Ferdinand and Miranda – and especially his warning to Ferdinand – may leave a somewhat unpleasant impression on a modern reader. But we should not forget that in this respect, Prospero reflects the anxiety of a typical Elizabethan father, especially one belonging to the nobility. In those times, much more than in ours, loss of virginity was viewed by society as a total disaster. This is reflected in Polonius' fear of Hamlet's interest in Ophelia, and very much more in the reaction of Hero's father in *Much Ado About Nothing*, when the father, believing that his daughter has lost her virginity, wishes her dead. This also explains, among other reasons, why parents were anxious to get their daughters married at a very early age. In fact we should take more kindly to early marriages in that period because of a law amongst the aristocracy by which 'an heiress who was demonstrated to have been unchaste was deprived of her inheritance.'[34] In view of this, parents were anxious that their daughters not be exposed to temptation.[35] Moreover, the fact that 'late in the reign of the first Queen Elizabeth, the proportion of bastard births could reach 9 per cent to 10 per cent over whole decades in certain parishes in Lancashire and Cheshire',[36] should be more than enough to explain the Elizabethan father's anxiety.

This anxiety is particularly visible in the last plays, which seem to have been written from a father's point of view. In these plays, as Betrand Evans has said, 'the worlds upon which Marina, Imogen, and Perdita are cast are such as might occur to the imagination of a father fearful for his own daughters after he is gone.' It is owing to such a fear that 'Of four heroines of the romances, three, Marina, Imogen and Miranda, narrowly miss being raped.'[37] It is not easy to explain why Shakespeare should be so obsessed with rape at this stage of his career. To claim that his concern for his own daughters' welfare is behind this obsession is, of course, mere speculation.[38] It is, however, clear that Prospero reflects this concern in a much more tangible form than any other father in Shakespeare. The chief merit of Prospero is that the moment he is assured of a suitable husband for Miranda he renounces his magic and drowns his book. He declares that his role is over and that all he has to do is to go to Naples —

> Where I hope to see the nuptial
> Of these our dear-belov'd solemnized;
> And thence retire me to my Milan, where
> Every third thought shall be my grave. (V.i.308–311)

This father is not possessive, as King Lear was. He does not wish that his daughter should 'love [her] father all.' He knows that she has a life of her own to live. It is enough comfort to him that she is safe and happy in the new world that she is entering.

VII

We may conclude with a few general observations. It is clear that Shakespeare is keen to prevant family disruption. Disruption does, of course, occur sometimes, but generally speaking, Shakespeare offers a sane point of view which recognizes both the urges of youth and the traditional role of old age. Not all fathers in his society are able to see the young people's point of view, but there is no doubt that the tendency of Shakespeare's plays is to accommodate the old and the young and allot an appropriate place to

each. Shakespeare avoids extreme positions, and barring one or
two cases, the movement is towards a compromise. The language
used by Proteus' father in *The Two Gentlmen of Verona* while
asking his son to go to Milan to join Valentine, sounds clearly
exceptional:

> Muse not that I thus suddenly proceed;
> For what I will, I will, and there an end. (I.iii.64–65)

In other cases – including that of Capulet – the arbitrariness of the
father's conduct is provided proper motivation. Some Elizabethan
fathers may have acted like Proteus' father, but they do not seem
to be Shakespeare's models.

In the case of children too, Shakespeare avoids both extreme
rebellion and extreme submission. Hero in *Much Ado about
Nothing* is a wholly submissive daughter, but by introducing
Beatrice Shakespeare deliberately undercuts her docile attitude.
Ophelia in *Hamlet* is quite similar to Hero. When her father tells
her that she is a 'green girl' (I.iii.102) who does not 'understand
[herself] so clearly / As it behoves [his] daughter and [her]
honour' (I.iii.96–7), she quietly submits. Her attitude to her
brother is not as submissive. When he warns her against 'the
trifling of [Hamlet's] favour' (I.iii.5) and advises her not to
encourage him, she retorts:

> But, good my brother,
> Do not, as some ungracious pastors do,
> Show me the steep and thorny way to heaven,
> Whiles, like a puff'd and reckless libertine,
> Himself the primrose path of dalliance treads
> And recks not his own rede. (I.iii.46–51)

Ophelia, however, never gets a chance to grow into adulthood and
is so badly let down by Hamlet that she does not know where to
look for strength.

It is instructive to compare what Mildred, a daughter in Chap-
man's *Eastward Ho,* says to her father with the usual attitude of
daughters in Shakespeare: 'Sir, I am all yours; your body gave me
life; your care and love, happiness of life; let your virtue still
direct it, for to your wisdom I wholly dispose myself.' 'For to your
wisdom I wholly dispose myself' – is not a position that Shakespeare demands from daughters in his plays. Even Hero is not
made to express such sentiments, though perhaps she is the only

daughter in Shakespeare whose conduct reflects them most accurately. Beatrice, of course, reflects an altogether different attitude to parental authority. When Hero's uncle says to her 'Well, niece, I trust you will be ruled by your father' (II.i.44–5), Beatrice anticipates Hero's docile answer and intervenes: 'Yes, faith: it is my cousin's duty to make curtsy and say, "Father, as it please you". But yet for all that, cousin, let him be a handsome fellow, or else make another curtsy and say, "Father, as it please me"' (II.i.46–49). Hibbard has asked: 'I should dearly like to know how the original audience for the play, somewhere about the year 1598, responded to that sally, which must have been at least as delightfully shocking as Liza Doolittle's "Not bloody likely" would be some three hundred years later.'[39] But surely, as Peter Malekin says, 'while an audience's normal emotional responses may be extended, they cannot be ignored.'[40] Moreover, Beatrice merely sums up the contemporary debate on the children's right to choose their spouses and she tries to be fair to both children and parents. She is, of course, putting it in provocative language, and largely from a child's point of view. Obey your parents, as far as possible, she says, but not when they impose an unfit marriage on you: when that happens, have the courage to say, 'Father, as it please me'. That most Elizabethan daughters were not able to say so is a different matter, but Beatrice is not alone in holding the views she does.

We are not surprised when a sensible girl like Rosalind says: 'But what talk we of fathers when there is such a man as Orlando.' (III.v.35). We do understand her state of mind. In the first flush of passion, all young men and women tend to forget that parents are also important. C. L. Barber's view that 'In the festive comedies proper, holiday liberty frees passion from inhibition and the control of the older generation' is wholly correct. But this need not mean that this 'sexuality' frees young men and women *wholly* from 'the ties of family'.[41] That is often only a temporary phase. Moreover, it is applicable to all young people in love, irrespective of whether they belong to 'the festive comedies proper' or to other kinds of plays. We have already seen this happen in *Romeo and Juliet*. We also see it in *Troilus and Cressida*. Cressida's statement on this question is, infact, even plainer than Rosalind's. When told by Pandarus that she has to go to her father and leave Troilus, Cressida replies:

I will not, uncle. I have forgot my father.
I know no touch of consanguinity,
No kin, no love, no blood, no soul so near me
As the sweet Troilus.   (IV.i.95–98)

In *As You Like It* Rosalind's statement about fathers and Orlando
is made in a state of excessive emotional exuberance. In her saner
moments she may not have made it. After all, it is not without
significance that before offering her hand to Orlando, Rosalind
asks her father's permission. Rosalind addresses herself to the
Duke and to Orlando, but first she speaks to the Duke:

To you I give myself, for I am yours.

Then she says the same thing to Orlando. It is appropriate that
Rosalind should offer herself in this way to her father and to the
man she is going to marry, for she belongs to both of them. The
interesting thing about *As You Like It* is that even in a superla-
tively successful 'romantic' play, Shakespeare does not distort
contemporary social reality. There is no distortion even with
Celia who is clearly a rebel against her father. In renouncing the
world, her father Frederick also renounces his role as a father, and
very appropriately that role is taken over by the banished Duke
who is now a father both to her and to Rosalind. The play ends in
all–round domestic harmony.

VIII

The treatment of the relationship between parents and children
in Restoration comedy offers a sharp contrast to that of Shakespeare's. Shakespeare's attempt was to reconcile the points of view
of parents and children. There were, of course, conflicts – sometimes leading to tragedy – but Shakespeare's consistent attempt
was to restore the affection between parents and children and thus
to work for family solidarity. In Restoration drama, the position
is completely changed. The comedy of the period especially,
espouses the point of view of youth, and by and large treats the
old with contempt.

The writers of 'conduct-books' in the period were still as conservative in their outlook as their predecessors in the earlier
period. They preached total obedience to parents in all matters,
and specially in the matter of marriage. In *The Whole Duty of
Man* (1659) – a very popular moral guide of the period – we are

told: 'of all the acts of *disobedience*, that of marrying *against the consent of the Parents*, is one of the highest. Children are so much the goods, the Possessions of the Parent, that they cannot, without a kind of *theft*, give away themselves without the allowance of those that have the right in them' (p. 291). The maximum concession that the moralists made was that both parents and children be allowed the right of veto in the choice of a spouse. We may notice that even this is quite an advance on the position taken by King James I when he declared that 'parents may forbid their children an unfit marriage, but they may not force their consciences to a fit.' King James seems to give the right of veto only to the parents, though he does reject forced marriages. Mary Astell was wholly dissatisfied with the position of daughters in the seventeenth century and complained in *Some Reflections on Marriage* that the power of veto granted to a daughter hardly gave her the right to choose a husband: 'all that is allowed her, is to Refuse or Accept what is offer'd.' But even this right placed her in a much happier position than her counterpart in the Elizabethan age.

Whatever the limitations of Restoration comedy, it is only fair to say that this comedy does make a spirited attempt to challenge orthodox views on the question of the children's right to choose their spouses. In Shakespearean comedy daughters did finally succeed in marrying the men of their choice, but we should not forget that in Shakespeare's world parental authority was a fact of life, and children were expected not to ignore it. One of the most typical situations occurs in *The Winter's Tale* when Florizel is about to offer his hand to Perdita in a formal 'contract' before witnesses. Florizel's father, Polixenes, who is in disguise, feels compelled to intervene at this stage and asks Florizel whether he has a father. When Florizel replies in the affirmative, he asks him whether he knows about his proposed marriage. When Florizel says: 'He neither does nor shall' (IV.iv.385), Polixenes replies:

> Methinks a father
> Is at the nuptial of his son a guest
> That best becomes the table.   (IV.iv.386–88)

Polixenes, without disclosing his identify yet, also reminds Florizel that his entering into a formal contract with Perdita without his father's knowledge and permission is 'a wrong / Something unfilial' (IV.iv.396–7) and states what Elizabethans would have regarded as an eminently reasonable and indeed enlightened position:

> Reason my son
> Should choose himself a wife; but as good reason
> The father – all whose joy is nothing else
> But fair posterity – should hold some counsel
> In such a business.   (IV.iv.397–402)

Florizel is not in a position to seek his father's 'counsel' but he recognizes the correctness of Polixenes' stand. Children in Restoration comedy, by and large, reject this position, and it is not an accident that over one third of all Restoration comedies contain successful clandestine marriages, mostly in defiance of parental bans.[42] Moreover, the mere fact that most comedies in the period often present the conflict between parents and children over love and marriage as their most prominent theme, must surely have some social significance.

The assertion by children of their right to choose their spouses must have been encouraged by the relaxed cultural climate of the period. How else can we explain the sudden decline – and almost disappearance – of the flogging of children both at school and at home after 1660? Stone's finding is that 'Flogging at the universities certainly died out altogether after 1660s – the last known case at Cambridge was in 1667.'[43] Much before Locke came to condemn flogging and all other kinds of physical punishment given to children, an anonymous pamphlet of 1669 put these words into the mouth of boys: 'our sufferings are of that nature as makes our schools to be not merely houses of correction, but of prostitution, in this vile way of castigation in use, wherein our secret parts . . . must be the anvil exposed to the immodest and filthy blows of the smiter.'[44] It seems strange that the question of corporal punishment in schools should have been raised in this somewhat indirect way by some of the contemporary writers. But even this showed a new awareness of the role of children in families. Most Puritan homes clearly believed that it was necessary to break the spirit of rebellion in the child by inflicting physical punishment, and thereby making him a suitable Christian. This naturally meant harsh treatment, often leading to physical torture. After the Restoration the situation seems to have changed quite radically, and people start frowning upon such treatment.

It seems clear that many parents in the later seventeenth century started showing greater concern for their children's welfare. One effect of this seems to have been a new tendency amongst affluent parents to withdraw their children from school and to educate them at home. There may also have been other reasons for this development. Stone, for instance, has said that the 'main cause for the withdrawal of the elite from the grammar school to the home was the same one as that which caused the withdrawal from the University, namely the fear of moral contamination from other boys, especially boys of lower social status.'[45] The almost brutal treatment meted out to children in many schools must also have been a powerful motive with some parents. In any case, it seems clear that many upper–class parents in the period started taking greater interest in the education of their children. This must have led to a more companionate relationship between parents and children, leading naturally to a greater assertion of independence by children, especially in the matter of the choice of their spouse. During the later years of the century there was the clear advice of John Locke to his contemporaries: 'he that would have his Son have a Respect for him, and his Orders, must himself have a great Reverence for his Son.'[46]

The kind of affectionate relationship recommended by Locke, however, reflected the thinking of the rising middle classes after 1688 and has hardly much relevance for the restored aristocracy after 1660. It is this aristocracy which set the tone of Restoration comedy. In their case the assertion of individuality by children tended not to cement but to disrupt family solidarity. Indeed the younger generation of this class was clearly in open rebellion against the older generation, and it is this rebellion that is depicted in Restoration comedy. This comedy is essentially sub-versive of conventional moral values, and shows youth in revolt against all traditional modes of behaviour. Though Congreve's *The Old Bachelor* comes very late in the period, its first few lines reflect most accurately the temper of the younger generation of the earlier period: 'Come, come, leave business to idlers, and wis-dom to fools; they have need of 'em: wit, be my faculty, and pleasure my occupation; and let Father Time shake his glass. Let low and earthly souls grovel till they have worked themselves six foot deep into a grave. Business is not my element – I roll in a higher orb.' Bellmour, the speaker of these lines, rejects more

than he mentions. He not only rejects all that made England great
in the two succeeding centuries, but also all that makes for a
civilized life. Congreve did not, of course, accept Bellmour as a
model. His own Mirabel (in *The Way of the World*) would have
found him boring, and Millamant might have taken him for a
distant cousin of Anthony Witwoud.

The attitude of young men like Bellmour – and the havoc that
they can play with normal social life – is perhaps best seen in
Thackeray's comments on Congreve:

Fathers, husbands, usurers are the foes these champions contend with.
They are merciless in old age, invariably, and an old man plays the part
in the dramas which the wicked enchanter or the great blundering giant
performs in the chivalry tales, who threatens and grumbles and resists – a
huge stupid obstacle always overcome by the knight. It is an old man
with a money-box: Sir Belmour his son or nephew spends his money and
laughs at him. It is an old man with a young wife whom he locks up: Sir
Mirabel robs him of his wife, trips up his gouty old heels, and leaves the
old hunks. The old fool, what business has he to hoard his money, or to
lock up blushing eighteen? Money is for youth, love is for youth, away
with the old people. When Mirabel is sixty, having of course divorced the
first Lady Millamant, and married his friend Doricourt's granddaughter
out of the rursery – it will be his turn and young Belmour will make a
fool of him.[47]

Thackeray is, of course, wrong about Mirabel, but his general
point about the attitude of the young towards the old is well
made.

IX

In a situation where most marriages are arranged, conflict
between parents and children is inevitable. In this period the
situation becomes particularly difficult owing to the declining
fortunes of the aristocracy and the landed gentry. The Restoration
was only a political arrangement bringing no appreciable economic advantage to members of this class. In such a situation,
parents are naturally anxious to improve the status of their family, or to prevent its decline, by a prudently arranged marriage, in
total disregard of their child's happiness. Indeed if any child
demanded that his or her wishes be consulted, parents are often
outraged. Their reaction is often understandable in view of their
feeling that the arrangements made by them for their children's
marriages could alone save their lands and honour. Whatever our

feelings regarding the right of children to choose their spouses, we cannot but sympathize with Henry, Lord Clarendon, who, on discovering that his son had married a woman of no portion without his consent, cried: 'O Lord! make me able to bear this irrecoverable blow. Good God! that my poor family should be brought into utter misery by him who was the only hopes of raising it. O Lord! my heart is even broke.'[48] Lord Halifax, in a letter to his brother Henry, dated March 1679/80, mentions his hopes of a better match for his son to further the interests of the family:

in the age we live in, and considering our sky looketh very changeable, and that we do not know what kind of weather we may have, the argument of alliance may grow much stronger, and it may so happen that in a shuffling and a distracted time, your nephew may by a wise and reasonable choice, by a thing well-timed, do a great deal towards the preservation of his family, if the times be such as to require it.[49]

These two illustrations refer to sons. But the marriages of daughters too, could be prudently arranged so that the interests of the family did not suffer much. Daughters did, of course, pose a threat, and like Merryman in Sedley's *Bellamira* (1687), many husbands were becoming conscious of the dangers of begetting girls 'without I know where to get the portions for them'. Merryman rightly said: 'In this age they [daughters] sour and grow stale upon their parents' hands' (III.iii). Parents, therefore, had to evolve strategies of their own. Dowries had to be given, but one way of saving on dowries was to palm off daughters to unworthy husbands. Such a practice must have been quite common, otherwise the many complaints made by women in Restoration comedy would not make sense. For instance, how does one explain the marriage of Mrs Pinchwife in *The Country Wife* or of Mrs Friendall in Southerne's *The Wives Excuse*? Such marriages were bound to lead to adultery, but considerations of this type were brushed aside by families which sought their own gain rather than the girl's happiness. It may sound strange to us to find Mrs Friendall's brother, Springtime, making this cynical comment on his sister's lot: 'She has satisfied her Relations enough in marrying this Coxcomb, now let her satisfie herself, if she pleases, with anybody she likes better' (I.i). But surely his statement merely highlights the total indifference of families to the lot of daughters after they had been disposed of in marriage.

Perhaps the most notorious example of a father planning to push his daughter into a hellish marriage purely for reasons of personal gain, occurs in Vanbrugh's *Aesop*. Aesop is old and ugly but he is the prince's favourite and so the father, Learchus, Governer of Cyzicus, wants to exploit the match to achieve a higher position for himself. His daughter makes it clear that she cannot accept Aesop as a husband but the father is determined that she should not only marry him but also love him. His attitude is best expressed here: 'We wise parents usually weigh our children's happiness in the scale of our own inclinations' (II.i). He is also confident that his daughter will obey him: 'my daughter will be governed, she's bred up to obedience' (II.i). Since the daughter is not able to oppose the designs of her father stoutly, her cause is taken up by her nurse, Doris. She reminds the father that such marriages lead inevitably to adultery. This, however, stings the father and the following conversation takes place between them:

LEAR : How, strumpet! would anything be able to debauch my daughter!
DOR : Your daughter? yes, your daughter, and myself into the bargain: a
    woman's but a woman; and I'll lay a hundred pound on nature's
    side. Come, sir, few words dispatch business. Let who will be the
    wife of Aesop, she's a fool, or he's a cuckold. But you'll never have a
    true notion of this matter till you suppose yourself in your daughter's
    place. As thus: You are a pretty, soft, warm, wishing young lady: I'm
    a straight, proper, handsome, vigorous, young fellow. You have a
    peevish, positive, covetous, old father, and he forces you to marry a
    little, lean, crooked, dry, sapless husband. This husband's gone
    abroad, you are left at home. I make you a visit; find you all alone;
    the servant pulls to the door; the devil comes in at the window. I
    begin to wheedle, you begin to melt; you like my person, and
    therefore believe all I say; so first I make you an atheist, and then I
    make you a whore. Thus the world goes, sir.   (III.i)

The daughter, of course, escapes this fate owing to Aesop's generosity, for he has only been testing the father. He arranges her marriage with the man she loves and denounces the father:

> . . . who's such a tyrant o'er his children
> To sacrifice their peace to his ambition.   (V)

The point that Vanbrugh – and indeed Restoration comedy in general – makes is that daughters are perfectly justified in rebelling against such parents. Not to do so would, in fact, be 'one continu'd Sin' (Mrs Behn's *The Town-Fop*, III.i).

There is another very interesting reason in this period why
children should rebel against their parents' wishes on the issue of
marriage. Arranged marriages were coming under attack owing
to a special feature of the new feminine culture emerging in the
later seventeenth century. Women were becoming much more
conscious of their figures as they were realizing that personal
beauty and deportment played no mean part in the marriage
market. If this were not so, playwrights and others – from Etherege to Addison – would not have found women's fashions such
an interesting subject for ridicule. Etherege puts this satirical
description in the mouth of Medley in *The Man of Mode*:

Then there is the *Art of Affectation*, written by a late beauty of quality,
teaching you how to draw up your breasts, stretch up your neck, to thrust
out your breech, to play with your head, to toss up your nose, to bite your
lips, to turn up your eyes, to speak in a silly soft tone of a voice, and use
all the foolish French words that will infallibly make your person and
conversation charming, with a short apology at the latter end, in the
behalf of young ladies, who notoriously wash, and paint, though they
have naturally good complexions.   (II.i)

Daughters fed on treatises like the *Art of Affectation* – we cannot
be too sure that Harriet herself had not mastered some of these –
were not likely to be deterred from insisting on the personal choice of a spouse. Harriet herself is an excellent example of this kind
of assertive daughter. She has no father, and her mother is not
very difficult to handle. But the point to note about her is her
declaration: 'Shall I be paid down by a covetous parent for a
purchase? I need no land; no, I'll lay myself out all in love' (III.i).
Such women could be fully depended upon to find some way to
assert their independence.

X

The protest of children against parental authority on the issue of
marriage is such a common theme in the contemporary drama
that it is perhaps best to choose only a few examples. A typical
example happens to be Thomas Porter's *The French Conjuror*
(1678). Porter's heroine, Clorinia, wishes· to marry her lover,
Dorido. In order to save himself a portion, however, her father
Avaritia intends to send her off to a nunnery. There is only one

course available to her and this is how her maid, Scintillia, persuades her to take it:

Madam, Love was never subject to any law, nor did ever call to its counsel Duty or Reason; and if so, why should you bring your Obedience to a doating old Father, in competition with the love and preservation of yourself and *Dorido*? Let the sacred knot be tied, Madam, and then farewell all dispute. Whether would you sacrifice yourself to a peevish old Father, or make yourself happy in an accomplish'd loving Husband? Come, be rul'd be me; stear the neerest course to your bliss.

(pp. 9–10)

The heroine gratefully accepts the advice and enters into a clandestine marriage.

This conflict between parental wish and the child's urge for personal fulfilment is seen at its best in Wycherley's *The Gentleman Dancing-Master* (1673). Hippolita is a prisoner in her father's house and we hear her protest in the very first scene: 'To confine a Woman just in her rambling Age! take away her liberty at the very time she shou'd use it! O barbarous Aunt! O unnatural Father!' She talks of her conflict with her aunt as between 'crabbed age and . . . youth' (I.i) and disagrees with her on almost every point, more particularly in her attitude to contemporary culture. The aunt regards fashionable society as dangerous for young girls and warns her niece of 'the fatal Liberty of this masquerading Age'. The niece, however, finds it 'a pleasant-well-bred-complascent-free-frolic-good-natur'd-pretty Age.' (I.i).

Hippolita's father wants her to marry her foolish cousin, a rich city-heir, but she is determined not to accept his choice. 'Fathers seldom choose well', she declares to her maid, 'I will no more take my Father's choice in a Husband, than I would in a Gown or a Suit of Knots' (I.i). It is clearly an indicator of the temper of the younger generation when we find another girl on the English stage in the same year, Hillaria in Ravenscroft's *The Careless Lovers* (1673), making a telling retort to her uncle: 'Do you think, Uncle, I ha'nt as much Wit to choose a Husband as you?' Wycherley is a much more consistent champion of the right of children to choose their spouses, and he therefore condemns contemporary mercenary marriages in the sharpest possible language. In *The Gentleman Dancing-Master* itself, he attacks 'the obstinacy and covetousness of Parents' (I.i) who marry off their daughters for their jointure:

For She whom Jointure can obtain—
To let a Fop her Bed enjoy,
Is but a lawful Wench for gain.   (II.i)

Such marriages never prosper, and Hippolita is perfectly justified in saying that in such cases, the daughter exchanges her father's 'slavery' for her husband's (II.i). Hippolita's clandestine marriage with the man of her choice shows her rejection of the mercenary and sordid values of her society. The play ends with this couplet spoken by Hippolita:

When Children marry, Parents shou'd obey,
Since Love claims more Obedience far than they.

In at least three of his plays Wycherley's main concern seems to be the conduct of parents and its impact on the conduct of children. In his first play, *Love in a Wood*, he shows us the consequences of a father locking up his daughter. Gripe – a 'seemingly precise, but a covetous, lecherous, old Usurer of the City', as the list of characters describes him – forbids Dapperwit, the man his daughter loves, from entering his house. The effect of this treatment is just the opposite of what is intended. The daughter meets him secretly and ultimately leaves home and marries him. Dapperwit is hardly an ideal husband but, as she confesses, because of her father's 'hard usage' of her, and 'to avoid slavery under him', she had agreed to 'stoop to [Dapperwit's] yoke' (V.i). Perhaps she does not know that her marriage with Dapperwit can become a real yoke. After all he is marrying her largely for her father's money and in case her father himself marries Lucy, as he has threatened, she may lose her importance in Dapperwit's eyes. And if it is also true, as she confesses to her father, that she is 'six months gone with Child' (V), then what choice has she? But that does not seem to concern anyone. The point that Wycherley makes is that a healthy approach to sex and marriage can develop only when parents trust their children and give them the freedom to choose their spouses. Where they deny them these rights, they run the risk of wrecking their lives.

The parents of Margery in *The Country Wife* have wrecked her life by pushing her into a mercenary marriage with Pinchwife, a lecherous old man of London. Pinchwife, who could 'never keep a Whore to [him] self' (I), believes that the only way to keep Margery faithful to him is to keep her under lock and key. So he treats her like a prisoner and Margery becomes a 'sullen Bird in a cage' (III). We know what happens to this marriage, but the best comment on the situation comes from Pinchwife's sister, Alithea: 'Brother, you are my only Censurer; and the honour of your Family shall sooner suffer in your Wife there, than in me, though I take the innocent liberty of the Town' (II). In the end, we find Alithea covering up for Margery (for whom she has sympathy): 'Come Brother your Wife is yet innocent you see, but have a care of too strong an imagination. . . . Women and Fortune are honest still to those that trust 'em' (V). Lucy's comment is equally pertinent: 'And any wild thing grows but the more fierce and hungry for being kept up, and more dangerous to the Keeper' (V). Alithea calls Lucy's statement 'a doctrine for all Husbands' (V). It is surely also a doctrine for all parents.

Another playwright with a similar doctrine to preach is Mrs Behn. Unfortunately, critics have tended to dismiss her plays as a compound of indecency and farce, and have failed to give her credit for highlighting some of the social evils of her times. There is no doubt that being a woman she is more acutely conscious of the crisis that daughters and wives face in her society than most of her contemporaries. She consistently condemns parents and guardians who force their children or wards to marry against their wishes. The theme of her first play, *The Forc'd Marriage* (1671), continues to haunt her almost throughout her career. The heroine of one of her later plays, *The Lucky Chance* (1687), laments:

> O, how fatal are forc'd Marriages!
> How many Ruins one such Match pulls on!
> Had I but kept my Sacred Vow to *Gayman*,
> How happy had I been – how prosperous he!
> Whilst now I languish in a loath'd embrace,
> Pine out my life with Age-Consumptions, Coughs.
>
> (I.ii)

It is clear that it is the mercenary and often totally un-understanding attitude of parents and guardians which is responsible for such marriages. There is, for instance, the case of Bellmour, the nephew of Lord Plotwell, in *The Town-Fop* (1677). Lord Plotwell wants Bellmour to marry Diana, his niece. But Bellmour is already 'contracted to Celinda'. He pleads with his uncle that he may be allowed to marry Celinda:

Oh pity me, my Lord, pity my Youth;
It is no Beggar, not one basely born,
That I have given my Heart to, but a Maid,
Whose Birth, whose Beauty, and whose Education
Merits the best of Men.   (II.iii)

But the uncle is not prepared to hear his pleas and threatens:
'Very fine! where is the Priest that durst dispose of you without
my Order? Sirrah, you are my Slave – at least your whole Estate is
at my mercy – and besides, I'll charge with an Action of 5000 £ for
your ten Years Maintenance: Do you know that this is in my
power too?' (II.iii). The nephew's revolt is natural in such circumstances, though in the process Diana suffers most.

There is another Diana, a daughter in *The Lucky Chance*
(1687), who revolts against a tyrannical father and speaks the
following couplet before she leaves his house to enter into a clandestine marriage with Bredwell, a 'Prentice' to him:

Father farewell – if you dislike my course,
Blame the old rigid Customs of your Force.   (V.i)

These 'rigid customs' are again attacked in *The Rover* (1677).
Florinda does not want to marry a man who has been chosen for
her by her father. When her brother tries to pursuade her to accept
their father's choice, she tells him: 'I hate *Vincentio*, and I would
not have a Man so dear to me as my Brother follow the ill Customs of our Country, and make a Slave of his Sister' (I.i). Her
younger sister, Hellena, is bolder still and encourages her to rebel
against both father and brother. Their father is away but their
brother is in the house and Florinda is nervous. But Hellena tells
her: 'We'll outwit twenty Brothers if you'll be ruled by me' (I.i). In
the end both sisters marry the men of their choice.

Almost everywhere in Mrs Behn's plays, daughters take a stand,
and though they do not always succeed and there is much suffering, the point made very well by the playwright is that this is a
problem that society must resolve to prevent women leading a life
of adultery. Most marriages in the period were arranged marriages, as we are told by Clarinda in *The Dutch Lover* (1673):

But as it most times happens
We marry where our Parents like, not we.   (V.i)

Often these are mercenary marriages. Hence children are forced to protest. This is what a daughter says in *The Dutch Lover*: 'I am contracted to a Man I never saw, nor I am sure shall not like when I do see, he having more Vice and Folly than his Fortune will excuse, tho' a great one; and I had rather die than marry him.' (I.iii).

XI

Etherege is not too concerned with the fate of such sons and daughters, and therefore he does not have any specific doctrine to preach regarding the parent–child relationship. He does, however, believe that children have a right to choose their spouses. The only play where this question is raised is *The Man of Mode*. Harriet has great affection for her mother – 'a great admirer of the forms and civility of the last age' (I.i) and consequently very conservative in outlook – but, as we have seen, she is determined not to accept an arranged marriage. Moreover, she is intelligent enough to handle her mother tactfully. But we cannot say the same of Young Bellair. His problem could have become quite serious if Etherege had not treated his father, Old Bellair, with such a pleasant humour that it removes any sense of threat from him. Old Bellair, we learn, has come to town and has found out that his son is courting 'an idle town flirt with a painted face, a rotten reputation, and a crazy fortune' (II.i.). He has written to him telling him that he has already made a match for him. The letter also contains the warning that he should 'resolve to be obedient to his will, or expect to be disinherited' (I.i.). Young Bellair is not a strong enough character, and when asked by Dorimant and Medley whether he would defy his father and marry Emelia, the woman he loves, all that he is able to resolve to do is 'not to marry at all' (I.i.). Later, when he meets his father, he requests him to be 'more indulgent' but the father remains adamant. Young Bellair tells Emelia and Lady Townley, his father's sister: 'He is firm in his resolution, tells me I must marry Mrs Harriet, or swears he'll marry himself, and disinherit me' (II.i). In the meantime, Old Bellair, an amorous old man of fifty–five, himself falls in love with Emelia who happens to be living in the same house where he has taken up his lodgings. Without realizing that Emelia is his son's choice, he is almost on the verge of making a proposal of marriage to her. Indeed, in the evening at Lady Townley's house, he comes 'singing and dancing up to

Emelia' and does make the proposal, though in a somewhat indirect way:

OLD BELLAIR: A dod sweetheart, be advised, and do not throw thyself
    away on a young idle fellow.
EMELIA: I have no such intention, Sir.
OLD BELLAIR: Have a little patience! Thou shalt have the man I spake of.
    A–dod he loves thee, and will make a good husband, but no words –
EMELIA: But Sir –
OLD BELLAIR: No answer – out a pise! Peace, and think on't.

                                    (IV.i)

But when at last Old Bellair learns that his son has married Emelia without his permission, after a momentary outburst both at his son and Lady Townley (who has obviously encouraged Young Bellair to go ahead with the marriage), he gives his blessings to the couple. The playwright brings him on the stage to speak the last line in the play: 'A–dod, the boy has made a happy choice.'

    Sir Sampson Legend in Congreve's *Love for Love* is not conceived in the same light humoured vein as Old Bellair in *The Man of Mode*, and he, therefore, does pose a real threat to his son, Valentine. Valentine is not without blame. He has lived an extravagant and somewhat dissolute life and has run into debt. However he has realised his mistake and is willing to make amends. But his father is unforgiving, indeed cruelly vindictive. In the second Act he enters 'with a paper' — a legal document which he has got prepared to disinherit Valentine. His tone is triumphant:

I'll make the ungracious prodigal know who begat him; I will, old Nostrodamus. What, I warrant my son thought nothing belonged to a father but forgiveness and affection; no authority, no correction, no arbitrary power; nothing to be done, but for him to offend, and me to pardon. I warrant you, if he danced till doomsday, he thought I was to pay the piper. Well, but here it is under black and white, *signatum, sigillatum,* and *deliberatum*; that as soon as my son Benjamin is arrived, he is to make over to him his right of inheritance. Where's my daughter, that is to be – ha! old Merlin! body o' me, I'm so glad I'm revenged on this undutiful rogue.

                                    (II.i)

When Valentine, who is not able to understand why his father should plan to ruin him, begs to be told the 'excuse for your barbarity and unnatural usage', Sir Sampson replies:

Excuse! Impudence! Why, sirrah, mayn't I do what I please? are not you my slave? did not I beget you? and might not I have chosen whether I would have begot you or no? 'Oons! who are you? whence came you? what brought you into the world? how came you here, sir? here, to stand here, upon those two legs, and look erect with that audacious face, hah? Answer me that? Did you come a volunteer into the world? or did I, with the lawful authority of a parent, press you to the service? (II.i)

Sir Samspon also tries to poison the mind of Angelica whom Valentine loves. Angelica, who is a highly intelligent girl, sees though the game and decides to humiliate and punish him. She tempts him to make an offer of marriage to her and then pretends to accept him. In the end she tears the paper that he wanted Valentine to sign and publicly offers her hand to Valentine. When he asks 'Oons, what is the meaning of this?' she gives the shattering reply:

Well, Sir Sampson, since I have played you a trick, I'll advise you how you may avoid such another. Learn to be a good father, or you'll never get a second wife. I always loved your son, and hated your unforgiving nature. I was resolved to try him to the utmost; I have tried you too, and know you both. You have not more faults than he has virtues; and 'tis hardly more pleasure to me, that I can make him and myself happy, than that I can punish you. (V.ii)

Sir Sampson leaves the stage fuming and fretting and in utter disgrace. But no one sympathizes with him. Indeed, even his second son, Ben, in whose favour he wanted to disinherit Valentine, treats him with scant respect: 'So he asked in a surly sort of manner, – and gad I answered' en as surlily; what tho'f he be my father? I an't bound prentice to 'en:— so faith I told'n in plain terms, if I were minded to marry I'd marry to please myself, not him'. (IV.iii)

XII

It would of course be wrong to claim that there are no parents in Restoration comedy who are affectionate or even reasonable in their dealings with their children. But it is somewhat surprising that even when Restoration comedy presents such parents and guardians, its intention seems to be to contrast their attitude with that of other parents and guardians who are clearly tyrannical. Indeed, the chief merit of this comedy is that it offers the *rationale* behind the children's rebellion against their parents – as it does the *ratio-nale* behind the wives' rebellion against their tyrannical, indifferent or inadequate husbands. In this respect, this comedy acquires a special social significance that we cannot often claim for Shakespeare's plays.

It is interesting to find Sir Charles Sedley presenting a portrait of a thoughtful father in *The Mulberry Garden* (1668) in the figure of Sir John Everyoung, though we cannot help noticing some unpleasant features of his character. Everyoung is quite different from the typical Restoration fathers in that he recognizes that children have a personality of their own and that parents, by their attitude, can help or hinder its development. He believes 'those women, who have been least used to liberty, most apt to abuse it when they come to't.' (I.i). Restoration comedy consistently claims that only those women who enjoy freedom can lay any claims to morality since they alone can make a distinction between love and fornication. As Hellena in Mrs Behn's *The Rover* says: 'I don't intend every he that likes me shall have me, but he that I like.' (III.i). This right to choose is indeed the essence both of freedom and of morality.

Sir John Everyoung freely permits his daughters to take 'their innocent diversion as the custom of the country and their age requires.' (I.i). This liberal attitude is contrasted by the playwright with the attitude of his brother, Sir Samuel Forecast. Forecast believes in strictness and he is convinced that daughters, like money, are never safe but under lock and key. So when his daughter Althea decides to marry Eugenio, he sternly announces: 'Eugenio shall never call a child of mine *wife* as long as I live!' (II.i). Clearly against her wishes, he commands that she marry Horatio. Althea states not only her own dilemma but also that of the seventeenth century woman:

> Under what tyranny are women born!
> Here we are bid to love, and there to scorn;
> As if unfit to be allowed a part
> In choosing him that must have all our heart;
> Or that our liking, like a head–strong beast,
> Were made for nothing, but to be oppressed;
> And below them in this regard we are,
> We may not fly the cruelty we fear.
> The horse may shake the rider from his back,
> The dog his hated master may forsake;

Yet nothing of their native worth impair,
Nor any conscious sting about them bear.
But if a virgin an escape contrive,
She must for ever in dishonour live,
Condemned within herself, despised of all,
Into worse mischiefs than she fled from, fall. (II.ii)

Althea's dilemma is resolved very honourably, but there is no doubt that for most daughters it was a real problem with no easy solution in sight. The solution had to come from parents, but parents in contemporary comedy had not yet acquired the kind of sensitivity to their children's problems which alone can offer solutions.

This sensitivity we see, perhaps at its best, in Shadwell's *The Squire of Alsatia* (1688). Here again we have a pair of brothers, Sir William Belford and Sir Edward Belford. Sir William has two sons, the younger of whom has been adopted by Sir Edward Belford. Shadwell asks a question which no one before him had asked as sharply, regarding the wisest way to adopt 'in the Education of a Son' (II.i). Sir William's methods clearly belong to an earlier period. He does not like the enlightened approach of Sir Edward and tells him how he has brought up his elder son:

Well, I have a son whom by my strictness I have form'd according to my heart; He never puts on his Hat in my presence; Rises at second Course, takes away his Plate, says Grace, and saves me the Charge of a Chaplain. When ever he committed a fault, I maul'd him with Correction; I'd fain see him once dare to be extravagant; No, he's a good youth, the Comfort of my Age; I weep for joy to think of him. (I.i)

Sir Edward's approach is entirely different. He tells his brother how he has brought up his adopted son:

You are his Father by Nature, I by Choice; I took him when he was a Child, and bred him with gentleness, and that kind of Conversation that has made him my friend; He conceals nothing from me, or denies nothing to me. Rigour makes nothing but Hypocrites. (I.i)

He also warns his brother that children should be governed 'by love': 'I had as lieve govern a Dog as a Man if it must be by fear; this I take to be the difference between a good Father to Children, and harsh Master over Slaves.' (I.i).

These two attitudes towards the upbringing of children are also reflected in the choice of the young men's spouses. Sir William believes that children have no right to a will of their own. When asked whether his son would like the girl he is selecting for him, he flares up: 'He like her! What's matter whether he like her, or not? Is it not enough for him, that I do? Is a Son, a Boy, a Jackanapes, to have a will of his own? That were to have him be the Father, and me the Son.' (IV.i). Sir Edward, on the other hand, respects the wishes of his adopted son and when he suspects that the boy is involved in some unsavoury intrigue, this is how he tries to reclaim him:

Dear *Ned*, thou art the greatest joy I have; And believe thy Father, and thy Friend, there's nothing but Anxiety in Vice: I am not streight Lac'd; but when I was Young, I ne'r knew any thing gotten by Wenching, but Duels, Claps, and Bastards: And every drunken fit is a short madness, that cuts off a good part of Life. (III.i)

He also advises him not to waste his time in fashionable follies but to take care 'to make some figure in the World, and to sustain that part thy Fortune, Nature and Education fit thee for' (III.i). The boy not only promises to follow this wise advice but also takes his father into confidence: 'But I must confess, I am most passionately in Love, and am with your consent, resolv'd to Marry: Tho' I will perish e'er I do't without it.' The father wisely leaves the choice to the son but reminds him: 'I know you have so much honour, you would do nothing below your self.' (III.i).

It may be added that Belford Junior is not an unblemished young man. Indeed, he has almost all the vices of a comtemporary youth. But the point that the palywright is making is that with the help and guidance of parents, young men can reclaim themselves and start life with renewed confidence. To make his moral instruction doubly clear, the playwright brings Belford Junior and Sir Edward on the stage at the end of the play:

BELF JUN: Farewell for ever all the Vices of the Age, / There is no peace
  but in a Virtuous Life, / Nor lasting Joy but in a tender Wife.
SIR EDW: You, that would breed your Children well, by Kindness and
  Liberality endear 'em to you: and teach 'em by Example.
  Severity spoils ten, for one it mends;
  If you'd not have your Sons desire your ends,
  By Gentleness and Bounty make those Sons your Friends.

Sir Edward is almost anticipating John Locke, and it is clear that after 1680 English comedy enters a new phase. After a period of abandoned libertinism, it now seems to sober down. And the impudent baiting of the older people seems to decline. It should, however, be noted that the earlier baiting serves its purpose. It brings a new awareness both to parents and children, and we may confidently claim that the later companionate family would not have been possible if Restoration comedy had not scoffed at some of the chief deficiencies of contemporary culture. Its irreverence, indeed, serves a positive purpose, and parents are made to recognize that children have an individuality of their own.

A good example of this recognition is to be found in Farquhar's *The Recruiting Officer* (1706). Justice Balance, who has serious doubts about the wisdom of Silvia marrying Captain Plume, tells her: 'I would rather counsel than command. I don't propose this with the authority of a parent, but as the advice of your friend.' When Silvia promises not to 'dispose of [herself] to any man without [his] consent,' he says: 'Very well; and to be even with you, I promise that I will never dispose of you without your consent.' (II.ii). Ultimately Silvia marries Captain Plume with her father's consent and blessings. It is only fair to conclude, therefore, that in the area of domestic relationships, Restoration comedy registers a clear advance in social terms over Shakespeare. However liberal Shakespeare's own views may have been, his world is largely dominated by the values of patriarchalism, with all their social implications. The comedy of the later seventeenth century seems to undermine these values and tries to replace them, however haltingly, by more enlightened values.

CHAPTER III

CRABBED AGE AND YOUTH

I

We have seen how the parent–child relationship is handled by Shakespeare and the Restoration comic playwrights. In this chapter we may consider their general approach to the tensions that exist between youth and age in their societies. These tensions are quite pertinent to any discussion of family relationships, as they are a sure indicator of the cultural level of a society. In this particular case, we have constantly to keep in mind that Shakespeare reflects the tensions inherent in a patriarchal society, whereas the Restoration playwrights face a somewhat different world in which this society is breaking down.[1]

C. L. Barber has said that in 'the usual comic movement' in Shakespeare, 'the old are dismissed, or got around, on a tide of young feeling, whether or not they are finally reconciled and included in the new society created by the initially disruptive sexual energies of the new generation.'[1] The burden of our earlier discussion has been that even while recognizing the conflict between the younger and the older generations, Shakespearean drama moves towards a reconciliation between the two. The old, it is true, are sometimes dismissed, but they are never dismissed with contempt. Shakespeare's plays nowhere give us the impression that 'age is unnecessary' (*King Lear*, II. iv.153). Indeed Shakespeare almost invariably treats old age with respect. Even when we withhold respect from certain older characters – and in fact laugh at them, as at Justice Shallow and Silence in *Henry IV Part II* – we do not forget that their being old is merely incidental.

One may, of course, treat this respect for old age as a normal feature of a patriarchal society. As Keith Thomas has said, in such a society 'the prevailing ideal was gerontocratic: the young were to serve and the old were to rule. Justification for so obvious a truth was found in the law of nature, the fifth commandment, and the proverbial wisdom of ages.'[2] Thomas has also established, on the basis of his researches in this area, that in early modern England men in their forties, fifties and sixties were visibly entrenched in the seats of power, no less in the villages than in Parliament, the Courts, and Privy Council. It was commonly believed in Shakespeare's time that youth was a period of irresponsibility and that wisdom came only with old age.[3] Youth, in fact, was often denounced as a dangerous period when restraint was most needed. Shakespeare himself seems to refer to this view when he makes the shepherd in *The Winter's Tale* say: 'I would there were no age between ten and three–and–twenty, or that youth would sleep out the rest; for there is nothing in the between but getting wenches with child, wronging the ancientry, stealing, fighting.' (III.iii.59–63).[4]

While this was the accepted point of view, we should not fail to recognize that the new economic and social forces emerging in contemporary society could not have left traditional attitudes to old age wholly unaffected. Among other things, the spread of education may have reduced the importance of the old, who were earlier regarded as repositories of oral knowledge. Further, as Keith Thomas states, the role of religious movements contributed to the subversion of the position of older people. He says: 'First it was the Lutheran children who mocked their Catholic parents: "my father is an old doting fool and will fast upon the Friday: and my mother goeth always mumbling on her beads. But you shall see me of another sort, I warrant you." Later it was the Puritans and sectaries who revolted against their elders.' He cites what the Elizabethan minister, Henry Smith, said: 'If there were any good to be done in these days, it is the young men that must do it, for the old men are out of date.'[5]

The real threat to the old, as always, is economic. The worst feature of old age is that it is not productive, and consequently children in all ages and cultures have found the old an economic burden. Elizabethan sons could not have been too different. This may explain the popularity in the period of the conventional wisdom of *Ecclesiasticus*: 'As long as thou livest and hath breath in thee, give not thyself over to any. Far better it is that thy children should seek to thee, than that thou shouldst stand to their courtesy.' What Foulke Robertes says in *The Revenue of the Gospel is Tythes* (1613) reflects to a large extent the essentials of the *King Lear* situation:

Hath any man ever seen a poor aged man live at courtesy in the house of his son with his daughter–in–law? Doth not the good father in a short time, either by his coughing or spitting or testiness or some . . . unto-wardness or other become troublesome either to his own son or to his nice daughter–in–law, with continuing so long chargeable and so much waited–on, or to the children, with taking up their room at the fire or at the table, or to the servants, while his slow eating doth scant their reversions?[6]

Daniel Rogers' advice to parents in *Matrimoniall Honour* (1642) was clearly to avoid staying with their children. For some time the old might justify their keep by acting as servants and household drudges. But 'when all strength and ability is gone, then they are no longer set by, but . . . despised, counted as burdens.'[7] The position was best summed up by what a preacher in the late seventeenth century said: Children were the staff of old age, 'but God sometimes beats men with these staves instead of supporting them thereby.'[8]

There may have also been ambitious young men who were too impatient to wait to inherit property or title. Shakespeare's Edmund is, of course, not typical, for he does not hesitate even to plan the murder of his father. But what he says may not be alto-gether without basis in the contemporary stituation: 'This policy and reverence of age makes the world bitter to the best of our times; keeps our fortunes from us till our oldness cannot relish them. I begin to find an idle and fond bondage in the oppression of aged tyranny, who sways, not as it hath power, but as it is suffer'd.' (*King Lear*, I.ii.45–51).

II

In *King Lear*, however, Shakespeare wholly rejects the kind of plea that Edmund makes on behalf of youth. The play clearly unholds the traditional Christian values and condemns people like Edmund who are impatient or arrogant. It presents a conflict between the older values and the new philosophy represented by Edmund, Goneril, and Regan, and shows how hollow, sterile and self–destructive this new philosophy is. In its rejection of the value and sanctity of human relationships, this new philosophy becomes monstrous and unnatural. Gloucester's words may have sounded foolish to Edmund, but most contemporaries of Shakes-peare would have seen an intimate relationship between the new philosophy of life represented by Edmund and the upheaval in nature and society:

These late eclipses in the sun and moon portend no good to us. Though the wisdom of nature can reason it thus and thus, yet nature finds itself scourg'd by the sequent effects; love cools, friendship falls off, brothers divide; in cities, mutinies; in countries discord; in palaces, treason; and the bond crack'd 'twixt son and father. This villain of mine comes under the prediction: there's son against father. The King falls from bias of nature: there's father against child. We have seen the best of our time: machinations, hollowness, treachery, and all ruinous disorders follow us disquietly to our graves.   (I.ii.100–112)

Edmund's own mocking remarks to Edgar also reflect the same thinking:

I promise you, the effects he writes of succeed unhappily; as of unnaturalness between the child and the parent; death, dearth, dissolutions of ancient amities; divisions in state, menaces and maledictions against king and nobles; needless diffidences, banishment of friends, dissipation of cohorts, nuptial breaches, and I know not what.
                                                                (I.ii.136–142)

It is this 'unnaturalness between the child and the parent' with which *King Lear* is really concerned. The question that Shakespeare asks in this play is not whether King Lear is right or wrong, nor whether he had 'poor judgement' (I.i.291) and 'hath ever but slenderly known himself.' (I.i.292). The question simply is:

> Is it not as this mouth should tear this hand
> For lifting food to't?   (III.iv.15–16)

— and whether it would 'become the house' if a father were to fall on his knees and say:

> Dear daughter, I confess that I am old;
> Age is unnecessary; on my knees I beg
> That you'll vouchsafe me raiment, bed and food.
>   (II.iv.151–153)

King Lear narrows the question to one of 'Filial ingratitude' (III.iv.14), but Cordelia sees the problem in its larger context. Consideration for old parents necessarily inculcates consideration for old age itself. Those who lack this consideration are deficient in compassion, which is the basis of all human culture. Cordelia condemns her sisters for lacking precisely this quality:

> Had you not been their father, these white flakes
> Did challenge pity of them. Was this a face
> To be oppos'd against the jarring winds?
> To stand against the deep dread bolted thunder?
> In the most terrible and nimble stroke
> Of quick cross lightning to watch – poor perdu –
> With this thin helm? Mine enemy's dog,
> Though he had bit me, should have stood that night
> Against my fire.   (IV.vii.30–38)

King Lear, then, is 'the tragedy, not of two families, but of an entire civilization.'⁹ Its real theme is summed up in Lear's question: 'Is there any cause in nature that makes these hard hearts?' (III.vi.79). The play explores how human beings degenerate into beasts and how the milk of human kindness in them dries up. When the kind–hearted king in *King Henry VI Part III* sees a father carrying the dead body of his son whom he had killed in ignorance and a son carrying the dead body of his father whom he had killed in similar circumstances, he cries out:

> O pity, pity, gentle heaven, pity!   (II.v.96)

The need and relevance of such pity goes unrecognized by characters like Goneril and Regan. When King Lear goes out into the storm, Gloucester pleads with Goneril and Regan to entreat him to return in view of the coming night and storm, but Regan is unmoved and advises Gloucester to shut his doors. When Gloucester hesitates, Cornwall gives firmer advice:

> Shut up your doors, my lord; 'tis a wild night.
> My Regan counsels well. Come out o' th' storm.
>   (II.iv.303–4)

When told how Goneril, Regan and Cornwall have treated Lear, Albany gives not only his own outrageous reaction, but the reaction of all civilized men and women in all ages and cultures:

> If that the heavens do not their visible spirits
> Send quickly down to tame these vile offences,
> It will come
> Humanity must perforce prey on itself
> Like monsters of the deep.   (IV.ii.46–50)

Ulysses in *Troilus and Cressida* gives a similar warning to men who renounce all moral and human obligations and live only for self–aggrandisement. In the lives of such men the first casualty is their humanity, their capacity for love and human sympathy. Consequently, everything that mankind has built over centuries – religion, family, and other human institutions, including the state – all become meaningless for them. Their lives are an epitome of the collapse of human civilization. Ulysses' picture of this collapse is most vivid:

> Strength should be lord of imbecility,
> And the rude son should strike his father dead;
> Force should be right; or, rather, right and wrong –
> Between whose endless jar justice resides –
> Should lose their names, and so should justice too.
> Then everything includes itself in power,
> Power into will, will into appetite;
> And appetite, an universal wolf,
> So doubly seconded with will and power,
> Must make perforce an universal prey,
> And last eat up himself.   (I.iii.114–124)

In *King Lear*, the universal chaos predicted by Ulysses is prevented only by the love of Cordelia for her father. We are reminded that the world of King Lear is still safe because there is a daughter:

> Who redeems nature from the general curse
> Which twain have brought her to.   (IV.vi.208–9)

Thus in *King Lear*, old age is finally invested with a grandeur and a dignity which is not to be found elsewhere in Shakespeare. This grandeur and dignity was perhaps the only answer to the contempt that Goneril and Regan show towards old age. For Goneril, old age stands for 'indiscretion' and 'dotage':

> How have I offended?
> All's not offence that indiscretion finds
> And dotage terms so.   (II.iv.190–1)

For Regan, it is just weakness – a condition which she treats with contempt:

> I pray you, father, being weak, seem so.   (II.iv.196)

Lear can appeal only to the heavens:

> O heavens,
> If you do love old men, if your sweet away
> Allow obedience, if you yourselves are old,

Make it your cause; Send down, and take my part.
                                    (II.iv.184–187)

The reply to this appeal comes from Cordelia who tells her father
that he deserves love and reverence:

O look upon me, sir,
And hold your hands in benediction o'er me.
          (*Lear falls to his knees*)
No, sir, you must not kneel.   (IV.vii.56–58)

It is unnatural[10] that parents should kneel to their children. As
Cordelia says, the natural order of things is that children should
kneel and their parents should hold their hands in benediction
over them. This natural order has been disturbed in the play and a
heavy price has to be paid both by parents and children before
conditions are created for its re-establishment.

Perhaps some speculation regarding Shakespeare's almost
invariable practice of not letting his evil characters live till they
are old may be in order, though it clearly seems to reject the
classical view that those whom the gods love die young. There is
something in the scene in *King Lear* where Gloucester is blinded
which makes us wonder whether Shakespeare sees a *natural* relationship between goodness and old age. Only such an interpretation makes sense of Gloucester's appeal to those who were present
at the scene:

He that will think *to live till he be old*
Give me some help.   (III.vii.68–9)
                                    (Italics mine)

Help did come from the first servant though it did not save Gloucester's eyes. But the mere fact that a servant of Cornwall should
have felt outraged enough at the inhumanity of his master and
Regan to risk his life is an important pointer to the birth of newer
forces in the bleak world of *King Lear* – forces that will finally
purge it of evil. The servant did die young but he died with the
blessings of all who saw his act of heroism. In a sense, his is not a
death at all, but a martyrdom, as is that of Cordelia later. It is the
evil characters who really die – die as human beings first, then as
beasts whose carcasses are thrown out for vultures to feed on. It is
one such evil character – Regan – about whom the third servant
says:

> If she lives long,
> And in the end meet the old course of death
> Women will all turn monsters.   (III.vii.99–101)

It is perhaps of some significance that at the end of the play,
Edgar says:

> The oldest hath borne most; we that are young
> Shall never see so much nor live so long.   (V. iii.323–4)

He seems to be saying that the old represented higher values of
life which the young perhaps may not be able to emulate. The
play seems to end not on a note of exultation but of weariness.

   Macbeth is not sure whether he will live long but he does know
that in his case old age will not have any of the traditional advan-
tages of that period of life:

> I have lived long enough: my way of life
> Is fallen into the sere, the yellow leaf;
> And that which should accompany old age,
> As honour, love, obedience, troop of friends,
> I must not look to have.
>
> (*Macbeth*, V.iii.22–26)

Macbeth knows how gracious old age can be if accompanied by
'honour, love, obedience, troop of friends', but he also knows that
it is not for him or for those who have lived an evil life to attain
such a gracious old age.

III

While the theme of age versus youth does not appear to be central
in any play other than *King Lear*, the question of the relation
between age and youth does appear in a muted form in other
plays. In these other plays, Shakespeare explores the values
upheld by old age through his presentation of older characters. In
this connection, Adam in *As You Like It* is an important figure.
Adam is a servant, and of an altogether different social class from
King Lear, and he has, therefore, to look out for himself. How
difficult old age could be – and what provision one should make
to face it – is best seen in what Adam says to Orlando:

> I have five hundred crowns,
> The thrifty hire I saved under your father,
> Which I did store to be my foster–nurse

> When service should in my old limbs lie lame
> And unregarded age in corners thrown.   (II.iii.38–42)

'And unregarded age in corners thrown' is a warning to all old men and women – a warning that men like Lear never care to understand owing to their social status. Adam, however, has to be careful not to be reduced to penury. In the very first scene of the play, he is dismissed by Oliver who calls him an 'old dog' (I.i.68). Adam sees this as an attack both on his age and on his loyalty: 'Is "old dog" my reward? Most true, I have lost my teeth in your service.' (I.i.69–70). But what he adds is more relevant for our purposes because it reminds us that times have changed and that the old conception of the family, which included servants, has also changed: 'God be with my old master, he would not have spoken such a word.' (I.i.70–1). He, however, recognizes his bond with the family and so advises Orlando to leave home to escape death. He even offers him all his savings in addition to his services (II.iii.46–55). Orlando's response to Adam's offer also indicates how the older values which Adam espouses are fast disappearing owing to the new mercantile forces entering society:

> O good old man, how well in thee appears
> The constant service of the antique world,
> When service sweat for duty, not for meed.
> Thou art not for the fashion of these times,
> Where none will sweat but for promotion,
> And having that do choke their service up
> Even with the having; it is not so with thee.
>   (II.iii.56–62)

It is important to recognize that in Shakespeare, save for *King Lear*, there is no evidence of 'unregarded age in corners thrown'. In this play itself a stage comes when Adam is too hungry and tired to go further, and pleads with Orlando to 'measure out [his] grave.' (II.vi.2). But Orlando will not desert him. Indeed, he tells Adam: 'If this uncouth forest yield anything savage, I will either be food for it, or bring it for food to thee' (II.vi.4–6). Orlando's request to Duke Senior and his companions shows his solicitude and affection for Adam, whom he treats almost like a father:

> Then but forbear your food a little while,
> Whiles, like a doe, I go to find my fawn,
> And give it food. There is an old poor man,
> Who after me hath many a weary step

Limped in pure love; till he be first sufficed,
Oppressed with two weak evils, age and hunger,
I will not touch a bit.

(II.vii.126–132)

IV

Orlando praises Adam for possessing the values typical of the
'antique world', but the old in Shakespeare do not represent only
the older values of feudal society. In *All's Well that Ends Well* it is
refreshing to watch the old representing more enlightened modern values than the young. The play raises the question about
where true nobility and honour reside, in birth or in merit. This
question, as M. C. Bradbrook says, was '*the* great topic of the
courtesy books, and in a court that included such a high proportion of self–made men as Elizabeth's did, the question was not
without practical consequences.'[11] Whatever the consequences,
there is no doubt that the age is sharply divided between those
who, like Sir Thomas Elyot, believe that true nobility is 'only the
prayse and surname of virtue'[12] and the others for whom no virtue
is higher than that of noble birth. For this latter category, marrying out of one's 'degree' is a debasing of the blood, which blem-
ishes successive generations. Most sixteenth century men are so
obsessed with considerations of 'degree' that Bertram's objection
to marrying the daughter of a physician would have sounded
quite natural to them. The king in that age, it is true, had the
right to marry his wards to whom he pleased – often they were
sold – but compelling a nobleman's son to marry a commoner
was certainly abuse of his authority. However highly respected
Helena's father may have been for his skill as a physician, he
belonged to a profession which was clearly not dignified. As
Bradbrook has said, it 'approximated too nearly to the barber–sur-
geon and the apothecary to receive much honour.'[13] Helena herself is perhaps conscious of this. In any case, she knows that
Bertram is 'above' her and that she does not belong to his 'sphere'
(I.i.85–87). But she also believes that by curing the King, she has
earned enough 'honour' to make her worthy of any noble man.

The point the play makes is that Bertram is a wholly conventional youth who is interested only in 'name' and not in substance. For him honour resides in birth. That virtue and honour
can be and indeed are independent of birth is a concept foreign to

his way of thinking, and it is not without significance that this
concept is at last expounded by the King in his famous speech:

> 'Tis only title thou disdain'st in her, the which
> I can build up. Strange is it that our bloods,
> Of colour, weight, and heat, pour'd all together,
> Would quite confound distinction, yet stand off
> In differences so mighty. If she be
> All that is virtuous, save what thou dislik'st –
> A poor physician's daughter – thou dislik'st
> Of virtue for the name; but do not so.
> From lowest place when virtuous things proceed,
> The place is dignified by th' doer's deed;
> Where great additions swell's, and virtue none,
> It is a dropsied honour. Good alone
> Is good without a name. Vileness is so;
> The property by what it is should go,
> Not by the title. She is young, wise, fair;
> In these to nature she's immediate heir;
> And these breed honour. That is honour's scorn
> Which challenges itself as honour's born
> And is not like the sire. Honours thrive
> When rather from our acts we them derive
> Than our fore-goers. The mere word's a slave,
> Debauch'd on every tomb, on every grave
> A lying trophy; and as oft is dumb
> Where dust and damn'd oblivion is the tomb
> Of honour'd bones indeed. What should be said?
> If thou canst like this creature as a maid,
> I can create the rest. Virtue and she
> Is her own dower; honour and wealth from me.
>
> (II.iii.115–142)

It is remarkable that Shakespeare should have given greater
sensitivity to his older characters in this play – the Countess of
Rousillon, the King of France and Lafew – and made Bertram
such an unpleasant character. The play does, of course, end on a
seemingly happy note, but we remain morally confused. Has an
unworthy husband been made worthy by a loving and forgiving
wife? Has he grown in self-knowledge? Dr Johnson said that
Bertram had merely been 'dismissed to happiness'. But what
about Helena? In the very first scene she had playfully asked
Parolles how a virgin could 'lose [her virginity] to her own liking'
(I.i.149). The question in fact was how an intelligent woman
could achieve a happy marriage in a status-ridden society. Diana

was not exaggerating when she described the situation of Helena
in these words:

> Alas, poor lady!
> 'Tis a hard bondage to become the wife
> Of a detesting lord. (III.v.63–65)

The lord may not stay detesting – in fact he claims that after
knowing all the facts he will 'love her dearly, ever, every dearly'
(V.iii.314) – but somehow one does not feel very comfortable.
Perhaps, knowing her world as she does – a world in which a
woman can get some sense of security only in marriage, and with
a woman like the Countess of Rousillon as her mother-in-law –
things may end well for Helena too. It is, however, strange that a
woman should be expected to find comfort in her mother-in-law
rather than in her husband. Such a situation is not altogether
unintelligible in a traditional society.

V

It would be wrong to idealize old age on the basis of *All's Well
that Ends Well*. Old age can be a very unpleasant period of one's
life and Shakespeare is not unaware of this fact. Not all men or
women grow wiser with old age. Indeed, as Jacques says in *As
You Like It*:

> And so, from hour to hour, we ripe and ripe,
> And then, from hour to hour, we rot and rot
>
> (II.vii.26–27)

Of course, both processes take place simultaneously. Luckier people may escape the rotting process, grow old with grace and die
with dignity. Others start rotting very early in life and never
ripen. Perhaps Polonius in *Hamlet* belongs to this latter category.
He symbolizes the rottenness of the state of Denmark. At least that
is Hamlet's view, and so at one stage Hamlet unfeelingly paints a
most terrible picture of old age:

old men have grey beards; that their faces are wrinkled; their eyes purg-
ing thick amber and plum-tree gum; and that they have a plentiful lack
of wit, together with most weak hams

(II.ii.196–198)

The picture that Hamlet paints of the physical and mental debil-
ity of the old may be correct enough, and yet it is difficult to

believe that Hamlet generally regards old people with contempt. Can we imagine, for instance, that he would have seen old age in a similar light in his own father – a father who, he claims, had 'Hyperion's curls; the front of Jove himself; / An eye like Mars, to threaten and command?' (III.iv.56–7). His purpose, in his comments on old age, is clearly to insult and humiliate Polonius.[14] He succeeds in doing this even though his description hardly fits Polonius.

There is another comment in Shakespeare on old age which cannot be taken seriously. This appears in *The Passionate Pilgrim*. (It is, of course, highly doubtful whether Shakespeare really wrote this.)[15] Here a wholly superficial contrast is offered between youth and age:

> Crabbed age and youth cannot live together:
> Youth is full of pleasance, age is full of care;
> Youth like summer morn, age like winter weather;
> Youth like summer brave, age like winter bare.
> Youth is full of sport, age's breath is short;
>   Youth is nimble, age is lame;
> Youth is hot and bold, age is weak and cold;
>   Youth is wild, and age is tame.
> Age, I do abhor thee; youth, I do adore thee.   (XII)

There is, naturally, a clear difference between old age and youth, and many of the things said here are correct enough – as they were in Hamlet's description of old age. But all this does not mean that old age is to be treated with contempt. Shakespeare's plays do often show conflict between the old and the young but their general tendency is to establish that youth and age can and must live together. For the young in Shakespeare, the old are not a different species: they are human beings like them, and though at times they can be quite exasperating, they are only what the young will be after some time. Shakespeare's age, unlike the present one, is not obsessed with the generation-gap. In this context the attitude of Prince Hal, now King Henry V, is quite instructive. In his rejection of Falstaff, he seems to emphasize Falstaff's age. Falstaff is called 'old' twice in the rejection scene; he is reminded 'how ill white hairs become a fool and jester', he is told that 'the grave doth gape for him' (*King Henry IV–Part II*, V.v.47 ff.). But it would be wrong to assume that Falstaff is rejected simply because he is old; he is rejected because he is Falstaff, 'The tutor and the feeder

of my riots' (V.v.63). If it was old age that was rejected, the new
King would not have told another old man, the Lord Chief
Justice:

> You shall be as a father to my youth;
> My voice shall sound as you do prompt mine ear;
> And I will stoop and humble my intents
> To your well-practis'd wise directions.
>
>   (V.ii.118–121)

The only old man in Shakespeare who is presented as wholly
ridiculous is Justice Shallow in *King Henry IV Part II*. He has
grown senile and talks of his imaginary exploits in youth. A
hilarious conversation takes place between him and Falstaff:

SHALLOW: O, Sir John, do you remember since we lay all night in the
windmill in Saint George's Field?

FALSTAFF: No more of that, Master Shallow, no more of that.

SHALLOW: Ha, 'twas a merry night. And is Jane Nightwork alive?

FALSTAFF: She lives, Master Shallow.

SHALLOW: She never could away with me.

FALSTAFF: Never, never; she would always say she could not abide Master
Shallow.

SHALLOW: By the mass, I could anger her to th' heart. She was then a
bona-roba. Doth she hold her own well?

FALSTAFF: Old, old, Master Shallow.

SHALLOW: Nay, she must be old; she cannot choose but be old; certain
she is old; and had Robin Nightwork, by old Nightwork, before I
came to Clement's Inn.

SILENCE: That's fifty-five years ago.

SHALLOW: Ha, cousin Silence, that thou hadst seen that that knight and I
have seen! Ha, Sir John, said I well?

FALSTAFF: We have heard the chimes at midnight, Master Shallow.

SHALLOW: That we have, that we have, that we have; in faith, Sir John,
we have. Our watchword was 'Hem boys' . . . Jesus, the days that we
have seen!

                                          (III.ii.189 ff.)

After Shallow has left the stage, Falstaff makes the devastating
comment: 'Lord, lord, how subject we old men are to this vice of
lying! This same starv'd justice hath done nothing but prate to
me of the wildness of his youth and the feats he hath done about
Turnbull Street; and every third word a lie' (III.ii.295-301). But
surely even in the case of Justice Shallow, it is not old age that

Shakespeare is laughing at. After all, Falstaff is as old as Justice Shallow, and he too laughs at him and has, indeed, already made up his mind to cheat him. Elisabeth Mignon has correctly pointed out that 'bumpkin Justice Shallow was no less ridiculous as a young man bent on hearing the chimes at midnight than as an old man reminiscing in garrulous fashion about having once heard the sound.' In fact, 'Shallow is not ridiculous simply because he is old, but because he is Shallow.'[16]

VI

Nothing shows Shakespeare's reluctance to treat old age with contempt so decisively as his portrayal of Falstaff in *The Merry Wives of Windsor*. There is a legend that the Queen commanded him to show the old knight in love. Now nothing exposes the vulnerability of old age so much as infatuation. It is in such situations that we see the truth of the saying that there is no fool like an old fool. If Shakespeare had shown Falstaff so infatuated, Falstaff would certainly have become an object of derisive laughter, which often happens to old lechers in Restoration comedy. But Shakespeare avoids this situation by showing that Falstaff's conduct is prompted, in Dr Johnson's words, 'not by the hope of pleasure, but of money.'[17] All that Falstaff does is to 'counterfeit love' in the hope of cheating the wives of two rich merchants. His failure to do so — and the various humiliations he suffers — provides real entertainment. But, as Dover Wilson has said, the spirit of this comedy is 'without bitterness, without malice, without even a trace of contempt.'[18] This is true because even though Falstaff is repeatedly deceived in the course of the play, he is nowhere self–deceived. Indeed, he gives us the impression that he is going through many of the humiliating experiences merely to add to our enjoyment of this excellent comedy. How else does one take his description of one such experience?

The rogues slighted me into the river with as little remorse as they would have drowned a blind bitch's puppies ... and you may know by my size, that I have a kind of alacrity in sinking.

(III.v.8ff.)

'Alacrity in sinking' is hardly a phrase that a baffled and defeated lover would have used. It is the language of a great humorist. So, even though Shakespeare obeyed the Queen, his artistic instinct did not fail him.

There is, however, a scene in *Henry IV Part II* where Falstaff could have been presented in an unsympathetic light as an old lecher. But the scene is handled with such delicacy that it becomes almost tender. The Prince and Poins want to surprise Falstaff in the company of Doll Tearsheet. So they enter disguised as drawers. Doll Tearsheet in the lap of Falstaff makes Poins ask the Prince: 'Is it not strange that desire should so many years outlive performance?' (II.iv.250-1) This is the usual way in which youth mocks old age. This mockery later becomes an obsessive theme in Restoration comedy, where men are judged only in terms of their sexual prowess. But Shakespeare has a much larger vision of humanity, and so what could only have been lechery in Restoration comedy becomes affection here:

FALSTAFF: Kiss me, Doll.
....

FALSTAFF: Thou dost give me flattering busses.
DOLL: By my troth, I kiss thee with a most constant heart.
FALSTAFF: I am old, I am old.
DOLL: I love thee better than I love e'er a scurvy young boy of them all.
FALSTAFF: . . . Thou't forget me when I am gone.
DOLL: By my troth, thou't set me a-weeping, an' thou say'st so. . .
FALSTAFF: . . . Farewell, good wenches. If I be not sent away post, I will see you again ere I go.
DOLL: I cannot speak. If my heart be not ready to burst! Well, sweet Jack, have a care of thyself.
FALSTAFF: Farewell, farewell.   (*Exeunt Falstaff and Bardolph*).
HOSTESS: Well, fare thee well. I have known thee these twenty–nine years, come peascod–time; but an honester and truer–hearted man — well, fare thee well.

(II.iv.252 ff.)

Falstaff is given almost a hero's farewell by the two women, and the warmth of their affection renders his age totally irrelevant — as it does Poins' silly prattle about 'desire' and 'performance'.

VII

It need not surprise us that almost every old man or woman in Restoration comedy is ridiculous in one form or another, and often worse. This comedy presents the youth culture of a particular set in Restoration society and regards older people as an embarrassing encumbrance. Indeed, it seizes upon 'senile folly to the exclusion of other aspects of old age' and almost nowhere recognizes its 'goodness, nobility and wisdom'.[19] Shakespeare had highlighted these other aspects of old age, but Restoration comedy clearly proclaims that 'Crabbed age and youth cannot live together.' The motto of many of its youthful heroes and heroines seems to be: 'Age, I do abhor thee; youth, I do adore thee.'

It is true that 'the very crabbedness of crabbed age is its passport into universal comedy.'[20] Yet this area of human relationships is presented in Restoration comedy with a kind of ruthlessness which is almost nowhere to be found in earlier comedy. Its main reason seems to be the obsession of the contemporary younger aristocracy with sex, though we should also take note of the general decline of respect for old age amongst the upper-classes in Restoration England. Keith Thomas has cited Bishop Tillotson's statement of 1683: 'Less care is commonly taken of the aged, and less kindness showed them.' Defoe's statement made in 1727, also cited by Keith Thomas, is much more perceptive in its understanding of the young people's attitude to the old: 'Young people look upon their elders as a different species. . . .They ascribe no merit to the virtue and experience of old age, but assume to themselves the preference in all things.'[21] In Restoration comedy, older people do have experience (though often of an unsavoury nature), but they certainly lack virtue of almost any kind.

Even though Etherege is never bitter, he sets the tone for the later comic playwrights in this respect. Whatever the faults of younger people in his plays, on the whole he presents the young as honest, spontaneous and generous, as against the middle-aged or the old who are generally hypocritical, lecherous and greedy. The best illustration of this is perhaps to be found in *She Wou'd if She Cou'd*. The two young ladies in the play, Ariana and Gatty, offer a sharp contrast to Lady Cockwood, as do the two young men, Courtall and Freeman, to Sir Oliver Cockwood and Sir Joslin Jolly. The young, whether men or women, are distinctly superior as human beings. They are frank, sincere and essentially innocent. However loudly the young women may claim to 'engage' (II.i) themselves in intrigues with young men, and whatever be the nature of the young men's 'employment' (II.ii), there is nothing unclean about them. As against this, we have the doings of Lady Cockwood and the two knights. The knights pride themselves on being 'bold, desparate old fellows among women and wine,' but we know that they make utter fools of themselves and become objects of laughter. It should be said to their credit that at worst they are only ridiculous, as against Lady Cockwood who, in her search for sexual gratification, can become vicious. She gloats over her scheme to 'daily poison' (IV.ii) the ears of the young ladies against Courtall and Freeman in the hope of appropriating them for herself. That she does not succeed is not for want of trying. She is the kind of woman who would do almost anything for personal ends if she really could.

In *The Man of Mode* again, the young are distinctly superior. At least there is no humbug about them. This generalization applies even to Dorimant to whom purely moral criteria cannot otherwise be easily applied. But the old people in this play, specially Lady Woodvill and Old Bellair, represent inferior values. In *She Wou'd if She Cou'd*, Etherege had presented the problem faced by the old in Restoration upper–class society. The marriage of Sir Oliver and Lady Cockwood is clearly an unsatisfactory one. Sir Oliver is so disgusted with his jealous and passionate wife that he has come to regard the institution of marriage itself as a curse: 'Well, a pox of this tying man and woman together, for better, for worse' (I.i). Both husband and wife want to find satisfaction outside marriage. The best that Sir Oliver may be able to manage is a chamber-maid or a prostitute. One experience that he narrates to Courtall is enough to indicate that he is past the age of any fulfilling experience: ' 'Twas my fortune t'other day to have an intrigue with a tinker's wife in the country, and this malicious slut betrayed the very ditch, where we used to make our assignations, to my lady' (II.ii). Lady Cockwood's luck is no better. The young man she is chasing, Courtall, has this to say about her: 'She is the very spirit of impertinence, so foolishly fond and troublesome, that no man above sixteen is able to endure her' (I.i). The fact is that neither Sir Oliver nor Lady Cockwood know how to age gracefully. In a world where sex dominates people's minds to the exclusion of all other goals in life, perhaps this sexual obsession is understandable. But sex is a game of youth, and when older people start playing it, they are bound to lose their sense of proportion and dignity.

We see this loss of dignity in Old Bellair and Lady Woodvill in *The Man of Mode*. Lady Townley — the only sensible person in the older generation, and in any case merely an amused observer

—understands her brother, Old Bellair, very well, and immediately senses his infatuation for Emelia. When she tells him that
he 'speaks very feelingly' (II.i) about Emelia, he replies: 'I am but
five and fifty, sister, you know, an age not altogether insensible'
(II.i). He then tells Emelia: 'Cheer up, sweetheart, I have a secret
to tell thee may chance to make thee merry; we three will make
collation together anon, i' the meantime — Mum, I can't abide
you, go, I can't abide you' (II.i). It is clearly an absurd situation. It
was perhaps not an altogether uncommon situation in the period,
and that, precisely, may be the reason why comic playwrights
make such fun of it. Lady Townley, however, does not let the
situation develop and arranges the marriage of Emelia and
Young Bellair without Old Bellair's consent or knowledge.

Lady Woodvill is not as foolish as Old Bellair but she is not
above temptation, and Dorimant, pretending to be Mr Courage,
a 'foppish admirer of quality' (III.iii) and a flatterer of old
women, easily exposes this weakness of her character and makes
her look ridiculous. Pretending to condemn the younger generation for its neglect of ripe beauty, Dorimant arouses the innate
flirtatious tendency in Lady Woodvill's character:

DORIMANT: They cry a woman's past her prime at twenty, decayed at four
and twenty, old and unsufferable at thirty.[22]
LADY WOODVILL: Unsufferable at thirty! That they are in the wrong, Mr.
Courage. At five and thirty, there are living proofs enough to con-
vince 'em.
DORIMANT: Ay madam! There's Mrs. Setlooks, Mrs. Droplip, and my
Lady Lowd! Shew me among all our opening buds a face that
promises so much beauty as the remains of theirs.
LADY WOODVILL: The depraved appetite of this vicious age tastes nothing
but green fruit, and loaths it when 'tis kindly ripened.
DORIMANT: Else so many deserving women, madam, would not be so
untimely neglected.   (IV.i)

Harriet should find the scene embarrassing, but that would be
against the spirit of youth in the comedy of manners. She, in fact,
finds it amusing and says to Medley: 'He [Dorimant] fits my
mother's humour so well, a little more and she'll dance a kissing
dance with him anon' (IV.i). Medley's ironical reply immediately
wins our approval: 'Dutifully observed, madam' (IV.i).

There is a daughter in Congreve in whose case too the amuse-
ment should have turned sour in the mouth, but there is no
evidence that it does. Mrs Fainall knows the cruel hoax involving

Lady Wishfort, her mother, and Waitwell, the servant of Mirabel in *The Way of the World*, but she seems to be clearly on the side of Mirabel. She tells him that his scheme will succeed 'for I believe my lady will do anything to get a husband' (II.ii). Even when Mirabel uses a cruelly contemptuous tone and says that her mother 'would marry anything that resembled a man, though 't were no more than what a butler could pinch out of a napkin' (II.ii), all she does is to offer a general comment: 'Female frailty! we must all come to it, if we live to be old, and feel the craving of a false appetite when the true is decayed' (II.ii). They dismiss the subject after Mirabel has added another insult: 'An old woman's appetite is depraved like that of a girl — 'tis the green sickness of a second childhood'. (II.ii).

We must not, of course, treat Lady Wishfort as tragic and ruin the pleasure that she provides. She is easily the most hilarious comic character in the whole comedy of manners and Congreve gives her some of his most delicious lines: 'I look like an old peeled wall. Thou must repair me, Foible, before Sir Rowland comes, or I shall never keep up to my picture.' — and, 'No, I hope Sir Rowland is better bred than to put a lady to the necessity of breaking her forms. I won't be too coy, neither — I won't give him despair — but a little disdain is not amiss; a little scorn is alluring.' — and, 'tenderness becomes me best — a sort of dying-ness — you see that picture has a sort of a — ha, Foible! a swim-mingness in the eye — yes, I'll look so — my niece affects it; but she wants features. Is Sir Rowland handsome? Let my toilet be removed — I'll dress above. I'll receive Sir Rowland here. Is he handsome? Don't answer me. I won't know: I'll be surprised, I'll be taken by surprise.' (III.i). While commenting on the character of Lady Wishfort, G. B. Street has said: 'To regard this poor old soul as mere comedy is to attain to an almost satanic height of contempt: the comedy is more than grim, it is savagely cruel.'[23] But such an approach to this character is completely out of place. We should not fail to recognize that at the end of the play the world of Lady Wishfort has not really collapsed. All that has happened is that her niece, Millamant, is now free to marry Mirabel. But otherwise the last act shows the family coming together — Mrs Fainfall, Millamant, Sir Wilful Witwoud and a new member of the family, Mirabel — to protect its interests. Lady Wishfort is not rejected as Sir Sampson Legend is rejected.

She may not preside over the family any more, as she has done in the past, but she continues as a senior member. She may still continue holding her 'cabal' meetings and discreetly searching for a decorous lover![24]

VIII

What Mrs Fainfall and Mirabel say about Lady Wishfort reflects the normal attitude of the young towards the old. Mrs Fainfall talks of the old feeling 'the craving of a false appetite when the true is decayed' and Mirabel compares this 'false appetite' to 'the green sickness of a second childhood' or the 'depraved' appetite of a girl. It is clear that the old are to be judged only in terms of appetite, false or depraved. The emphasis is laid so heavily on this aspect of their character that all their other qualities are forgotten. Even Lady Wishfort talks of this kind of appetite when she reminds Waitwell (disguised as Sir Rowland) that he must not attribute her 'yielding to any sinister appetite, or indigestion of widowhood' (IV.ii).

This indigestion of widowhood is perhaps seen at its most sinister in Lady Flippant in Wycherley's *Love in a Wood*. She is described in the list of characters as 'an affected Widow, in distress for a Husband' and the very first line in the play where she speaks to Mrs Joyner, 'a Match–maker, or precise City–Bawd', she betrays her impatience: 'Not a Husband to be had for money'. She further complains that Mrs Joyner has failed her though she herself used 'more Industry to get her a Husband' than any 'Woman breathing'. Her industry is, of course, evident: 'Have I not constantly kept Covent-Garden-Church, St. Martins, the Play-Houses, Hide-Park, Mulbery-Garden, and all other of the publick Marts where Widows and Mayds are expos'd?' (I.i). It is clear from what she says later that her need is not for a husband alone. After one of her fruitless visits to St James' Park, she laments: 'Unfortunate Lady, that I am! I have left the Herd on purpose to be chas'd, and have wandered this hour here; but the Park affords not so much as a Satyr for me, (and that's strange) no Burgundy man, or drunken Scourer, will reel my way' (V.i). J. H. Smith has rightly called her 'brazen and nymphomaniac'.[25]

The 'monstrous regiment of women' hovering round Horner in

The Country Wife is no better, though it conducts its affairs with a sophistication that Lady Flippant lacks. Wycherley's world is so obsessed with sex that even a girl of fourteen — Hippolita, the heroine of *The Gentleman Dancing-Master* — at times leaves a somewhat uncomfortable impression in our minds, and we wonder whether she too possesses similar tendencies in her character, and whether, if differently placed, she would behave like some of these women. This is not a pleasant thought, but then in Wycherley life is often presented as too raw.

Our speculation may be quite unfair to Hippolita, but the point is that where men and women become desperate about sex, they become a menace both to themselves and to others. With the old (Lady Flippant is not really old, and as she claims, 'my Person's in good repair' (I.i); but in this comedy one is either in the first flush of youth or faded) a desparate search for sexual satisfaction can almost become a disease, as it has in the case of Lady Flippant. It is not correct to say that this is necessarily a female disease, as Mrs Fainall seems to suggest when she talks of 'Female frailty', though women are perhaps more self–conscious about being vulnerable to the ravages of time. We should recognize that in Restoration comedy superannuated beauties are no more ridiculous than men like Wycherley's Pinchwife or Congreve's Fondlewife, whose very names are a sufficient judgment on them. Both have married — or bought — young wives, and both are utterly inadequate as husbands.

The author of *The Whole Duty of Man* perhaps had such marriages in mind when he gave this advice to married people in his *The Ladies Calling* (1673):

The humors of youth and age differ so widely, that there had need be a great deal of skill to compose the discord into a harmony. When a young Woman marries an old man, there are commonly jealousies on the one part and loathings on the other, and if there be not an eminent degree of discretion in one or both, there will be perpetual disagreements.

(Part II, p. 85)

The young had often no freedom to choose their spouses yet the old surely could show this 'eminent degree of discretion' by not marrying persons who were too young for them. But Restoration comedy is full of old men who completely lack discretion.

There is the case of Fondlewife himself. This is how he reasons with himself:

Tell me, Isaac, why art thee jealous? Why art thee distrustful of the wife of thy bosom? — because she is young and vigorous, and, I am old and impotent. Then, why didst thee marry, Isaac? — because she was beautiful and tempting, and because I was obstinate and doting, so that my inclination was, and is still, greater than my power. And will not that which tempted thee, also tempt others, who will tempt her, Isaac? — I fear it much. But does not thy wife love thee, nay, dote upon thee? — Yes — Why then! — Ay, but to say truth, she's fonder of me than she has reason to be; and in the way of trade, we still suspect the smoothest dealers of the deepest designs — that she has some designs deeper than thou canst reach, th' hast experimented, Isàac. (*The Old Bachelor*, IV.i.)

That Letitia has designs is shown by the playwright immediately after Fondlewife has left home and Bellmour walks in to supply the place of Vainlove, Letitia's lover!

Then there is Sir Sampson Legend in *Love for Love*, who makes a fool of himself by falling in love with Angelica. Angelica, it is true, leads him on, but he richly deserves to be exposed:

SIR SAMPSON: . . . I am not so old neither to be a bare courtier, only a man of words: odd, I have warm blood about me yet, and can serve a lady any way — Come, come, let me tell you, you women think a man old too soon, faith and troth, you do! — Come, don't despise fifty, odd, fifty, in a hale constitution, is no such contemptible age.

ANGELICA: Fifty a contemptible age! not at all, a very fashionable age, I think, — I know very considerable beaux that set a good face upon fifty: — fifty! I have seen fifty in a side-box, by candle-light, out-blossom five-and-twenty.

SIR SAMPSON: Outsides, outsides; a pize take 'em, mere outsides! hang your side-box beaux! no, I'm none of those, none of your forced trees, that pretend to blossom in the fall, and bud when they should bring forth fruit; I am of a long-lived race, and inherit vigour: none of my ancestors married till fifty; yet they begot sons and daughters till fourscore; I am of your patriarchs, I, a branch of one of your antediluvian families, fellows that the flood could not wash away . . .
(V.i)

Sir Sampson is shown at his most heroic — and consequently most ridiculous—when he tells her that he would do anything for her 'incomparable beauty': 'If I had Peru in one hand, and Mexico in t'other, and eastern empire under my feet, it would make me only a more glorious victim to be offered at the shrine of your beauty' (V.i). Sir Sampson is, of course, a fool — as also a knave — but when old age starts offering itself as a 'victim' at the 'shrine' of youth, solely out of infatuation, we seem to have entered an altogether different world from that of Shakespeare.

IX

Restoration comedy has a natural tendency to show old age in embarrassing situations. There is, for instance, Aldo, the father of Woodall in Dryden's *The Kind Keeper* (1678). He meets his son but does not recognize him. The son has been bred abroad and has just returned. Moreover he goes under a false name. Aldo starts telling the young man in confidence how he helps women who have been cast away by their gallants and who are in need of help and comfort. The following conversation takes place between them:

WOOD: Sure you expect some kindness in return.
ALDO: Faith, not much: Nature in me is at low water-mark; my Body's a
    Jade, and tires under me, yet I love to smuggle still in a Corner; pat
    'em down, and pur over 'em; but after that I can do 'em little harm.
WOOD: Then I'm acquainted with your business: you wou'd be a kind of
    Deputy-Fumbler under me   (I.i)

'Deputy-Fumbler' is a humiliating enough description for a man who is too old for normal sex but who finds other ways of satisfying his sexual urge. Aldo, however, is a decent enough man, described in the list of characters as an honest. good-natured and free-hearted old gentleman of the town. It is in Shadwell's Snarl in *The Virtuoso* (1676) that we see old age at its ugliest. He is described in the list of characters as 'an old, pettish fellow, a great admirer of the last age and a declaimer against the vices of this, and privately very vicious himself'. Every time he meets Miranda and Clarinda — his granddaughters — he starts attacking women for 'their washing, painting, patching, and their damn'd ugly, new fashion'd Dresses' (I.ii). In his eyes these two girls, too, are sluts who 'take more pains to lose Reputation than those [ladies of the last age] did to preserve it' (I.ii). He suspects every woman of indulging in extra-marital sex and is afraid that 'the next age will have very few that are lawfully begotton in't, by the mass' (I.ii). He describes the last age as 'an Age of innocence' (I.ii) and in a totally hypocritical pose declares: 'By the mass, my heart bleeds to see so great a decay of conjugal affection in the Nation' (III.ii). His heart really bleeds only for his mistress, Mrs Figgup, whom he secretly meets at a convenient place. The kind of sexual pleasure that Snarl derives from these meetings is a clear sign of sickness:

SNARL: Ah poor little Rogue! in sadness, I'll bite thee by the lip, i'
faith I will. Thou has incen'st me strangely, thou hast fir'd my
blood, I can bear it no longer, I' faith I cannot. Where are the
Instruments of our pleasure? Nay, prithee do not frown, by the Mass,
thou shall do't now.

FIGG: I wonder that should please you so much that pleases me so
little?

SNARL: I was so us'd to't at *Westminster*-School, I cou'd never leave it off
since.

FIG.: Well: look under the Carpet then if I must.

SNARL: Very well, my dear Rogue. But dost hear, thou art too gentle. Do
not spare thy pains. I love Castigation mightily — So, here's good
provision.

    Pulls the Carpet, three or four great Rods fall down. (III.ii)

One effect of the contemptuous attitude of the comic playwrights to old age is that the role of parents gets degraded. In
Wycherley's *Love in a Wood* (1672), a mother (Mrs Crossbite) acts
as a bawd to her daughter (Lucy) and when the daughter protests
against her old lover (Dapperwit) being supplanted by a lecherous old man (Alderman Gripe) this is what the mother says: 'He
has taught you to talk indeed; but Huswife, I will not have *my
pleasure* disputed' (III) (Italics mine). Another mother in Shadwell's *A True Widow* (1679) plans to sell her two daughters as
mistresses to fashionable gentlemen. When the elder daughter,
Isabella, declines an offer of 'a Thousand pounds down, and
three Hundred pounds *per Annum* during life' (II), her mother
describes her as a 'perverse' girl who would 'rather marry a
Groom, than be Mistress to a Prince'. When Lady Busy, 'half
Bawd, half Match-maker', reminds Isabella that her mother and
she 'have known the World' and that ' 'tis fit the Young should
submit themselves to the gravity and discreation of the Old' (II),
Isabella gives the sarcastic reply: 'Yes, where they can find it.' It is
a strange world where the mother wants to corrupt her daughters
and where one of the daughters resists and is finally happily
married. The other daughter becomes the mistress of two persons,
and failing to achieve a 'Settlement or a Marriage', has to be
disposed off in marriage to a wholly unworthy man.

Dryden's *The Kind Keeper* also has a mother, Mrs Overdon,
who is out to exploit her daughter's youth. She brings her to Aldo
and this is the conversation that takes place:

MRS OVER: Ask blessing, *Pru:* he's the best Father you ever had.

ALDO.: Bless thee, and make thee a substantial, thriving Whore. Have
your Mother in your eye, *Pru*; 'tis good to follow good example:

How old are you, *Pru*? hold up your head, Child.

PRU.: Going o' my sixteen, Father *Aldo*.

ALDO.: And you have been initiated but these two years: loss of time, loss of precious time. Mrs *Overdon*, how much have you made of *Pru*, since she has been Man's meat?

MRS OVER.: A very small matter, by my troth; considering the charges I have been at in her Education: poor *Pru* was born under an unlucky Planet; I despair of a Coach for her. Her first Maiden-head brought me in but little: the weather-beaten old Knight that bought her of me, beat down the price so low; I held her at an hundred Guinnies, and he bid ten; and higher than thirty he wou'd not rise.

ALDO.: A pox of his unluckie handsel: he can but fumble, and will not pay neither.

PRU.: Hang him; I cou'd never endure him, Father: he's the filth'st old Goat; and then he comes every day to our house, and eats out his thirty Guinnies; and at three Months end, he threw me off.

MRS OVER.: And since then, the poor Child has dwindled, and dwindled away: her next Maiden-head brought me but ten; and from ten she fell to five; and at last to a single Guinny: she has no luck to keeping; they all leave her, the more my sorrow.

ALDO.: We must get her a Husband then in the City; they bite rarely at a stale Whore at this end o' th' Town, new furbish'd up in a taudry *Manto*.

MRS OVER.: No: pray let her try her fortune a little longer in the World first: by my troth, I shou'd be loth to be at all this cost, in her *French*, and her *Singing*, to have her thrown away upon a Husband.

ALDO.: Before *George*, there can come no good of your swearing, Mrs. *Overdon*: Say your Prayers, *Pru*, and go duly to Church o' Sundays, you'l thrive the better all the week. Come, have a good heart, Child; I'll keep thee my self: thou shalt do my little business; and I'll find thee an able young Fellow to do thine.   (IV.i)

What Norman Holland has said about the adaptation of Beaumont and Fletcher's *The Chances* (1627) by George Villiers, Duke of Buckingham, applies not only to plays like Wycherley's *Love in a Wood*, Shadwell's *A True Widow*, and Dryden's *The Kind Keeper* but also to quite a few other plays in the Restoration period:

The change perfectly exemplifies the Restoration comic idea of the relation of parents to children. Their influence is never beneficial: in this play, it is corrupting; in others, repressive. Those who appear to be guides are in nature not. The use of a girl's mother for her bawd also sets a tone of universal social corruption surrounding the action, and this is an axiom of Restoration comedy — that one operates in a very fallen age indeed.'[26]

Holland's 'axiom of Restoration comedy' is a generalisation, but there is a great deal of substance in it. It is rarely that Restoration comedy lends dignity to old age. Every parent or guardian is not, of course, like Mrs Crossbite of Wycherley, or Shadwell's Widow, or Dryden's Mrs Overdon. But by and large the old in Restoration comedy fail to arouse any feelings of love and admiration. Indeed, they often arouse only feelings of contempt. This was perhaps inevitable in a comedy which reflected the values of a decadent youth culture.

CHAPTER IV

HUSBANDS AND WIVES (I):
SHAKESPEARE

I

Laurence Lerner observes that 'if we are to believe the poets, love
and marriage exist in a state of conflict: love exists outside marriage, or ceases when marriage begins or enters marriage only to
destroy it.'[1] This is clearly a generalization and whether or not it
is true of poets in general, it is not at all certain whether it is true
of Shakespeare. The impression that one gathers from Shakespeare's plays is that it is his constant endeavour to reconcile love
and marriage. It may, of course, be pointed out that in a play like
Antony and Cleopatra love exists outside marriage and Antony's
attitude towards Cleopatra can be contrasted with his attitude
towards Octavia. And yet in the final acts of the play, love and
marriage come together when Cleopatra says in perhaps her fin-
est moment:

> Husband, I come.
> Now to that name my courage prove my title![2]   (V.ii.285-6)

There is also no evidence in Shakespeare that love ceases after
marriage. Rosalind mentions the possibility: 'men are April
when they woo, December when they wed: maids are May when
they are maids, but the sky changes when they are wives' (*AYLI*,
IV.i.131-34). But these remarks are addressed to the man she is
going to marry and are meant not only to tease but also to 'educate' him — to undercut the excesses and extravagances of romantic love. The impression left by the play is clearly that they shall
live happily ever after. Indeed, that is the impression left by all
Shakespeare's comedies. It is not without significance that the
heroines of Shakespeare's comedies do not rush into marriage
without exploring the personalities of the men they marry. They
recognize that if marriage is not to amount to 'wooing, wedding
and repenting' (*Much Ado*, II.i.62) if the relationship is to be a
permanent and stable one, then there must be mutual understanding and more than superficial laking. There is one comedy,

The Comedy of Errors, where Shakespeare shows love drying up after marriage — at least that is the wife's complaint — but even here the point the play makes is not that love necessarily ceases when marriage begins but rather that immature people (especially those who are inordinately jealous for no apparent reason) create unnecessary difficulties for themselves.

Lerner states that in *Romeo and Juliet* Capulet has 'no affection for his wife' and that he comes nearest to affection only 'when he calls on her to share his grief — "O heavens! O wife, look how our daughter bleeds" — and that even here he is simply including her in a feeling that is paternal and familial, for he calls her, as he always does, simply "wife"'[3]! But surely Lerner misunderstands the husband-wife relationship in the Elizabethan patriarchal society where calling her 'wife' was the only approved mode of address available to a husband. It certainly did not denote any lack of affection. Further, Shakespeare's chief concern in the play is to depict the love between Romeo and Juliet and not between the older people.

Lerner's last claim that love destroys marriage in the case of Romeo and Juliet or Othello and Desdemona[4] is also not tenable. The passion of these couples was, of course, too intense, but they could have survived as loving husbands and wives if external circumstances and agents had not conspired against them. To claim that their marriages are destroyed from within is clearly erroneous.

Since we are contrasting Shakespeare's handling of the husband–wife relationship with its treatment in Restoration comedy, we may notice that almost nowhere does Shakespeare depict the battle of the sexes which is a common theme in the Restoration Comedy of Manners. He clearly regards the roles of the sexes as complementary and feels that as man is incomplete without woman, so woman is incomplete without man. In *King John*, a citizen mentions this aspect of the man–woman relationship while recommending marriage between Blanch and the Dauphin:

> He is the half part of a blessed man,
> Left to be finished by such as she;
> And she a fair divided excellence,
> Whose fulness of perfection lies in him.[5]   (II.i.437-40)

This theme is present in one form or another in almost all the comedies of Shakespeare where the plays end in marriage.

II

One significant difference between Shakespeare's plays and Restoration comedy is that the constant theme of the latter is 'rivalry between the sexes which was overtly playful but frequently descended into sadism'. Indeed, the 'sophisticated relationships between men and women' in Restoration literature 'frequently appear as cold-blooded exploitation by the stronger party, whether man or woman.'[6] It is remarkable that Shakespeare's world should be free from this virus. Critics have sometimes suspected that rivalry between the sexes exists in *Much Ado About Nothing*. But we must not forget that this is wholly on the surface and is meant only as an amusing pose both on the part of man and woman. Surely it would be ridiculous to treat Beatrice's retort to Leonato seriously when he jocularly suggests that he hopes 'to see [her] one day fitted with a husband':

Not till God make men of some other metal than earth. Would it not grieve a woman to be over-master'd with a piece of valiant dust, to make an account of her life to a clod of wayward marl? No, uncle, I'll none: Adam's sons are my brethren; and, truly, I hold it a sin to match in my kindred
(II.i.50-55)

This woman, however, takes no time to change her mind and gladly decides to requite Benedick when she learns that he loves her. Benedick's anti-female posture is equally ridiculous:

That a woman conceived me, I thank her; that she brought me up, I like-wise give her most humble thanks; but that I will have a recheat winded in my forehead, or having my bugle in an invisible baldrick, all women shall pardon me. Because I will not do them the wrong to mistrust any, I will do myself the right to trust none; and the fine is, for the which I may go the finer, I will live a bachelor.

(I.i.206-213)

Of course, he will do nothing of the kind and will give up this state of bachelorhood at the earliest opportunity, and suddenly recognize 'that the world must be peopled', as if that is his personal responsibility! The only defence of his earlier boast that he can offer is: 'When I said I would die a bachelor, I did not think I should live till I were married.' (II.iii.219-20). The play clearly establishes that the earlier postures of Beatrice and Benedick are merely a reaction to the conventional and extravagant behaviour of romantic lovers. Indeed they take no time to recognize that their salvation lies only in coming together. Not only their salvation but the salvation of others too, as Benedick claims: 'Prince, thou art sad; get thee a wife, get thee a wife.' Lest the Prince should laugh at this zeal of a new convert, Benedick adds: 'There is no staff more reveren'd than one tipp'd with horn.' (V.iv.118-119).

A superficial reading of *The Taming of the Shrew* can give the impression that here at any rate Shakespeare shows rivalry between the sexes, depicting at some length the cold-blooded exploitation by the stronger party of the weaker one — the weaker being the woman. This is clearly a wrong impression. Even though the real theme of this play is essentially the same as that of the other romantic comedies of Shakespeare, namely, establishing a genuine personal relationship between man and woman, it is worked out through a series of farcical situations which distort our response. Outwardly the play shows the taming of a shrew — a taming that involves cruelty and humiliation. Katherine suffers first at the hands of her family and then at the hands of a husband whom she is compelled to marry in somewhat awkward circumstances. She fights back as long as she can but a stage comes when she is completely exhausted for lack of food and sleep. Petruchio claims that whatever he does, he does 'in reverend care of her' and that he is doing it to cure her of her shrewishness:

> This is a way to kill a wife with kindness,
> And thus I'll curb her mad and headstrong humour.
>
> (IV.i.192-3)

This claim may be true enough, but at a more basic level of human psychology it is truer still that the play exposes Petruchio's own immaturity. Petruchio suffers excessively from an inflated male ego. He is determined that the woman he has married must accept him as her lord and master, and that the world should see and applaud this male dominance. Indeed, he is almost as infantile in his obsession as Sly the tinker:

SLY: Are you my wife, and will not call me husband? My men should call me 'lord', I am your goodman.
PAGE: My husband and my lord, my lord and husband; I am your wife in all obedience. *(Induction,* ii.102-5)

Once Kate comes to understand the real need of Petruchio — a
need that is clearly born of a sense of inadequacy — she changes
her strategy, and even while permitting him 'to indulge his
dream of total mastery, subverts her husband's power without
attempting to challenge it, and she does so in a gamesome spirit,
without hostility or bitterness.'[7] It is, of course, not a new situation in the man-woman relationship, nor is Kate's strategy a new
one. As Nevill Coghill has wisely said, 'like most of those wives
that are the natural superiors of their husbands, she allows Petruchio the mastery in public.'[8]

Kate's superiority is seen in her wit–combat with Petruchio in
her very first meeting with him — indeed in her very first words
to him. As soon as she enters, Petruchio hails her:

PET.: Good morrow, Kate — for that's your name, I hear.
KATH.: Well have you heard, but something hard of hearing: They
    call me Katherine that do talk of me.   (II.i.181-3)

This superiority is more particularly evident in later scenes when
she has fully understood Petruchio's real nature and decides to let
him indulge in his fantasy of complete domination over her. So
when he declares that old Vincentio is a 'Fair lovely maid', Katherine improves on him in her description of the old man:

> Young budding virgin, fair and fresh and sweet,
> Whither away, or where is thy abode?
> Happy the parents of so fair a child;
> Happy the man whom favourable stars
> Allots thee for his lovely bed-fellow.   (V.i.36-40)

When Petruchio reprimands her and tells her that Vincentio is
not a maid but an 'old, wrinkled, faded, withered' man, she
catches the hint and shows again her inventive skill:

> Pardon, old father, my mistaking eyes,
> That have been so bedazzled with the sun
> That everything I look on seemeth green.   (V.i.44-46)

Her famous speech in the last scene should be read in the context
of what has been said above. Only in an apparent sense is it an
expression of servile submission. Such submission was the lot of
most women in that period — or even today in most societies
where women have no economic independence — but here the
speech serves a wholly different purpose. Petruchio, as we have

seen, has still to outgrow the desire to dominate the woman. He
has yet to acquire confidence both in himself and in the woman
he has married. As Coppelia Kahn has said: 'Such voluntary surrender is, paradoxically, part of the myth of female power, which
assigns to woman the crucial responsibility for creating a mature
and socially respectable man.'[9] This Katherine can do by reminding Petruchio that husband and wife have different roles to play
in life, and that only foolish people quarrel about the superiority
or inferiority of either of the two roles. The fact is that both roles
are necessary for a happy married life. Unless a man and a woman
recognize the difference in the roles that they are required to play
— whether by nature or by society — we can have neither a stable
family life nor an orderly society. As Katherine says:

> Thy husband is thy lord, thy life, thy keeper,
> Thy head, thy sovereign; one that cares for thee,
> And for thy maintenance commits his body
> To painful labour both by sea and land,
> To watch the night in storms, the day in cold,
> Whilst thou liest warm at home, secure and safe;
> And craves no other tribute at thy hands
> But love, fair looks, and true obedience —
> Too little payment for so great a debt.   (V.ii.145-53)

The speech is apparently addressed to women, but its real aim is
to educate Petruchio. By the time the play ends, the husband and
wife have come to realize that there can be no rivalry between
them nor any exploitation of one by the other. So this too, like the
other comedies of Shakespeare, ends on a note of fulfilment. We
are left with a sense that, (to use Coppelia Kahn's words again) —
'Truly, Petruchio is wedded to his Kate.'[10]

Germaine Greer has described Kate's speech as 'the greatest
defence of Christian monogamy ever written' and has rightly
asserted that it 'rests upon the role of a husband as protector and
friend, and it is valid because Kate has a man who is capable of
being both.' When she describes Shakespeare as 'one of the most
significant apologists of marriage as a way of life and a road of
salvation',[11] the implication is that Shakespeare celebrates the
institution of marriage and treats it as the only means available to
man or woman for achieving happiness and fulfilment. Indeed,
his message is clear, namely, that it is through marriage alone
that men and women can become integrated human beings.

III

Shakespeare's emphasis on the sanctity of marriage can be fully appreciated only in the context of the state of marriage which prevailed amongst the English nobility in the earlier part of the sixteenth century, and the climate created by the religious reformers of the period in favour of an ideal Christian marriage. On the state of marriage in England in the earlier part of the century, we have the well-known statement of Lawrence Stone:

In the early sixteenth century open maintenance of a mistress — usually of lower class origin — was perfectly compatible with a respected social position and a stable marriage. Peers clearly saw nothing shameful in these liaisons, and up to about 1560 they are often to be found leaving bequests to bastard children in their wills. In practice, if not in theory, the early-sixteenth-century nobility was a polygamous[12] society, and some contrived to live with a succession of women despite the official prohibition on divorce.[13] Presumably, in deference to Puritan criticism of the double standard, this casual approach to extra-marital relationships disappeared after 1560 and between 1610 and 1660 evidence for the maintenance of regular, semi-official mistresses becomes rare.[14]

There are several bastards in Shakespeare, and in *King Lear* we have the notorious case of Gloucester who boasts with impunity of a bastard son — 'there was good sport at his making, and the whoreson must be acknowledged' (I.i.23-24). It is, however, indicative of Shakespeare's attitude to such a casual approach to extra-marital relationships that Gloucester's legitimate son should at last have to say to Edmund:

> The gods are just, and of our pleasant vices
> Make instruments to plague us:
> The dark and vicious place where thee he got
> Cost him his eyes.
>
> (V.iii.170-3)

Moreover, Gloucester's is an exceptional case, and on the whole, the most distinguishing feature of Shakespeare's plays is their purity of tone. For one thing, there are no rakes[15] in Shakespeare — or almost none — and he more or less enjoins on both men and women a respect for the marriage bond. Women were always expected to live chaste and spotless lives — both before and after marriage — but the remarkable fact about Shakespeare is his 'adherence to a single standard of sexual morality' for men and women alike. Harbage, who makes this point, names Romeo, Orsino, Orlando, Malcolm, Florizel and Ferdinand as leading

lives as stainless as the heroines of the plays in which they appear.
He also says that the lecherous men in Shakespeare — 'Falstaff,
Shallow in his youth, Lucio, Patroclus — are either comic or
contemptible' and, further, that 'those perhaps not lecherous in a
comic way but so infatuated as to become lawlessly involved —
Claudio, Cassio, Troilus, Antony — are all viewed as pitiable.'[16]
Harbage is perhaps overstating the case, and we cannot say that
there is no double standard in Shakespeare or that in every case
there is an 'adherence to a single standard of sexual morality'. But
the fact is that the general tendency of Shakespearean drama is
towards equality between the sexes in this most crucial sphere of
conduct.

It is remarkable that this should be so in an age when, as Ruth
Kelso says, 'The ideal set up for the lady is essentially Christian in
its character, and the ideal for the gentleman essentially pagan.'[17]
Chastity was the chief, if not the only, quality required of a lady,
whereas it was not even included among the virtues required of a
gentleman. The age, indeed, must have found it very appropriate
that Spenser chose to embody chastity in a Lady-Knight, depart-
ing from his usual practice of embodying a particular virtue in a
knight. Shakespeare's rejection of this aristocratic doctrine must
owe a great deal to the new climate created by the religious
reformers who denounced contemporary social evils, more particularly the callous and cold-blooded exploitation of woman by
man. It is not without significance that the impact of the religious reformers was felt even by King James who gave this advice
to his son in 1599: 'Ye must keepe your bodie cleane and unpol-
luted, while [i.e. till] ye give it to your wife whome to onlie it
belongeth: For how can ye justlie crave to be joyned with a pure
Virgin, if your bodie be polluted? Why should the one halfe be
cleane, and the other defiled.'[18] It is true that at times the
preachers' stand sounded somewhat contradictory as they
emphasized, on the one hand, obedience to parents, especially in
the choice of a spouse, and on the other marriages based on love
between two parties. But it is fair to add that in spite of all their
insistence upon obedience to parents, they consistently emphasized the conditions under which husbands and wives could lead
chaste and contented lives. Marital fidelity is the most important
feature of such lives, and they clearly recognized that love between
husband and wife alone could provide a viable basis for fidelity.

Most conduct-books in the period emphasize the conditions under which chastity in marriage can become a reality. They, therefore, define marriage in intelligible and realistic terms. Since they cannot but accept the Bible as their sole guide, they refine upon the relationship between Adam and Eve for human guidance. This refinement is to be seen at its best in Bullinger, one of the most popular writers in the sixteenth century, whose writings influenced almost all contemporary conduct-books. This is what he has to say about the origin of marriage: 'God made the man Adam altogether perfect, set him in the Paradise or garden of pleasure, and afterwards sayd immediately: It is not good that man should be alone.' Adam, having looked upon all the beasts, 'found . . . none that he could set his harte upon, none lyke him selfe, none that he myght dwell by as by an helper and comforter'. He knew that he was alone, and 'woe', says Henry Smith, quoting Solomon, to all such 'as theeves steale in when the house is emptie; like a Turtle, which hath lost his mate, like one legge when the other is cutte off, like one wing when the other is clipte, so had the man bene if the woman had not bene joyned to him.' William and Malleville Haller from whose article on 'The Puritan Art of Love' these quotations have been taken, add this comment: 'Thus the first need that befell man, even before he had sinned, was for woman and the first intervention of divine providence in his especial behalf was to create a wife for him and to establish wedlock as the prime source and pattern of all human relationships to come.'[19]

The relationship between husband and wife, then, is a very special one and it is based on the conviction that God made them for each other and that they alone are fit for each other. This idea of fitness is to be seen in Henry Smith's description of 'a fitte wife': 'Therefore a godly man in our time thanked the Lord that he had not onely given him a godly wife, but a fitte wife: for he sayd not that she was the wisest, nor the holiest, nor the humblest, nor the modestest wife in the world, but the fittest wife for him.'[20] Such husband and wife are indeed so 'fit' for each other that John Wing in *Crowne Conjungall* (1620) described them as 'the sweetest, and most pleasing objects, upon earth; to take up each others eyes, from all the world besides, that no other in this regard may once be thought worth looking upon.'[21] Perhaps even a better description of such a couple occurs in Daniel Rogers' *Matrimoniall Honour* (1642):

Husbands and wives should be as two sweet friends, bred under one constellation, tempered by an influence from heaven, whereof neither can give any great reason, save that mercy and providence first made them so, and then made their match; saying, see, God hath determined us, out of this vast world, each for other; perhaps many may deserve as well, but yet to me, and for my turne, thou excellest them all, and God hath made me to thinke so (not for formality sake to say) but because it is so.[22]

Thomas Becon who had written a long preface to the English translation of Bullinger's book and who later wrote a book of his own entitled *Book of Matrimony* (1564), sums up contemporary religious thinking on the question in his well-known description of matrimony:

[Matrimonye is] an hie, holye and blessed order of life, ordayned not of man, but of God, yea and that not in this sinneful world, but in paradyse that most joyful garden of pleasure: which [Matrimonye] hath ever ben had in great honour and reverence among all nacions: wherein one man and one woman are coupled and knit together in one fleshe and body in the feare and love of God, by the free, lovinge, harty, and good consents of them both, to the entent that they two may dwel together, as one fleshe and body of one wyl and mynd in all honesty, vertue and godliness, and spend theyr lyves in the equal partaking of all such thinges, as God shal send them with thankes gevynge.[23]

While Becon has only ideal marriages in mind (which seem to have been made in heaven), his statement does provide general guidelines for a happy married life. He makes three points: one, that the marriage between two persons is based on free, loving and hearty consent; second, that they live together in a state of harmony based on a perfect compatibility between their bodies, minds and wills – a compatibility that should ensure a life of 'honesty, vertue and godliness'; and, third, that they share their joys and sorrows – or whatever God sends them – with 'thankes gevynge'.

It is remarkable that all the three points made by Becon are present in Shakespeare's conception of marriage. As we have already seen, he clearly rejects arranged marriages, and however difficult it was in his age (and in quite a few of his plays), the marriages in Shakespeare are by and large based on the free, loving and hearty consent of the partners. Sometimes parents have to be defied; sometimes daughters have to elope with their lovers; sometimes they even risk their lives to achieve a love-marriage. But there is hardly any case in Shakespeare where there is a forced marriage. Consequently, nowhere do we have the kind of situation that is almost constantly present in Restoration comedy where a woman is normally advised to find 'a gallant, to supply the defects of a husband'. (Edward Ravenscroft, *London Cuckolds* (1682), II.i). As Valentine in *The Two Gentlemen of Verona* claims, the person one loves is different from all others: 'whose worth makes other worthies nothing / She is alone.' (II.iv. 161–62).

Compatibility between bodies, minds and wills, however, is not easy to achieve. The two persons may not lack free, loving and hearty consent, but such consent alone may not ensure harmony. As Germaine Greer has said, Shakespeare 'recognised it [i.e. marriage] as a difficult state of life, requiring discipline, sexual energy, mutual respect and great forbearance.'[24] Shakespeare's men do not realize this fact but his women do, and accordingly, they search for a stable basis on which to put their relationship. Being realistic, they recognize that neither 'romanticism' nor sexual attraction can sustain a marriage. They therefore 'use wit and realism in the service of passion to mock male folly, to educate men, and to achieve a fruitful union with them. Rosalind, Viola, Portia and the women in *Love's Labour Lost* all have active roles in their plays, grounding male idealism in reality and effecting a reconciliation of sex with love, wit with affection, male with female.'[25] It is important that they do so because it is quite possible that from being a goddess of the romantic lover, the woman might end up by becoming only a super menial. In times when divorce was impossible – or more or less impossible – and when adultery could lead to banishment or death, it was vital for a woman to make a sensible choice.

Shakespeare's heroes are often too immature to become suitable husbands. Orlando in *As You Like It* is clearly one of them. He is a 'fancy-monger,' (III.ii.337) and fits admirably the picture of a lover drawn by Jaques in his description of 'the seven ages of man':

> And then the lover,
> Sighing like furnace, with a woeful ballad
> Made to his mistress' eyebrow.   (III.vii.147–149)

He hangs verses on trees in praise of his beloved and becomes an object of ridicule. He is not the only lover in Shakespeare who

writes bad verses in praise of his mistress. Even Hamlet does so –
and, of course, Benedick tries, though mercifully, he just cannot
rhyme well. But Rosalind bluntly reminds Orlando that most
lovers live in a world of fancy and are often attracted by the mere
idea of being in love; that their professions of eternal loyalty are
mere lies and that 'men have died from time to time, and worms
have eaten them, but not for love.' (IV.i. 93–94). Her most perceptive comment is to be seen in the distinction that she draws
between romantic love and marriage:

ROSALIND : Now tell me how long you would have her, after you have
possess'd her.
ORLANDO : For ever and a day.
ROSALIND : Say 'a day' without the 'ever'. No, no, Orlando; men are
April when they woo, December when they wed: maids are May
when they are maids, but the sky changes when they are wives. I
will be more jealous of thee than a Barbary cock–pigeon over his
hen, more clamorous than a parrot against rain, more newfangled
than an ape, more giddy in my desires than a monkey. I will weep
for nothing, like Diana in the fountain, and I will do that when
you are disposed to be merry; I will laugh like a hyen, and that
when thou art inclined to sleep.   (IV.i.127–139)

Orlando, clearly baffled by what Rosalind has said, asks, 'But will
my Rosalind do so?' adding: 'O, but she is wise'. Thereupon
Rosalind launches another attack on his conventional view of a
wise woman:

The wiser, the waywarder. Make the doors upon a woman's wit,
and it will out at the casement; shut that, and 'twill out at the
key–hole; stop that, 'twill fly with the smoke out at the
chimney.

(143-147)

The question that Rosalind jocularly raises is a serious one. She
reminds Orlando that marriage cannot be based on romantic love
alone and further that a successful marriage with an intelligent
and articulate woman is still more difficult to maintain.[26] Rosalind is clearly rejecting the Elizabethan stereotype of a modest,
virtuous, obedient and docile Elizabethan wife.

    Beatrice also rejects this type. Like Rosalind, while she is capa-
ble of intense love and devotion, she demands qualities in the
man of her choice which she can admire. These are somewhat
unconventional qualities in that age as they seem to lay heavy

emphasis on his *mind* and heart. By contrast, however intelligent otherwise, in this regard Benedick looks for the same qualities in a wife as other Elizabethan husbands: 'Rich she shall be, that's certain; wise, or I'll none; virtuous, or I'll never cheapen her; fair, or I'll never look at her; mild, or come not near me; noble, or not I for an angel; of good discourse, an excellent musician, and her hair shall be of what colour it please God' (*Much Ado*, II.iii.25-31).[27] Women in Shakespeare do not *directly* state what qualities they expect in a good husband, but in their own way they do assess the men they decide to marry. Men, of course, are not concerned with what qualities they need to possess to make good husbands. Don Pedro, for instance, is quite content to describe Benedick as not 'the unhopefullest husband that I know' (II.i.341) simply because 'he is of a noble strain, of approved valour, and confirm'd honesty' (342-3).[28] But these qualities by themselves are not enough. Even Bertram of *All's Well that Ends Well* was of a 'noble strain' and of 'approved valour'. His mother and Helena did not doubt his honesty too, though it was not confirmed. And yet he made a totally unworthy husband. So a woman in Shakespeare has to be careful. Beatrice, in any case, is a very perceptive person and she cannot be easily impressed by what appears on the surface. She has to probe, and only then decide.

V

At one stage, Beatrice hints at the chief deficiency of Benedick's character: 'He were an excellent man that were made just in the mid-way between him [Don John] and Benedick: the one is too like an image and says nothing, and the other too like my lady's eldest son, evermore tattling.' (II.i.6-10). This is yet another instance of Beatrice's 'merry war' with Benedick, but it is also perhaps an expression of her impatience with what she regards as Benedick's lack of seriousness. This impatience may also explain her somewhat unkind remark later that Benedick is 'the Prince's jester' (II.i.120). That she is concerned with this seriousness as a *quality* that a potential husband should possess —a seriousness that is born of intellectual and emotional maturity — is subtly indicated in her subsequent exchange with Don Pedro:

BEATRICE: . . . I may sit in a corner and cry 'Heigh-ho for a husband'!
DON PEDRO: Lady Beatrice, I will get you one.

BEATRICE: I would rather have one of your father's getting. Hath your grace ne'er a brother like you? Your father got excellent husbands, if a maid could come by them.

DON PEDRO: Will you have me, lady?

BEATRICE: No, my lord, unless I might have another for working-days: your grace is too costly to wear every-day. . .　　　　　(II.i.287-296)

The importance of Beatrie's last remark here has rarely been noticed. Critics have come to feel that in these remarks, to use Beatrice's own words, there is 'all mirth and no matter'. The only person who took this remark seriously was Bernard Shaw. In *Getting Married — A Disquisitory Play*, he raises the question of an imaginative and cutivated woman *wanting a Sunday husband as well as a weekday one*. The play deals with the situation of Reginald who has married a girl thirty years younger than himself. Soon his young wife feels bored with him and falls in love with a young man of her own age named Sinjon Hotchkiss. The decree of divorce has not been made absolute yet when Reginald, against the wishes of the members of the family, comes to attend the wedding of his niece at the house of his brother, Bishop Bridgenorth. The Bishop's second brother, the General, is already there. To their surprise, Reginald's wife, Leo, also appears on the scene. After the General has learnt from Reginald and Leo that the divorce preceedings are wholly a case of collusion, he asks them in some surprise why they have done this and brought disgrace to the Bridgenorth family. Leo gives a reply which shatters the General's sense of respectability:

LEO: Oh, how silly the law is! Why cant I marry them both?

THE GENERAL: (*Shocked*) Leo!

LEO: Well, I love them both. I should like to marry a lot of men. I should like to have Rejjy for every day, and Sinjon for concerts and theatres and going out in the evenings, and some great austere saint for about once a year at the end of the season, and some perfectly blithering idiot of a boy to be quite wicked with. I so seldom feel wicked; and, when I do, it's such a pity to waste it merely because it's too silly to confess to a real grown–up man.

When the Bishop comes out of his study, the following conversation takes place between him, his wife and Leo:

MRS BRIDGENORTH: And now she says she wants to marry both of them, and a lot of other people as well.

LEO: I didn't say I wanted to marry them: I only said I should like to marry them.

THE BISHOP: Quite a nice distinction, Leo.

LEO: Just occasionally, you know.

THE BISHOP: (*sitting down cosily beside her*) Quite so. Sometimes a poet, sometimes a Bishop, sometimes a fairy prince, sometimes somebody quite indescribable.

LEO: Yes: That's just it. How did you know?

THE BISHOP: Oh, I should say most imaginative and cultivated young women feel like that. I wouldn't give a rap for one who didn't. Shakespeare pointed out long age that a woman wanted a Sunday husband as well as a weekday one. But, as usual, he didn't follow up the idea.[29]

Perhaps Shaw is stretching the point. Perhaps he is also utilizing a stray remark in Shakespeare only to attack the Victorian conception of marriage and the absurd divorce laws in existence at that time. It is not easy to believe that Shakespeare could have been attacking the contemporary notions of marriage. That was not his habit. It may, however, be conceded that in Beatrice's remark Shakespeare did articulate, though in a somewhat indirect and tentative way, a woman's wish for an ideal husband —something that Shaw makes the theme of the discussion between Leo and the Bishop. However, neither Shakespeare nor Shaw could find a suitable answer to the question raised by Beatrice and Leo. Beatrice does not, of course, take Don Pedro's proposal seriously and turns it into a jest. But she is clear in her mind that men like Don Pedro, whatever their status in society, can never make suitable husbands for women like her. She wants in her husband's personality the richness and variety that most men lack and which most women do not even demand. Ultimately she finds these in Benedick. Marriage for most men and women in Shakespeare's times was a routine affair, and what William Stout said in 1699 could perhaps stand as an epitaph for many sixteenth and seventeenth century couples: 'they lived very disagreeably but had many children.'[30] Beatrice wants to avoid this fate and if she could speak freely to Benedick, she might have said to him what in the late seventeenth century Dorothy Osborne wrote in a letter to William Temple: 'there are a great many ingredients must goe to the makeing mee happy in a husband, first . . . our humors must agree.'[31]

VI

In a society where most marriages were arranged, it is difficult to see how the woman could discover whether her humour and the humour of the man she was to marry would agree. So Shakespeare's heroines have not merely to reject arranged marriages, but also to reverse the usual sex–roles in courtship that the age had chalked out for them. It is interesting to watch how Shakespeare violates the contemporary code that women are to be seen, not heard.[32]

Since a reversal of sex roles in courtship is a violation of 'degree', Shakespeare often takes advantage of disguise. When Rosalind sees Orlando for the first time in the Forest of Arden, she is dressed as a boy, and though her first reaction is one of bafflement — 'Alas the day! what shall I do with my doublet and hose?' (*As You Like It*, III.ii.204-5)—she quickly recovers and decides to exploit her disguise: 'I will speak to him like a saucy lackey, and under that habit play the knave with him.' And she does play the knave superbly! After talking in a bantering tone about how time 'travels in diverse paces with diverse persons' (III.ii.290), she comes to the real point of this encounter: 'There is a man haunts the forest that abuses our young trees. . . .If I could meet that fancy–monger, I would give him some good counsel, for he seems to have the quotidian of love upon him.' (III.ii.331ff.). And then Orlando's 'education' begins.

Another person who is badly in need of education of this kind is Orsino in *Twelfth Night*. Viola is in love with him but her situation is hopeless. Her problem is that Orsino is in love with Olivia and she is in disguise as his page. But this is not her real problem: her real problem is the immaturity of Orsino who understands neither himself nor the lady he claims to love. Viola, who is one of the few heroines who is specifically praised for possessing 'a *mind* that envy could not but call fair' (II.i.24-25) (Italics mine), realizes that he is so obsessed with self–love (almost like Malvolio) that the first task of an intelligent woman must be to cure him of this obsession and bring him back to sanity. She also notices that this obsession with self–love often finds expression in his denigration of women and their capacity for love and devotion. At one stage he feels that Viola is insulting him by saying that any woman can love him as much as he loves Olivia:

> no woman's heart
> So big to hold so much; they lack retention.
> Alas, their love may be call'd appetite —
> No motion of the liver, but the palate —
> That suffer surfeit, cloyment, and revolt;
> But mine is all as hungry as the sea
> And can digest as much. Make no compare
> Between that love a woman can bear me
> And that I owe Olivia   (II.iv.94ff.)

Viola, taking advantage of her disguise, speaks as a man and exposes the hollow claims of men like Orsino. First she invents the story of her sister who suffered in love — a fate that she is afraid might be hers — and then comes to the real attack which is likely to set Orsino thinking:

> We men may say more, swear more, but indeed
> Our shows are more than will; for still we prove
> Much in our vows, but little in our love.   (II.iv.115ff.)

Viola is saying more or less the same thing to Orsino that Rosalind had said to Orlando. In both cases the woman has to make the man understand that romantic love is not enough, that while extravagant declarations may make the period of courtship exciting, marriage is quite different and requires a stable relationship based on constancy and understanding.

There are cases where the woman cannot take shelter behind a disguise, and in such cases Shakespeare has to evolve other strategies. The point to notice, however, is that even a daughter like Desdemona — 'A maiden never bold, / Of spirit so still and quiet that her motion / Blush'd at herself' (*Othello*, I.ii.93-95) —takes the initiative in courtship. Carol Neely has rightly said:

During courtship she hides, as they ['the comedy heroines'] did, behind a sort of disguise — not literal male dress but the assumption of a pose of docility and indifference which conceals her passion from both her father and Othello. . . .Eventually, though, she takes the lead in the courtship as the heroines do; she finds an excuse to be alone with Othello, mocks him by speaking of him 'dispraisingly' (III.iii.73), and traps him into a proposal using indirection not unlike Rosalind's with Orlando.[33]

In some cases, 'indirection' cannot serve the purpose, and so the woman decides to speak first even though she recognizes, as Cressida does, that it is man's privilege to do so:

> But, though I lov'd you well, I woo'd you not;
> And yet, good faith, I wish'd myself a man,

> Or that we women had men's privilege
> Of speaking first.   (*TC*, III.ii.123ff.)

Cressida also gives reasons why women hesitate to speak first:

> Women are angels, wooing:
> Things won are done; joy's soul lies in the doing.
> That she belov'd knows naught that knows not this:
> Men prize the thing ungain'd more than it is.
> That she was never yet that ever knew
> Love got so sweet as when desire did sue;
> Therefore this maxim out of love I teach:
> Achievement is command; ungain'd, beseech.
> Then though my heart's content firm love doth bear,
> Nothing of that shall from mine eyes appear.   (I.ii.278ff.)

Cressida's reasons are largely those of a coquette and cannot apply to all women in Shakespeare. Juliet is a much more typical Shakespearean heroine. She confesses her love for Romeo thinking that she is alone. Romeo, however, overhears what she has said and when he appears before her, she naturally feels embarrassed. But not for long. After telling him that it is 'the mask of night' which hides her 'maiden blush', she frankly confesses her feelings. Miranda is even more straightforward:

> Hence, bashful cunning!
> And prompt me plain and holy innocence!
> I am your wife, if you will marry me!
> If not, I will die your maid.   (*The Tempest*, III.i.81ff.)

Dusinberre has pointed out that Shakespeare's women do not employ coyness as a feminine guile — a weapon of the coquette. They are chaste and 'chastity requires frankness'.[34] Perhaps the most frank of them is Helena in *All's Well that Ends Well*. She does not mind bandying words with Parolles and when Parolles asks whether she is 'meditating on virginity' she does not shrink back but instead asks him a counter–question: 'Man is enemy to virginity: how may we barricade it against him?' (I.i.106-7). The argument between Helena and Parolles is not without purpose and Helena puts her problem in a nutshell when she asks him: 'How might one do, sir, to lose it to her own liking?' (I.i.141-2). That is precisely what she ultimately does but it involves her in pursuit of a man in most awkward circumstances. Indeed, when she accepts the impossible conditions Bertram puts before her, she reverses the sex roles to such an extent that she almost resembles a Knight performing impossible feats in expectation of winning the

Lady. Coleridge felt uncomfortable while commenting on her. 'It must be confessed', he said, 'that her character is not very delicate.'[35] George Eliot too seems to have been surprised at Shakespeare's daring in creating such a character. She saw the same pattern in other plays too and wrote that 'it is remarkable that Shakespeare's women almost always *make love*, in opposition to the conventional notion of what is fitting for a woman.'[36] It is a pity that George Eliot failed to write a book on Shakespeare in the English Men of Letters Series, as, at one stage, she had undertaken to do, and though Sir Walter Raleigh who later accepted the assignment did an excellent job, a book on Shakespeare by the most intelligent — and also perhaps the most liberated — woman in the period would have greatly enriched our understanding of Shakespeare's women.

It is not surprising that in our own times Germaine Greer should admire Shakespeare more or less for the same reasons as George Eliot might have done. Shakespeare, she says, 'was as much concerned in his newfangled comedies to clear away the detritus of romance, ritual, perversity and obsession as he was to achieve happy endings.' She clearly prefers Julia and Viola to Silvia (*The Two Gentlemen of Verona*) and Olivia (*Twelfth Night*), and says: 'The girls in men's clothing win the men they love by a more laborious means, for they cannot use veils and coquetry: they must offer and not exact service, and as valets they must see their lovers at their least heroic.' Her further comment on the kind of women Shakespeare prefers is worth quoting in full:

When the choice lies between the ultra-feminine and the virago, Shakespeare's sympathy lies with the virago. The women in the tragedies are all feminine – even Lady Macbeth (who is so often misinterpreted as a termagant), especially Gertrude, morally unconscious, helpless, voluptuous, and her younger version, infantile Ophelia, the lustful sisters, Goneril and Regan opposed by the warrior princess Cordelia who refuses to simper and pander to her father's irrational desire. Desdemona is fatally feminine, but realizes it and dies understanding how she has failed Othello. Only Cleopatra has enough initiative and drive to qualify for the status of female hero.[37]

There is exaggeration here – and even distortion, at least in the case of Desdemona[38] – but the point being made is that Shakespeare's ideal woman is positive, strong and self-sufficient, and that whenever she fails to be that, she ends tragically.

VII

However, it needs to be emphasized that all the qualities that these women possess are directed towards one simple, traditional goal: to achieve a companionate marriage and to raise a family. The woman is the pillar on which the structure of the family is to stand: man, however masterful, plays only a secondary role. The woman has to possess exceptional qualities or else the structure will collapse. Shakespeare clearly recognizes that it is for the woman to hold the balance, however precarious it may be at times, between 'realism and romanticism, lust and love, desire and illusion, love and friendship, cuckoldry and marriage, masculinity and femininity.'[39] It is this central importance of woman which may explain why most contemporary humanist and Puritan writers write their conduct books from a man's standpoint, reminding him what remarkable qualities women can possess and how they should be loved and cherished. All women do not, of course, possess these qualities, and they can also be a hindrance rather than a help in life's journey. But a genuine 'help-meet' is God's own blessing and it is such a 'help-meet' that Erasmus has in mind when he says in his *In Laude and Prayse of Matrymony* (1532):

It is an especyall swetnes to have one with whom ye may communycate the secrete affectyons of your mynde, with whom ye may speake even as it were with your owne self, whome ye may savely truste, whyche supposethe your chaunces to be his, what felycyte (thynke ye) have the conjunction of man and wyfe, than whych no thynge in the unyversall worlde may be founde outher greater or fermer.[40]

In *The Excellency of Good Women* (1613), Barnaby Rich expressed the same idea in a somewhat more contemporary idiom:

A man that wanteth a friend for pleasure, a servant for profit, a counsellour to advise him, a comforter to cherish him, a companion to solace him, a helper to assist him, or a spirituall instructor to informe him, a good and vertuous wife doth supply all these occasions.[41]

It is clear that Erasmus and Barnaby Rich are at one with Thomas Becon in their demand that husband and wife should share their joys and sorrows with thanks-giving. Erasmus' emphasis on the husband and the wife communicating the secret affections of their

minds to each other is especially relevant for our purposes. In
Shakespeare, wives regard it as their natural right to know what is
troubling the minds of their husbands. Lady Percy, like most
women in the History plays, has only a minor role in *Henry IV,
Pt I*, but Shakespeare makes her confront Hotspur before his
departure for the war:

> O my good lord, why are you thus alone?
> For what offence have I this fortnight been
> A banish'd woman from my Harry's bed?
> Tell me, sweet lord, what is't that takes from thee
> Thy stomach, pleasure, and thy golden sleep?
> . . . .
> Why hast thou lost the fresh blood in thy cheeks
> And given my treasures and *my rights of thee*
> To thick-ey'd musing and curs'd meloncholy?
> . . . .
> Some heavy business hath my lord in hand,
> And I must know it, else he loves me not.
>
> > (II.iii.33ff.)
> > (Italics mine)

Another wife, Portia in *Julius Caesar*, also wants to know the
cause of her husband's grief, and as his wife she claims the *right*
to know. Hence she persists in the face of his denials:

> No, my Brutus;
> You have some sick offence within your mind,
> Which by *the right and virtue of my place*
> I ought to know of; and upon my knees
> I charm you, by my once-commended beauty,
> By all your vows of love, and that great vow
> Which did incorporate and make us one,
> That you unfold to me, your self, your half,
> Why you are heavy . . .
> BRUTUS: Kneel not, gentle Portia.
> PORTIA: I should not need, if you were gentle Brutus.
> Within the bond of marriage, tell me, Brutus,
> Is it excepted I should know no secrets
> That appertain to you? Am I your self
> But, as it were, in sort or limitation?
> To keep with you at meals, comfort your bed,
> And talk to you sometimes? Dwell I but in the suburbs
> Of your great pleasure? If it be no more,
> Portia is Brutus' harlot, not his wife.   (II.i.266ff.)
> > (Italics mine)

VIII

The examples of companionate marriage that we have given may, however, give a one-sided picture. Not many marriages in Elizabethan times were really companionate. Nor could most wives freely and confidently discuss their husbands' problems with them – and certainly not as a matter of 'right'. The Elizabethan age – in spite of the Queen on the throne – was essentially a man's age and the wife was expected to be wholly obedient to her husband. It was a normal part of Elizabethan culture that the husband took most decisions and the wife accepted them as a part of her duty. In Maynard Mack's words, it is fathers who dominate Shakespeare's stage and the 'almost total authority granted them by law and custom' made them 'the initiators and prohibitors of action, the dispensers and withholders of wealth and privilege (including the privilege of marriage), and the meters-out of unappealable decrees both wise and unwise.'⁴² It need not, surprise us, therefore, that Capulet in *Romeo and Juliet* assigns only minor duties to his wife. He does not even consult her about fixing the day of his daughter's marriage to Paris and all that he wants her to do is to prepare Juliet 'against this wedding day' (III.iv.32). The thought that she should have been consulted does not even cross Lady Capulet's mind and she tells Juliet that she has 'a careful father' (III.v.107). When Juliet, in her moment of agony, appeals to her, 'I pray you tell my lord and father, madam, / I will not marry yet' (120), all that she says is: 'Here comes your father. Tell him so yourself.' (124). She does try to stop Capulet's outburst, but to no purpose. In fact the nurse shows more resilience in this scene, as elsewhere in the play. Of course this need not be treated as evidence of any lack of affection either between Capulet and Lady Capulet or between the mother and the daughter. It merely shows that the wife accepts the wisdom of her husband's action. Her parting words to Juliet are only an echo of her husband's harsh 'decree':

> Talk not to me, for I'll not speak a word.
> Do as thou wilt, for I have done with thee.

> (III.v.203–4)

All this does not show that she is her husband's chattel. It only shows a cultural pattern. Lady Capulet is no different from any other typical Elizabethan wife who was expected to have 'just the proper amount of obedience and humility and yet . . . possess the spirit and capacity to be a real help–meet of her husband.'[43] The trouble starts when this balance is lost and the wife becomes either too interfering or too lifeless. Lady Macbeth is the most disturbing example of an interfering wife, and in the process of asserting her will she destroys her husband. So does Cleopatra, who, though not technically Antony's wife, imposes her judgment on him and leads him to destruction. The woman was expected to have initiative but she could become a menace when she aspired to be a female hero. Indeed, a too dominating mother could also pose a threat to her son, as Volumnia does in *Coriolanus*.

Obedience to her husband, and humility, then, are the natural attributes of an Elizabethan wife. One thing, however, should be clearly recognized: the doctrine that some of the conduct-books preached for the guidance of women in that age was very harsh indeed. 'Obedience, to win praise', says Ruth Kelso in her summary of the doctrine, 'had to be complete, unquestioning, and included the acceptance of correction, even blows, in all humility, subjection, fear, sweetness, and patience without provoking either parents or, later, husband by talking back, babbling, or running away.'[44] Shakespeare rarely exposes his women to this indignity although he does expect them to obey their husbands in all humility and with patience.

It is not easy to believe that Beatrice would acquire these qualities, and yet she must if she has to make a good wife. Indeed, the development of Beatrice from 'Lady Disdain' (I.i.101) to a loving and obedient wife is one of the most important themes of *Much Ado*. It is also not without significance that in her very first confession of love for Benedick, Beatrice talks of '*Taming* [her] wild heart to [his] *loving* hand' (III.i.112) (Italics mine). It must be admitted that she is too sparkling an example of a liberated young lady to be typical of Elizabethan or of any earlier time. But to say, as has recently been done, that she has no relationship with Elizabethan culture and that she only expresses 'a masculine wish for such a woman and thus serves as a critique of prevailing culture'[45] is quite misleading. One can understand that such views are expressed only in reaction to Juliet Dusinberre's statement that real city women in Shakespeare's time were 'a race of everyday Beatrices'.[46] Both approaches ignore the complexity of the changing pattern of Elizabethan culture and the often conflicting influences under which Shakespeare works. Beatrice does represent an ideal but an ideal which Shakespeare and some of his forward–looking contemporaries regard as capable of realization in their society.

It is not Beatrice alone but all women in Shakespeare – except perhaps Adriana in *The Comedy of Errors* whose case needs a separate examination – who accept male authority. Men take it for granted that there is no question of their wives disobeying them. Even a man like Iago who recognizes neither family nor religion – nor any other kind of duty outside his self-interest – can never imagine that his wife would not accept his command in all circumstances. Emelia too recognizes this, but for the first time in her life she is confronted with a new moral situation, and so when Iago says, 'I charge you get you home', she has no option but to defy him:

> Good gentlemen, let me have leave to speak.
> 'Tis proper I obey him, but not now.
> Perchance, Iago, I will ne'er go home.
> *(Othello*, V.ii.197ff.)

Another wife – a noble shrew herself, if we like – also defies her husband but she does as Emelia had done – in obedience to a higher duty. Paulina in *The Winter's Tale* confronts Leontes in his palace with the new–born child and when Leontes asks her husband in anger, 'What, canst not rule her?', Paulina replies:

> From all dishonesty he can: in this,
> Unless he take the course that you have done —
> Commit me for committing honour – trust it,
> He shall not rule me.   (II.iii.44ff.)

Both Emelia and Paulina do, however, recognize the husband's right to rule the wife, though in their particular circumstances that right ceases to operate. It should have ceased to operate in the case of Imogen too, but the doctrine is so ingrained in the psyche of women that even when the husband is behaving in a monstrous way, the wife regards it as her duty to obey him. When she reads Posthumus' letter to Pisanio ordering him to 'take away her life', she urges him to carry out his master's command:

> Come fellow, be thou honest:
> Do thy master's bidding: when thou see'st him,
> A little witness my obedience.   (III.iv.65–67)

When Pisanio refuses, she tells him:

> Why, I must die;
> And if I do not by thy hand, thou art
> No servant of thy master's.   (75–77)

Showing this kind of obedience is, of course, going too far, but
the point is that once Imogen realizes that she has lost the love of
Posthumus she no longer attaches any importance to her life. It is
for this love that she disobeyed her father and incurred his dis-
pleasure – a course of action in which Posthumus seems to see
nothing unusual:

> And thou Posthumus, thou didst set up
> My disobedience 'gainst the King my father
> And make me put into contempt the suits
> Of princely fellows, shalt hereafter find
> It is no act of common passage, but
> A strain of rareness.   (89–94)

Desdemona would not make even this kind of complaint,
though her step in marrying Othello is even 'rarer'. She not only
disobeys her father but also refuses 'many proposed matches / Of
her own clime, complexion, and degree, / Whereto we see in all
things nature tends.' (III.iii.227–29). In fact her clandestine marriage with Othello is such a shock to her father that this 'match
was mortal to him, and pure grief / Shore his old thread in
twain.' (V.ii.204–5). She is the most obedient of wives and tells
Othello: 'Whate'er you be, I am obedient (III.iii.89). Even when
Othello strikes her in the presence of guests, all that she says is, 'I
have not deserved this.' (IV.i.241). And yet this 'heavenly true'
(V.ii.136) woman is 'falsely, falsely murdered' (V.ii.117) by the
man whom she had defended before the Venetian Senate against
her father's charge, and about whom she had said:

> I saw Othello's visage in his mind
> And to his honours and his valiant parts
> Did I my soul and fortunes consecrate.   (I.iii.252–54)

Othello makes mockery even of her obedience:

> Sir, she can turn, and turn, and yet go on,
> And turn again. And she can weep, sir, weep.
> And she's obedient; as you say, obedient,
> Very obedient . . .   (IV.i.265–68)

A reader's or a spectator's response is well expressed in Emelia's comment: 'What should such a fool / Do with so good a wife?' (V.ii.236–7).

IX

One woman in Shakespeare who challenges man's right to demand obedience from his wife is Adriana in *The Comedy of Errors*. She asks: 'Why should their liberty than ours be more?' (II.i.10). Her sister, Luciana, gives a sensible reply: 'Because their business still lies out o'door' (II). But the irritated Adriana states: 'Look when I serve him so he takes it ill.' (12). How can she serve him so? She has no outdoor business. She is merely a housewife. Why should she, then, claim equality with her husband in such a small matter as coming late for dinner? We soon realize that the cause of her irritation – and her demand for equality – lies much deeper. Though this was an arranged marriage, there was a time when the husband loved her passionately, though now that love has declined:

> The time was once when thou unurged wouldst vow
> That never words were music to thine ear,
> That never object pleasing in thine eye,
> That never touch well welcome to thy hand,
> That never meat sweet-savoured in thy taste,
> Unless I spake, or looked, or touched, or carved to thee.
> How comes it now, my husband, O how comes it,
> That thou art then estranged from thyself?
> Thyself I call it, being strange to me,
> That, undividable, incorporate,
> Am better than thy dear self's better part.
>
> (II.ii.112–122)

The play asks, though somewhat obliquely, whether the husband alone is responsible for this state of affairs. On the whole, he is a decent and considerate man. Adriana, however, is a nagging wife. It is, of course, true that her husband has started visiting a courtesan now and then, though it is clear that he is not having a sexual relationship with her (as was the case in Shakespeare's sources). It is also clear that the wife knows about these visits. But her handling of the situation is most inept. When asked by the Abbess, whether she ever 'reprehended' him, she replies that she did both in 'private' and 'in assemblies too' (V.i.60–61).:

It was the copy of our conference.
In bed he slept not for my urging it;
At board he fed not for my urging it;
Alone, it was the subject of my theme;
In company I often glanced it;
Still did I tell him it was vile and bad.   (V.i.62–67)

The Abbess rightly says that this conduct of the wife has driven
the husband mad. There is no doubt that Adriana is a difficult
wife and has not learnt that it is the responsibility of both the
husband and the wife to mend the relationship if strains start
developing. It is not that she has no case. Indeed her statement on
the double standard would have been fully approved by the contemporary religious reformers:

How dearly would it touch thee to the quick,
Shouldst thou but hear I were licentious,
And that this body, consecrate to thee,
By ruffian lust should be contaminate!
Wouldst thou not spit at me, and spurn at me,
And hurl the name of husband in my face,
And tear the stain'd skin off my harlot brow,
And from my false hand cut the wedding ring,
And break it with a deep-divorcing vow?
I know thou canst, and therefore see thou do it!
I am possessed with an adulterate blot.
My blood is mingled with the crime of lust;
For if we two be one, and thou play false,
I do digest the poison of thy flesh,
Being strumpeted by thy contagion.
Keep then fair league and truce with thy true bed,
I live unstained, thou undishonoured.   (II.ii.128–145)

The reformers, however, would also have advised her to show a
patience which she lamentably lacks. Her sister rightly accuses
her of 'Self-harming jealousy' (II.i.102). Her tongue is utterly
uncontrollable and she can use a language which is wholly
incomprehensible:

He is deformed, crooked, old, and sere;
Ill–faced, worse–bodied, shapeless everywhere;
Vicious, ungentle, foolish, blunt, unkind,
Stigmatical in making, worse in mind.   (IV.ii.19–22)

When reminded by her sister that if he is all this she has no reason
to regret his lack of love, she immediately concedes:

> Ah, but I think him better than I say.   (IV.ii.25)

Her immaturity is apparent, and though her husband has given her an excuse, she has to learn to behave differently. It is also clear that she has raised the question of equality only because she is feeling frustrated. What she really wants is not equality but her husband's love. The lesson both for the husband and the wife is clear: it is love from the husband that earns the wife's obedience. Where this love is lost, the woman is bound to raise the cry of equality. The play does not show the 'education' of the husband, but it does make the wife recognize her true role, as is clear from what she tells the Abbess:

> I will attend my husband, be his nurse,
> Diet his sickness, for it is my office,
> And will have no attorney but myself.
> And therefore let me have him home with me.
>
> (V.i.98–101)

It is this recognition of her 'office' as a wife – and a similar recognition recommended to the husband by Luciana of *his* 'office' (III.ii.2) – that shall ensure a happy future for them both. The play ends on a note of harmony and does not disturb the normal Shakespearean pattern, as it seemed to, when, in reply to Luciana's statement that a husband is 'the bridle' of his wife's 'will', Adriana had said: 'There's none but asses will be bridled so.' (II.i.13–14).

X

It is easy to dismiss Adriana but the question raised by her is disquieting. The disquietude is caused by the feeling that a husband can *demand* as a matter of *right* obedience and fidelity from a wife even when he is himself totally indifferent to her – indeed that he can beat her with a rope's end if she fails to perform her wifely duty. The religious reformers did emphasize that husbands too had duties towards their wives, but in actual life husbands could forget them with impunity. It is refreshing to see that in *The Comedy of Errors* Shakespeare makes the point sharply that a wife's obedience depends on the husband's love, and that where this love is lacking the wife is bound to rebel. He may not applaud the rebellion – indeed may even condemn it in deference to contemporary opinion – but he does remind us that marriage is a bond which binds both man and woman equally and that if the man forgets this, he does so at the cost of domestic harmony.

Adriana also raises the question of the double standard and asks whether a woman too can find comfort outside marriage to relieve the boredom at home. She knows what her husband would do to her if she were to visit a man 'wild, and yet, too, gentle'. But what can she do to him? One course of action is recommended by Emelia in *Othello*:

> Why, we have galls; and though we have some grace,
> Yet have we some revenge. Let husbands know
> Their wives have sense like them; they see and smell,
> And have their palates both for sweet and sour
> As husbands have. What is it that they do
> When they change us for others? Is it sport?
> I think it is. And doth affection breed it?
> I think it doth. Is't frailty that thus errs?
> It is so too. And have not we affections,
> Desires for sport, and frailty, as men have?
> Then let them use us well; else let them know
> The ills we do their ills instruct us so.   (IV.iii.84–101)

But Desdemona rejects Emelia's advice not only as unacceptable but as wholly profane. She would rather die than violate her code of conduct.

Since marriage was the only 'career' available to a woman in Elizabethan times – unless she was a queen – and since divorce was well-nigh impossible, she was expected to evolve her own strategy to make the married state as tolerable, comfortable and happy as possible. If things went wrong in spite of her efforts, she was not expected to think of revenge, as Emelia suggests, or of asserting her individuality as Adriana does. Both approaches would be wrong according to the contemporary conduct-books. William Gouge in his *Of Domesticall Duties* (1622) categorically states: 'A wife must be milde, meeke, gentle, obedient, though she be matched with a crooked, perverse, prophane, wicked Husband.'[47] That most women cannot accept this advice is also clear from the fact that the women in Gouge's parish, Blackfriars (where he preached between 1608 and 1622, the year of the publication of his sermons) protested against 'his exposition of wifely subjection'. The protest, however, failed to take into account the fact that Gouge was merely expounding the scriptures. Hence he said:

Though an husband in regard of evill qualities may carry the Image of the devill, yet in regard of his place and office he beareth the Image of God; so doe Magistrates in the commonwealth, Ministers in the Church, parents and masters in the familie.[48]

What should an Elizabethan woman do? Following the scriptures would, of course, be safest, but it is not easy and human nature revolts against a situation where 'Ignorance and Folly (the Ingredients of a Coxcomb, who is the most unsufferable Fool) tyrannises over Wit and Sense.'[49] She has only two options: either to 'have patience and endure' (*Much Ado*, IV.i. 253) or decide not to marry at all. But the second is hardly an option. Apart from the fact that marriage is the only career available to her in that age, deciding not to marry would mean her denying her womanhood.[50] We have, for instance, the case of Moll Cutpurse in Dekker and Middleton's *The Roaring Girl*. At one stage she says: 'A Wife, you know, ought to be obedient, but I fear I am too headstrong to obey, therefore I'll ne'er go about it' (II.ii). But the step that Moll takes is clearly an exceptional one and the play makes it clear that she has not only to deny her sex but has to function *as a man* in order to survive in her world. If she were to function as a woman, she would have been destroyed straightaway. Virginia Woolf has pertinently asked: 'What would have happened had Shakespeare had a wonderfully gifted sister, named Judith?' First, she would never have acquired the knowledge, skill and experience of her brother, but if she were foolish enough – or goaded enough by her genius – to travel to London in search of fame, she would have ended with a child by Nick Greene and 'killed herself one winter's night' and been buried 'at some crossroads where the omnibuses now stop outside the Elephant and Castle.'[51]

Martha Andersen-Thom's complaint that the framework within which Shakespeare's heroines have to operate is 'obviously hierarchical and patriarchal', and that 'Women are happily granted freedom when they function to refresh, to integrate, and to balance but not when they threaten to upset that structure,'[52] is, therefore, a perfectly valid one. It is, however, remarkable that despite the constraints imposed on him by the times in which he was writing, Shakespeare is able to raise questions which are surprisingly modern. These questions do show that Shakespeare is aware of the predicament of women in his times though he cannot, of course, find a satisfactory answer to them. Dusinberre's view that 'Shakespeare saw man and woman as equal in a world which declared them unequal',[53] is correct to a large extent. It is also largely correct that Shakespeare tried to apply a 'single standard of sexual morality' to men and women in his plays. But he cannot change the world in which he operates. He has indeed to operate within two conflicting world–views – one which is traditional and asks the wife to treat her husband as a God, and the other which sees a change in men and institutions and visualizes a more humane and equal basis for human relationships. Placed as he is, Shakespeare clearly cannot satisfy the modern feminists[54] though they should recognize that he does not share the anti-feminist prejudices of his contemporaries. Indeed, as Virginia Woolf claimed, he possesses a genuinely 'androgynous' mind which refuses to accept the modern cult of 'pitting of sex against sex, of quality against quality; all this claiming of superiority and imputing of inferiority, belong to the private-school stage of human existence where there are "sides" . . .'[55] Shakespeare thus is neither a feminist nor an anti-feminist. He looks at women as human beings first and as women only secondarily, and he is aware of the grave disabilities from which they suffer. His advice to women would have been that they should recognize these disabilities but, in the interest of domestic harmony, should try to get round them with intelligence, tact and patience. His advice to men would have been the same. Indeed, he would have fully endorsed what Dod and Cleaver said in *A Godly Forme of Household Government*: 'as the wife ought with great care to endeavour, and by all good means to labour to bee in favour and grace with her husband; so likewise the husband ought to feare to be in disgrace and disliking with his wife.'[56]

It would be too much to expect Shakespeare to *attack* the powers that his society had given to husbands over their wives. But there seems no doubt that in all cases where husbands treat their wives harshly, Shakespeare's sympathies are invariably with the wives who are morally superior to the men who reject them. It is a cruel fact of history that in all patriarchal societies, including that of Shakespeare, a husband, on mere suspicion of infidelity, could cast off his wife with the full approval of society, and such a wife would find no protection anywhere. Much before Othello's suspicions are confirmed, he declares:

> If I do prove her haggard,
> Though that her jesses were my dear heart-strings,
> I'd whistle her off, and let her down the wind
> To prey at fortune.   (III.iii.257–60)

'To prey at fortune' – that is the crux of the matter in a society where women have no economic independence. Christopher Hill cites Francis Bacon's view that in that period 'Wives were left wholly to the tyranny of their husbands.' Hill also quotes an anonymous contemporary lawyer who said: 'The law of England is a husband's law.'[57] These two statements may perhaps refer more particularly to the laws governing inheritance, but they seem equally relevant in other spheres of a woman's life too.

XI

It is a painful fact that at the slightest provocation, Shakespeare's men have a tendency to denigrate the female sex and to treat as property even the women they claim to love. As Bernard Shaw has pointed out in his Preface to *Getting Married*, even Antony and Othello, Shakespeare's most infatuated and passionate lovers, 'betray the commercial and proprietary instinct the moment they lose their temper: "I found you", says Antony, reproaching Cleopatra, "as a morsel cold upon Caesar's trencher." Othello's worst agony is the thought of "keeping a corner in the thing he loves for others' uses." But this is not what a man feels about the thing he loves, but about the thing he owns.' Leontes' attitude to Hermione in *The Winter's Tale* is no better than that of Othello towards Desdemona. 'And many a man there is', he says,

> That little thinks she [his wife] has been sluic'd in his absence,
> And his pond fish'd by his next neighbour.

(I.ii.192)

Imogen in *Cymbeline* is also called a 'pond', not by her husband but by Iachimo, who tells Posthumus: 'You may wear her in title yours; but you know strange fowl light upon neighbouring ponds.' (I.iv.84ff.). In *The Rape of Lucrece*, as has been pointed out by Coppelia Kahn, 'The frequent references throughout the poem to Lucrece as 'treasure', 'prize', 'spoil', and the comparison of Tarquin to a thief (134–140, 710–11, to cite two of many examples) constitute a running, metaphorical commentary on marriage as ownership of women.'[58] In *Troilus and Cressida*, too, the same terms are used, but the imagery is more markedly commercial. Cressida is 'a pearl' and Troilus 'the merchant' (I.i.103–6) who wishes to possess her, while Helen is 'a pearl / whose price hath launch'd above a thousand ships / And turn'd crown'd kings to merchants' (II.ii.81–83). The entire Trojan debate, it will be remembered, turns on the question of the 'value' of Helen.

That Elizabethan husbands should treat their wives as property is not surprising[59] if we remember, as Keith Thomas points out, that under the contemporary law (which had come down from Anglo-Saxon times), a man was punished for adultery 'not for unfaithfulness to his wife, but for violating the rights of another husband.'[60] Christopher Hill mentions the writings of several theologians popular with contemporary Puritans which equated adultery with theft 'because the wife is the husband's property.' He also mentions how the law treated men and women differently in the case of murder. Since a woman was both a man's property and his subject, the killing of a husband amounted to 'petty treason' in the eyes of the law. Consequently, Hill says, 'women were still burnt for husband-murder' whereas 'murdering one's wife was only a hanging matter.'[61] It is especially in relation to sexuality that men's possessive instincts are aroused most. It is in this context that they become most savage towards women.[62] It is notable that almost all women in Shakespeare – whether in comedies or tragedies – accept their sexuality as a normal part of their life and are frank about it. For them love is not divorced from sexuality, as it it in the case of most men in Shakespeare's comedies or tragedies. We are not, therefore, surprised at Rosalind talking of her 'child's father' (*AYLI*, I.iii.10) after her very first meeting with Orlando, or at Perdita speaking of Florizel's 'desire to breed by me' (*WT*, IV.iv.103). The chief role of women in Shakespeare is indeed to expose male fantasy and to provide men 'an initiation into the realities of love, sex, marriage and children.'[63] Marriage is a 'blessed bond of board and *bed*' (*AYLI*, V.iv.136) (Italics mine) but men talk only in terms of 'sighs and tears', 'adoration, duty, and observance' (Ibid., V.ii.78,88). Romeo talks of 'love's light wings' (*RJ*, II.ii.66) and uses all the hyperbolic armoury of romantic love, whereas Juliet contemplates:

> how to lose a winning match,
> Play'd for a pair of stainless *maidenhoods*.   (III.ii.12–13)
> (Italics mine)

Othello tells the Senate:

> She lov'd me for the dangers I had pass'd;
> And I lov'd her that she did pity them
>
> (*Othello*, I.iii.167–8)

But Desdemona states:

> . . . I did love the Moor to *live* with him,
> ....
> So that, dear lords, if I be left behind,
> A moth of peace, and he go to the war,
> The *rites* for why I love him are bereft me
>
> (I.iii.248, 255–57)
> (Italics mine)

On reaching Cyprus and meeting Desdemona, Othello exclaims:

> If it were now to die
> 'Twere now to be most happy
>
> (II.i.187–8)

Desdemona immediately supplies the corrective:

> The heavens forbid
> But that *our loves and comforts* should increase
> Even as our days do grow.
>
> (II.i.191–93)
> (Italics mine)

Later, of course, Othello becomes so obsessed by Desdemona's infidelity that he murders her. This terrible act is caused precisely by the male possessive instinct. Othello believes that Desdemona has violated the most important tenet of the contemporary doctrine laid down for wives, namely, chastity, and he regards it as his moral and social duty to punish her. As we have already seen, chastity was not even included among the virtues required of a gentleman. Lord Halifax in his *The Lady's New Year Gift: Or, Advice to a Daughter* (1688) had tried to explain the double standard: 'the root and excuse of this injustice [i.e. demanding chastity from women but permitting infidelity in men] is the preservation of families from any mixture which may bring a blemish to them.'[64] Dr Johnson goes further: 'confusion of progeny constitutes the essence of the crime; and therefore a woman who breaks her marriage vows is much more criminal than a man who does it. A man, to be sure, is criminal in the sight of God; but he does not do his wife a very material injury, if he does not insult

her;[65] ... [if] The man imposes no bastards upon his wife.' Dr
Johnson also states that female chastity is of the greatest importance because 'upon that all the property of the world depends.'[66]
Juliet Dusinberre, seizing on this idea of property, says: 'At the
heart of the double standard lay the concept of virginity as a
property asset. Virginity is more cherished among the upper
classes who have more property to dispose of ... Fear of a bastard
intruding on the succession of property dictated virginity in
brides and faithfulness in wives.'[67]

But surely the treatment of women by Shakespeare's men is not
always prompted by the 'confusion of progeny' or the fear of a
bastard inheriting the property. There is only one play in Shakespeare where a man is obsessed by the thought of his wife's impos-
ing a bastard on him – that is *The Winter's Tale*. The moment the
thought crosses Leontes' mind that Polixenes and his wife might
be lovers, he starts talking of 'mingling bloods' (I.ii.108). And
then his mind goes to his son who might also be a bastard and he
asks the boy:

> Mamillius,
> Art thou my boy?
>
> (I.ii.119–120)

This thought works like poison in him, and he starts asking what
a man can do in this 'bawdy planet' (I.ii.201) where 'contempt
and clamour will be [his] knell.' (I.ii.189–190). When the boy tells
him, 'I am like you, they say,' (I.ii.208) he is somewhat comforted.
But he leaves us in no doubt that what has hurt him most is the
feeling that Hermione's unfaithfulness gives 'scandal to the blood
o' th' Prince, my son, / Who I do think is mine and love as mine.'
(I.ii.330–31). Soon another child is born, who, he is sure, is a
bastard. When Paulina brings the child before him, he rejects it
publicly, threatens it, and orders it destroyed. He justifies his
behaviour by stating:

> Shall I live on to see this bastard kneel
> And call me father? better burn it now
> Than curse it then.   (II.iii.154–156)

It is significant that when Hermione comes to plead her case, it is
not her life she asks for but her honour, for this alone can secure
legitimacy to her children.

XII

The lives of Othello and Posthumus are not complicated by the existence of supposed bastard children. But on mere suspicion of infidelity on their wives' part, they are prepared to take extreme steps. An Elizabethan husband had, of course, no legal right to kill his wife, but society assumed – as many societies do even today – that a wife accused of adultery could be given almost any punishment by her husband. It has been said that according to the English code, Othello's honour could have been vindicated if he had killed Cassio and divorced Desdemona. Desdemona did in fact make the plea that he might banish her instead of killing her. But Othello rejected her plea. In Venice, we are told by a contemporary of Shakespeare who visited Venice in 1589, the punishment for an unfaithful wife was 'deathe, but not by the lawe, but by the bloody hand of her husband.'[68] In fact, as Giovanni della Casa said in 1537, a Venetian husband 'who has a wife who is immodest and adulterous, and does not get rid of her, that man... shall surely be dishonoured and damned.'[69] So Othello dispenses Venetian justice. It is surprising that no one in the play challenges Othello's *right* to kill Desdemona. Even Emelia, who gives expression to our outraged feelings, is shocked precisely because Othello is a 'gull' and a 'dolt' (V.ii.162), who has 'killed the sweetest *innocent* that e'er did lift up eye.' (Italics mine) (V.ii.198–9). In fact, '*Othello* is a tragedy, not because it shows us a man killing his wife, but because a man kills his innocent wife.'[70] So also in *Much Ado*, no one blames Claudio for 'killing' Hero. Beatrice is, of course, outraged, but again that is because she is convinced that Hero is blameless. It is not without significance that before accepting Beatrice's command to 'kill Claudio', Benedick wants to be assured that Hero is really innocent: 'Think you in your soul the Count Claudio hath wrong'd Hero?' (IV.i.325).

While the women in Shakespeare are not self-assertive as the modern feminists would like them to be, surely they are not passive victims. Germaine Greer is clearly unfair when she dismisses Desdemona as 'fatally feminine'. A woman who takes the lead in courtship, defies her father, and boldly defends her marriage to a foreigner before the whole Senate of Venice can in no sense be described as a weakling. Indeed Carol Neely has claimed that—

Desdemona's spirit, clarity, and realism do not desert her entirely in the latter half of the play as many critics and performances imply. In the brothel scene, she persistently questions Othello to discover exactly what he accuses her of and even advances a hypothesis about her father, linking with herself the 'state-matters' which may have transformed Othello. Throughout the scene she defends herself as 'stoutly' (III.i.45) as she had earlier defended Cassio:

> If to preserve this vessel for my lord
> From any hated foul unlawful touch,
> Be not to be a strumpet, I am none.   (IV.ii.85–87).

She does, of course, fail to mend the relationship. But she continues searching for ways to do so. As Carol Neely perceptively remarks:

Her naivete and docility in the willow scene are partly a result of her confusion and exhaustion but perhaps also partly a protective facade behind which she waits, as she did during courtship, while determining the most appropriate and fruitful reaction to Othello's rage. The conversation and the song with its alternate last verses explore alternate responses to male perfidy-acceptance 'Let nobody blame him, his scorn I approve' – or retaliation: 'If I court moe women, you'll couch with moe men' (IV.iii.51, 56). Emilia supports retaliation – 'The ills we do, their ills instruct us so' (I.103) though, like Bianca, she practices acceptance. Desdemona's final couplet suggests that she is groping for a third response, one that is midway between 'grace' and 'revenge', one that would be more active than acceptance yet more loving than retaliation: 'God me such usage send, / Not to pick bad from bad, but by bad mend!' (II.104–5) . . . Her earlier command to have the wedding sheets put on her bed seems one expression of this positive usage. Just before her death, as in the brothel scene, she strives to 'mend' Othello's debased view of her, transforming the 'sins' he accuses her of into 'loves I bear to you'; but he recorrupts them: 'And for that thou diest' (V.ii.40–41)[71]

Another wife whose life is threatened is Imogen in *Cymbeline*. She is as innocent as Desdemona and yet is accused by her husband of being false to his bed. Her reaction to the accusation is as surprised as that of Desdemona:

> False to his bed? What is it to be false?
> To lie in watch there, and to think on him?
> To weep 'twixt clock and clock? If sleep charge nature,
> To break it with a fearful dream of him,
> And cry myself awake? That's false to's bed,
> Is it?   (III.iv.38–43)

It need not surprise us that Imogen's husband, Posthumus, like

Othello, also thinks of 'cord, or knife, or poison' (V.v. 214) to kill the alleged lover of his wife, Iachimo. He would not have, of course, hesitated to use these methods to kill his wife too, if he were not in banishment. On learning that Iachimo had made him a cuckold, his first thought is:

> O that I had her here to tear her limb-meal!
> I will go there and do't, i'the court, before
> Her father.   (II.iv.147–149)

Realizing that he cannot go to the court to kill Imogen, he sends a letter to his servant, Pisanio, to 'murder her'. (III.ii.11).

In a fit of frenzy, Posthumus also behaves like Othello and almost loses his hold on reality. In such moments, these men are so tormented that they derive a special satisfaction by denouncing women's morals. Posthumus states that 'We are all bastards'[72] (II.v.2), for all women are false:

> For there's no motion
> That tends to vice in man, but I affirm
> It is a woman's part. Be it lying, note it,
> The woman's; flattering, hers; deceiving, hers;
> Lust and rank thoughts, hers, hers; revenges, hers;
> Ambitions, covetings, change of prides, disdain.
>   (II.v.20–25)

As against this, Imogen's anguish is expressed in words which are at once reasonable and moderate. This immediately establishes her moral superiority and generosity of spirit:

> So thou, Posthumus,
> Wilt lay the leaven on all proper men:
> Goodly and gallant shall be false and perjur'd
> From thy great fall.   (III.iv.59–62)

Of course, when he hears that Imogen is dead, Posthumus sees the terrible implications for wives of such an attitude in their husbands:

> You married ones,
> If each of you should take this course, how many
> Must murder wives much better than themselves
> For wrying but a little.   (V.i.2–5)

The wives may be better than their husbands – as indeed they always are in Shakespeare – but the individual husband need not give thought to this when he decides to be his own justicer.

XIIJ

Othello, Leontes and Posthumus claim to have a 'cause' of some sort, though it is wholly illusory, but what about Henry VIII? Shakespeare's difficulty in *Henry VIII* is that he cannot present the king in an unsympathetic light, and yet, at the same time, has to show the sufferings of an ideal wife. At one stage he shows the dilemma of the king who is reluctant to part from her but has to do so to satisfy his 'conscience':

> Would it not grieve an able man to leave
> So sweet a bedfellow? But conscience, conscience;
> O 'tis a tender place, and I must leave her.   (II.ii.141–3)

But the play casts doubts on these motives. The Duke of Suffolk has already informed us through an aside that it is not the king's 'conscience' but a baser passion that is responsible for the divorce:

> No, his conscience
> Has crept too near another lady.
>
>   (II.ii.15–16)

So the king has to redeem himself in our eyes and he does it in the trial scene. The Queen rebukes Cardinal Wolsey for his 'arrogancy, spleen and pride' (II.iv.108) and refuses to accept him as her judge. After telling the court that she would appeal to the Pope, she 'curtsies to the King and offers to depart.' Her departure, however, would defeat the very purpose of the trial. So the King orders her to return. But she pays no attention to this and after telling the assembly that she would never 'upon this business my appearance make / In any of their courts' (II.iv.130–1), she walks out. The King could have seen defiance in her conduct. Instead, he says:

> Go thy ways Kate;
> That man i' th' world who shall report he has
> A better wife, let him in nought be trusted
> For speaking false in that. Thou art, alone –
> If thy rare qualities, sweet gentleness,
> Thy meekness saint–like, wife–like government,
> Obeying in commanding, and thy parts
> Sovereign and pious else, could speak thee out –
> The queen of earthly queens. She's noble born;
> And like her true nobility she has
> Carried herself towards me.   (II.iv.133–143)

The King's praise confirms what Katherine had said about herself in lines which provide the best description, in the whole of Shakespeare, of an ideal Elizabethan wife and her predicament:

> Alas, sir,
> In what have I offended you? What cause
> Hath my behaviour given to your displeasure
> That thus you should proceed to put me off
> And take your good grace from me? Heaven witness,
> I have been to you a true and humble wife,
> At all times to your will conformable,
> Ever in fear to kindle your dislike,
> Yea, subject to your countenance – glad or sorry
> As I saw it inclin'd. When was the hour
> I ever contradicted your desire
> Or made it not mine too? Or which of your friends
> Have I not strove to love, although I knew
> He were mine enemy? What friend of mine
> That had to him deriv'd your anger, did I
> Continue in my liking? nay, gave notice
> He was from thence discharg'd? Sir, call to mind
> That I have been your wife in this obedience
> Upward of twenty years, and have been blest
> With many children by you. If, in the course,
> And process of this time, you can report,
> And prove it too against mine honour, aught,
> My bond to wedlock or my love and duty,
> Against your sacred person, in God's name,
> Turn me away and let the foul'st contempt
> Shut door upon me, and so give me up
> To the sharp'st kind of justice.   (II.iv.19–44)

Dr Johnson was so impressed by the 'meek sorrows and virtuous distress of Katharine' that he thought that in this play 'the genius of Shakespeare comes in and goes out with Katharine.' It is true that she determines the tone of the play and it does not surprise us when we see people asking anxiously about her welfare even when they have come to see the coronation of Anne. Indeed, even Anne calls her 'So good a lady that no tongue could ever / Pronounce dishonour of her (by my life, / She never knew harmdoing)' (II.iii.3–5). But, of course, she has no friends to speak for her and her enemies are too 'cunning' (II.iv. 104). So she has to speak for herself:

> Bring me a constant woman to her husband,
> One that ne'er dream'd a joy beyond his pleasure,
> And to that woman, when she has done most,

Yet will I add an honour – a great patience.

> (III.i.134–137).

Her great patience is seen at its best in her last moments. She has sympathy even for Wolsey, her greatest enemy, and concern for all her dependants. Her last thought is for the King: 'Remember me / In all humility unto his highness' (IV.ii.160–1) she says to Lord Capucius, and then adds:

> Tell him in death I bless'd him,
> For so I will.   (163–4)

We are reminded of Desdemona's last words:

> Commend me to my kind lord. O, farewell.
>
> (*Othello*, V.ii.126)

XIV

The chief merit of these suffering women in Shakespeare is that they are model wives. They combine in their characters all the qualities that go to make an ideal spouse for an Elizabethan nobleman. In *Othello* we have no doubt at all that Desdemona is perfectly capable of achieving a companionate marriage. Indeed she has been trained precisely for this task. Othello himself concedes that she is a highly cultured lady, fit in all respects to preside over a cheerful noble house:

> . . . my wife is fair, feeds well, loves company,
> Is free of speech, sings, plays, and dances well.
>
> (III.iii.188–9)

So are the others. They combine in an excellent measure social graces, virtuous disposition and a queenly dignity which nothing can damage. Desdemona rightly says:

> Unkindness may do much;
> And his unkindness may defeat my life
> But never taint my love.
>
> (IV.ii.160–2)

This love, we should note, is almost radically different from the love in Restoration drama. So perhaps is Elizabethan marriage from the companionate marriage of the late seventeenth and early eighteenth centuries. There are marriages in Shakespeare too, as we have seen, which can be described as companionate, but their *basis* is largely different from that of marriages in the later period. It needs to be recognized that by and large, as enjoined by religion and custom, the Elizabethan wife regards herself *incomplete* without her husband, and her conception of love is simply that of *merging* her personality in that of her husband. It is not surprising that Katherine in *Henry VIII* surrenders her personal preferences and wishes in *all* matters to those of her husband. Indeed she lives, as she rightly says, 'subject to [his] countenance – glad or sorry / as [she] saw it inclin'd' (II.v.27–28). This attitude is born of her understanding of the contemporary 'bond of wedlock or [a wife's] love and duty' (II.v.40). Imogen's understanding of this bond is no different. She regards killing herself as the only honourable course of action the moment she discovers that her heart, 'the innocent mansion of [her] love', is empty after her 'master' 'who was indeed / The riches of it' (*Cymbeline*, III.iv.69–72) has left it. Desdemona is clear in her mind that she too has lived 'subject to [Othello's] countenance – glad or sorry / As [she] saw it inclin'd.' She rightly claims that to Othello's 'honours and his valiant, parts / *Did I my soul consecrate*' (I.ii.253–4). (Italics mine). Her life was so much merged in his that neither her senses nor her mind 'Delighted them in any other form' (IV.ii.156). Her chief concern is that whatever may happen to her, her love for her husband should not be 'tainted'.

The attitude of these women would have delighted the heart even of John Sprint who, in a sermon in 1699, said that 'a good Wife [should] endeavour to frame her outward Deportment, and her inward Affections according to her Husband's: to rejoyce when he rejoyces, to be sad when he mourns, to grieve and be troubled when he is offended and vexed.'[73] Sprint perhaps had in mind late seventeenth century women who had different ideas about the bond of wedlock, but his ideas were a normal part of an Elizabethan woman's doctrine. The remarkable thing about Shakespeare, however, is that he gives most of his heroines, both in the comedies and the tragedies, very positive and often sparkling personalities of their own. And yet, in deference to the contemporary conservative world–view, he is reluctant to let them function on their own as individuals. Indeed his basic assumption remains the same as stated in the lines cited earlier in this chapter from *King John*:

And she a fair divided excellence,
Whose fulness of perfection lies in *him*.   (II.i.439–40)
(Italics mine)

About the husband too, of course, the theory was the same,
namely, that he was 'the *half* part of a blessed man' (II.i.437)
(Italics mine) to be completed by his wife, but in actual practice
the men in Shakespeare are allowed all the freedom that they need
to grow and develop into powerful individuals, often quite inde-
pendently of women. This whole question of woman being
incomplete without man, in whom alone her salvation lies – and
consequently her role being wholly subservient to his – will come
under question in the Restoration period.

CHAPTER V
HUSBANDS AND WIVES(II):
RESTORATION COMEDY OF MANNERS

I

It would be wrong to claim that the Restoration woman has liberated herself from the Elizabethan notion that a woman is only half herself, the other half — and clearly the more important half — being the man she marries. Most women, in this period too, subscribe to 'the horrible merging, mingling self-abnegation of love' and have not achieved that 'single, *separate being*, with its own laws'[1] (Italics mine) which is the real sign of equality and freedom. Generally speaking, however, their position is quite considerably improved as compared to the position of the Elizabethan woman. This improvement is reflected in Restoration comedy, where the general tendency clearly is towards recognition of a woman's individuality.

Guy Montgomery, in fact, has claimed that the new world of the Restoration age emerged from chaos, and 'proposed to men and women an equality scarcely known before to English society.'[2] C. V. Wedgewood specially contrasts the position of women in Shakespeare and Restoration comedy in her well-known remarks:

The old system of chivalry, in which women were chattels — precious chattels, but chattels nonetheless — to be protected and possessed, had in an attenuated form governed the moral outlook of the upper classes well into the seventeenth century. A new morality had not yet been worked out to fit a society which now finally came unmoored from feudalism and chivalry. With all their cynicism, the morals of the fast set in the later seventeenth century represent a move towards greater justice between men and women. The capacity to meet a man on equal terms, which had been the prerogative of an occasional Brunhild or Britomart, was now open to any woman of quick wits. It can hardly be sustained that the morality depicted by Wycherley, Etherege, Congreve and Vanbrugh is an advance on that depicted by Spenser, Shakespeare, Massinger, or even Ford. But at least theirs is a society in which neither Hero nor Imogen could be so scandalously mistreated by their lovers with the full approval of society.[3]

146

tions soon lose their relevance. However loudly Petruchio may proclaim that 'wealth is the burden of my wooing dance' (*The Taming of the Shrew*, I.ii.66), the burden of the play is to show how two somewhat stubborn individuals can convert this marriage into a companionate one. In *The Merry Wives of Windsor*, Fenton did at one time covet Anne's father's wealth (III.iv.12) but that time is long past and 'tis the very riches of thyself / That now I aim at' (III.iv.17-18). Indeed, his is a genuine marriage of love.

In the Restoration age the situation is radically changed. Now the mercenary consideration becomes the chief motive for marriage amongst the upper-class. Indeed, as P. F. Vernon has pointed out, in the later seventeenth and early eighteenth centuries, marriages of convenience became 'so widespread. . .as to indicate that the aristocracy had come to accept a new view of the nature and function of marriage.' 'A carefully arranged marriage', he adds, became 'the readiest means of accumulating landed property, and so, inevitably, a new attitude to marriage arose.'[8] It is this new attitude to marriage that we have to keep in mind while considering the difficulties that women face in this period in achieving a companionate marriage. What Dorimant says to Mrs Loveit is a lie, but it correctly depicts the situation that the Restoration upper-class is facing: 'Believe me, a wife, to repair the ruins of my estate that needs it.' (*The Man of Mode*, V.ii). Dorimant's remark to Young Bellair again does not reflect his true state of mind, but it certainly reflects the attitude of the younger aristocracy:

> The wise will find a difference in our fate,
> You wed a woman, I a good estate.   (IV.ii)

The reasons for this increasing emphasis on the money-motive are to be found in the increasing wealth of the city merchants and the dwindling fortunes of the landed aristocracy. The crisis must have got intensified by the reduction of eligible husbands owing to losses caused by the civil war. There is enough evidence to show that some of the rich merchants were paying very large dowries and causing real concern amongst members of the older aristocracy. Writing in 1685, Sir William Temple rightly bewailed the new situation: 'I think I remember within less than fifty years, the first noble families that married into the city for downright money, and thereby introduced by degrees this public

grievance which has since ruined so many estates by the necessity
of giving great portions to daughters.'⁹ Marriage in the period
had become so mercenary that a courtesan in Mrs Behn's *The
Rover: Or, The Banish't Cavaliers* (1677), when abused by the
rover for her trade, snubs him in these words: 'Pray, tell me, Sir,
are not you guilty of the same mercenary Crime? When a Lady is
proposed to you for a Wife, you never ask, how fair, discreet, or
virtuous she is; but what's her Fortune — which if but small, you
cry — She will not do my business — and basely leave her, tho'
she languish for you.' (II.i). The rover himself concedes
that it is a 'barbarous custom'. Mary Astell's comment on this
barbarous custom is equally pertinent: 'What qualifications do
they look after in a Spouse? What will she bring? is the first
Enquiry: How many Acres? or how much ready Coin?'¹⁰ Defoe's
Moll Flanders was wholly correct when she complained that the
marriage-market had become 'unfavourable to our sex.'¹¹

III

A comedy that treats marriage as merely a commercial contract
where neither compatibility of temperament and age nor affection plays any part, is bound to present an unpleasant picture of
husband-wife relationships. At times, the picture is so unpleasant
that we are left in no doubt that the playwrights are attacking a
serious contemporary social evil. Some plays merely ridicule
greedy parents and guardians, or unsuitable and inadequate husbands. But there are other plays like Southerne's *The Wives
Excuse* (1692) where the problem of an unhappy marriage is presented in such grim terms as to make it almost a problem play.
That play comes rather late in the period, but even in its earlier
phase Restoration comedy presents marriage, in the words of a
character in Shadwell's *Epsom Wells* (1673), as 'the worst of Pri-
sons' — indeed an 'Ecclesiastical Mouse-trap'(I.i). A character in
Mrs Behn's *The Town-Fop* (1677) goes even further and describes
mercenary marriages as an 'Adultery' (II.iii) — in fact 'one continu'd Sin' (III.i). All this is not an exaggeration when applied to
marriages where '*Hymen* and Priest wait still upon Portion, and
Jointure' (*The Rover*, V.i). P. F. Vernon is wholly correct in
stating that where marriages 'yoked together, without regard for
human feelings, young and old, intelligent and stupid, sensitive
ladies and miserly businessman', — 'all unions without affection'

— they were bound to lead to 'mutual distrust, possessive tyranny, jealousy and contempt.'[12]

How can marriages of this type provide any satisfaction to the parties — or even become tolerable? The situation becomes particularly difficult when no divorce is possible. Rochester's view expressed to Burnet on his death-bed is not to be brushed aside lightly: 'The restraining a man from the use of Women, Except one in the way of Marriage, and denying the remedy of Divorce, he thought unreasonable Impositions on the Freedom of Mankind.'[13] Rochester, of course, never cared to look at the question from the woman's point of view, whom in any case he described as the 'silliest part of God's creation'. But men in Rochester's times — as perhaps in all periods in history — have found an answer in extramarital relationships. The male attitude is well stated by Dorilant in Wycherley's *The Country Wife* (1675): 'A mistress should be like a little country retreat near the town, not to dwell in constantly but only for a night and away, to taste the town better when a man returns' (I.i). Male adultery, Dorilant claims, does not threaten the institution of marriage; indeed it strengthens it. Such marriages were naturally not satisfactory from the woman's point of view, but they met the needs of society adequately. William Stout commented on a marriage in 1699: 'they lived disagreeably but had many children' and surely the most important thing that an upper-class husband demanded of his wife in the sixteenth and seventeenth centuries was an heir!

What really distinguishes Restoration comedy from earlier comedy, specially Elizabethan comedy, is its acceptance of the fact that married women too need the kind of 'retreat' that Dorilant mentions. Jeremy Collier was outraged at this defiance by contemporary comedy of the most sacred tenet of sexual morality in the mind of a male: 'It may not be amiss to observe that there are no Instances of debauching Married Women, in *Plautus*, nor *Terence*, no nor yet in *Aristophanes*. But on our Stage how common is it to make a Lord, a Knight, or an Alderman a Cuckold?'[14] But surely we cannot blame the wife of Sir Jasper Fidget or of Mr Pinchwife — and the innumerable other wives in Restoration comedy — for finding some solace outside marriage. For Sir Jasper his wife is only a bothersome encumbrance — at best a social ornament — and for Pinchwife Margery is no more than a substitute for a whore. Sir Jasper is indifferent, Pinchwife is hostile. In these marriages there is no trust, no understanding and, of course, no love.

Lady Fidget states her complaint in these words:

> Why should our damned tyrants oblige us to live
> On the pittance of pleasure which they only give?

(The Country Wife, V.iv)

What Jacinta, the woman of Julia in Mrs Behn's *The False Count* (1682), says could serve as a reply to Lady Fidget's complaint: 'Hang't, why should we young women pine and languish for what our own natural Invention may procure us; let us. . .lay our Heads together, and if *Machiaval* with all his Politicks can outwit us, 'tis pity but we all lead Apes in Hell, and die without the *Jewish* blessing of Consolation' (II.i). Julia, of course, would accept Jacinta's advice and outwit her husband, but there is no doubt that her situation is much worse than that of Lady Fidget. She is 'married to a Thing, fit only for his Tomb; a Brute, who wanting sense to value [her], treats [her] more like a Prisoner than a Wife' (I.ii). In her husband's mind she is worse than a prisoner: he calls her his 'Slave' (I.ii), his 'Property' (IV.ii), and his 'Goods and Chattels' (V.i). Hellena in *The Rover* has still not had such an experience as she is unmarried, but she can well imagine what it would be like: 'the Giant stretches itself, yawns and sighs a Belch or two as loud as a Musket, throws himself into Bed, and expects you in his foul Sheets, and e'er you can get your self undrest, calls you with a Snore or two — And are not these fine Blessings to a young Lady?' (I.i). Otway's Mrs Goodville in *Friendship in Fashion* (1678) knows this at first hand: 'I have not seen him this Fortnight; he never comes homes till Four in the Morning, and then he sneaks to his separate Bed, where he lies till Afternoon, then rises and out again upon his Parole: flesh and blood can't endure it.' (II.i). The wife of Spruce in James Carlisle's *The Fortune Hunters* (1689) puts the wife's point of view sharply: 'Bless me how unreasonably we are accus'd for Cuckolding our Husbands, when certainly, either by vanity, Folly, Pride, or ill Nature, they draw it upon themselves.' (pp. 58-9). Constant in Vanbrugh's *The Provok'd Wife* (1697) sums up this point of view at the end of the century:

A man of real worth scarce ever is a cuckold, but by his own fault.

Women are not naturally lewd; there must be something to urge 'em to it. They'll cuckold a Churl, out of Revenge; a Fool, because they despise him; a Beast, because they loath him. But when they make bold with a Man they once had a well grounded Value for, 'tis because they first see them neglected by him. (V.iv)

However sensible Constant's defence of the woman's conduct in Restoration Comedy may be, it provides no solution to the marriage problem. It does not help women to achieve what Mariana in Thomas Wright's *The Female Vertuoso's* (1693) describes as a genuinely satisfying marriage: 'When I reflect on Marriage, all I can see in it, is a dear Husband that will love me, pretty Children that will play about me, and a House of my own to manage' (p.1). The women who cuckold their husbands — whatever their reasons, whether satisfaction of sexual hunger or alleviation of a sense of injury — have surely missed that 'best state of pleasure and delight' which Shadwell's Woodly in *Epsom Wells* (1673) regards as the fruit of a 'Marriage that does the *hearts and wills unite*' (I.i) (Italics mine). Consequently they are also destined not to achieve 'the perfection of the mind and inward Graces' which the heroine of D'Urfey's *The Bath, Or, The Western Lass* (1701) describes as 'most essential to the happiness of Life' (p.3). Being conscious of this, some of the women in Restoration comedy are not able to accept adultery as a way out of their problems. However strong the temptation, a sensitive woman probably feels that to become someone's mistress hurts her self-respect. Perhaps Dryden's Cleopatra belonged to this category:

> Nature meant me
> A Wife, a silly harmless household Dove,
> Fond without art. (*All for Love*, IV)

Mrs Friendall in Thomas Southerne's *The Wives Excuse* (1692) was certainly meant to be a wife. She would have preferred to 'please her Husband, instruct her Children, have a Vigilant Eye over Domestick Affairs, keep a good Order in her Family, and stand as a Living Pattern of Virtue, and Discretion to all about her' (Thomas Wright's *The Female Vertuoso's*, p. 25). But she gets no chance and her husband destroys all her dreams. Must she take a lover, as most women in her circumstances in Restoration comedy might have done? Lovemore who has been pursuing her, regards it as inevitable.[15] But she rebukes him: '*Mr. Lovemore*, you might have known me better, than to imagine your sly flattery could softly sing me into a consent to anything my virtue had abhorr'd. But how have I behav'd myself? What have I done to deserve this? What encouragement have I given you?' When Lovemore gives the cheeky reply that 'A lover makes his hopes', Mrs Friendall says: 'Perhaps 'tis from the general encouragement of being a married woman, supported on your side by that honourable opinion of our sex, that because some women abuse their husbands, every woman may.[16] I grant you indeed, the custom of *England* has been very prevailing in that point; and I must own to you an ill husband is a great provocation to a wife. . . .I won't justify his faults, but because he does not take that care of me he shou'd, must not I have that regard to myself I ought? What I do is for my own sake.' (pp. 64-5). What she tells Mr Lovemore later in the play may sound somewhat exceptional in Restoration comedy, yet it is as valid a point of view as any other: 'Every woman carries her cross in this world: a husband happens to be mine, and I must bear it, as well as I can' (p. 81). And when the cross happens to be a particularly nasty piece of goods like Mr Friendall, life becomes a real hell. In her case the only solution would have been a divorce with the right to remarry. But a divorce of this kind was well-nigh impossible in that period, and so the play has to end on a bleak note. Mrs Friendall has to bear 'a slavery for life', and when they agree to separate, all that she can say to her husband is: 'I must be still your wife, and still unhappy' (pp. 88-9).

The fate of Mrs Sullen in Farquhar's *The Beaux' Stratagem* (1707) is not very much better, though on the surface it lacks the grimness of Mrs Friendall's situation. Mrs Oldfield (who played this role) protested that Farquhar 'had dealt too freely with the character of *Mrs Sullen*, in giving her to *Archer* without a proper Divorce, which was not a Security for her Honour.'[17] But in this Farquhar was being realistic, at least to the extent that no 'proper Divorce' with the right to remarry could really be provided. Irrespective of whether Mrs Sullen becomes Archer's mistress or resists him, the fact, in her case as well, is that for all the airy talk of happy parting at the end of the play, there is not going to be much happiness for her. Like Mrs Friendall, she must still be Mr Sullen's wife, and still unhappy. Her description of the misery of her married life, though at once humourous and brutal,[18] is quite applicable to many a marriage in Restoration comedy:

O Sister, Sister, if ever you marry, beware of a sullen, silent Sot, one that's always musing, but never thinks. . . .He came home this morning at his usual Hour of Four, waken'd me out of a sweet Dream of something else, by tumbling over the Tea-table, which he broke all to pieces; after his Man and he had rowl'd about the Room like sick Passengers in a Storm, he comes flounces into Bed, dead as a Salmon into a Fishmonger's basket; his Feet cold as Ice, his Breath hot as a Furnace, and his Hands and his Face as greasy as his Flannel Night-cap — O, Matrimony! — He tosses up the Clothes with a barbarous swing over his Shoulders, disorders the whole Economy of my Bed, leaves me half naked, and my whole Night's Comfort is the tuneable Serenade of that wakeful Nightingale, his Nose! O, the Pleasure of counting the meloncholy Clock by a snoring Husband! (II.i)

The real answer to Mrs Sullen's problem — or of Mrs Friendall's — lies in what Mrs Oldfield called 'a proper Divorce', which would naturally include the right to remarry. It is not without significance that Farquhar raises the question of divorce so sharply in this play. This was a very live topic during these years and 'the first very small step' had already been 'taken towards a modification of the institution of matrimony with the introduction of divorce by Act of Parliament in 1697, though the procedure was too long and costly, not to say unpleasant, to be of use to most people.'[19] But even the Act of Parliament insisted on adultery being one of the grounds for divorce, and Mr Sullen for all his hoggishness, is not an adulterer, as Mr Friendall clearly is. So what should Mrs Sullen do? Only Milton's grounds of mental and spiritual incompatibility can help her. Milton had declared that 'natural hatred whenever it arises, is a greater evil in marriage than the accident of adultery, a greater defrauding, a greater injustice.'[20] Hence Mrs Sullen's argument:

O sister, casual violation is a transient injury, and may possibly be repaired, but can radical hatreds be ever reconciled? No, no, sister, nature is the first lawgiver, and when she has set tempers opposite, not all the golden links of wedlock nor iron manacles of law can keep 'em fast'. (III.iii)

IV

Before we look into the fortunes of the lovers in the 'gay couple' comedies, we may notice another feature of Restoration comedy which militates against companionate marriage. An arranged marriage — even a mercenary one — need not be too much of a disaster if the individuals concerned have a reasonable attitude

towards each other. In Vanbrugh's *Aesop* (1697), the lovers are
given the following advice:

> When one is out of Humour, let the other be dumb.
> Let your Diversions be such, as both may have a share in 'em
> (V.i)

The advice about diversions is not easy to follow. When Amanda
in *The Relapse* asks Berinthia, who is now a widow, how she and
her husband lived together — this being an arranged marriage —
this is the reply that Berinthia gives:

> He loved the country — I the town.
> He hawks and hounds — I coaches and equipage.
> He eating and drinking — I carding and playing.
> He the sound of a horn — I the squeak of a fiddle.   (II.i)

This is clearly an extreme case but even normally men and
women in that society had to spend most of their time in different
spheres. But surely the first advice — 'when one is out of humour,
let the other be dumb' — should not be too difficult to follow.
And yet it becomes difficult in a situation where man and woman
start asserting superiority over each other. This frequently happened owing to a conflict in this period between the traditional
ideas regarding a woman's place in the home and her new awareness of personal identity. The mere fact that a woman could seek
satisfaction outside marriage is itself an evidence of this new
awareness.

In certain respects the position of a Restoration woman has
certainly improved. She is no more the obedient, silent and docile
woman of the Elizabethan age. She has higher expectations from
marriage and a new pride in her sex. What Ravenscroft's heroine
in *The Careless Lovers* (1673) says is perhaps quite typical: 'But
Uncle, it is not now as it was in your young days. Women then
were poor, sneaking, sheepish creatures. But in our age we know
our strength and have wit enough to make use of our talents.'
This improvement in the position of women owes a great deal to
the developments in England during the Civil War and the inter-
regnum. Indeed it was during this period that the very founda-
tions of the old patriarchal family came to be challenged, paving
the way for the emergence of 'the new woman'. Among other
developments, Keith Thomas mentions —

the Civil Marriage Act and the lively discussion of polygamy and of marriage within the forbidden degrees, the unusual part played by women in war, litigation, pamphleteering and politics, the appearance in English of continental feminist writings, and the attacks, sometimes by women themselves, on their limited educational opportunities, their confinement to domestic activity, their subjection to their husbands and the injustices of a commercial marriage market.[21]

However much the post-Restoration establishment might try to silence the voice of dissent in politics or in the field of domestic relations, it was impossible to restore the old order. Indeed, as Clarendon lamented, some basic changes had taken place in English culture: 'Children asked not blessing of their parents . . . .The young women conversed without any circumspection or modesty. . . .Parents had no manner of authority over their children.'[22]

From all this we must not, of course, conclude that Restoration women had achieved equality with men or that the age had accepted the concept of equality between the sexes. Indeed even the most sympathetic of seventeenth century writers, John Locke, never countenanced this concept. The moral writers demanded from contemporary women the same virtues as their counterparts did in Elizabethan times — 'piety and devotion, meekness, modesty, and submission.'[23] The argument was still the old theological one: 'And since Gods assignation has thus determined subjection to be the women's lot, there needs no other argument of its fitness, or for their acquiescence. Therefore whenever they oppose it the contumacy flies higher than the immediate Superior, and reaches God himself.'[24] Defiance of the authority of the husband by the wife had also serious social implications. John Sprint, in a sermon in 1699, attributed all dissensions in families and in married life to 'the Indiscretion and Folly, if not to the Obstinacy and Stubbornness of disobedient Wives.'[25] He, of course, comes very late in the period, and his attack on the insubordination of women is itself evidence of their improved position. But Sprint's statement, though it sounds extreme, is as true of the *theoretical* position of women in the earlier period as now. A good wife, he says, 'should be like a Mirrour which hath no Image of its own, but receives its Stamp and Image from the Face that looks into it: So should a good Wife endeavour to frame her outward Deportment, and her inward Affections according to her Husband's: to rejoyce when he rejoyceth, to be sad when he mourns, to grieve and be troubled when he is offended and vexed.'[26]

Restoration comic playwrights wholly reject John Sprint's ideal of a wife who is 'like a Mirrour which hath no Image of its own'. They create women who have a personality of their own and who expect to be treated as man's equal. Indeed they demand esteem from the men they marry as they recognize that no companionate marriage is possible without mutual esteem. Where this esteem is lacking and the man treats his wife as a slave, the relationship degenerates into conflict and misery.

It is a notable feature of Restoration comedy that it consistently ridicules men who behave as tyrants and treat their wives as property. These men are usually cuckolded by their wives and treated with contempt by their male friends and acquaintances. There is, of course, the classic case of Mr Pinchwife in *The Country Wife* (1675). But an even better example of a husband who keeps a merchant's daughter, Betty, deliberately uneducated so that she can become a wholly obedient and submissive wife, is Sir Salomon in John Caryll's *Sir Salomon: Or, The Cautious Coxcomb* (1671). Caryll provides an excellent parody of the conventional duties of a wife as enumerated by contemporary moralists in a scene which his audience must have found hilarious:

SIR SALO: . . .First tell me, what you were made for?

MRS BETTY: To be your Wife, forsooth.

SIR SALO: And what's the Duty of a Wife?

MRS BETTY: To honour, and obey her Husband; and love no man but him.

SIR SALO: Now, What are the particular duties; which I expect from her, who is to be my Wife?

MRS BETTY: First, to watch, and observe all the motions of your Eyes, and Countenance, and accordingly to stand, go, run, sit still, speak, or be silent: Secondly, To detest and abhor going to *Court, Hide-Park, Mulberry-Garden,* or the *Play-Houses.* Thirdly, To Visit, and be visited by none of a remoter degree, than an Uncle, or an Aunt; Fourthly To write and receive no Letters, to accept and give no Presents, but such as you see and allow of: Lastly, To warm Napkins, make Cawdles, dress Issues, give Glisters, and the like; Still remembering, that the office of a Nurse inseparably belongs to the duty of your Wife.

(p.19)

Caryll's Sir Salomon is not the only self-opinionated husband in Restoration comedy. There is Shadwell's Fribble in *Epsom Wells.* He is an egregious fool but he tells his wife: 'Know your Lord and Master, and be subject to my Government: I though but a Haberdasher will be as absolute a Monarch over you, as the

great Turk over his Sultan Queen' (II.i). He, however, forgets that
even the king had ceased to be 'absolute', and wholly lacks the
capacity to be a master in his house. D'Urfey's Toby in *Madam
Fickle: or the Witty False One* (1676) is even worse. He does not
even know the name of the woman he is going to marry but this is
how he talks:

Hang't I will marry — I fancy there's a great deal of pleasure in't. First to
command a Family, and sit at the upper end of the Table. Then to make
my Wife serve instead of a *Vallet de Chambre*, and never pay her no
Wages neither: Then to command her this way, that way, t'other way,
and every way; for this thing, that thing, t'other thing, and everything.
Udshash 'tis very pretty.

A woman in William Joyner's tragedy, *The Roman Empress*
(1670), challenges man's right to tyrannize over women and even
denounces the arbitrary man-made laws which society imposes on
them:

> He makes lawes
> Partial t' himself, rigid to us: his vows
> He breaks, ours must be kept; his vices
> Pass only for his gallantries; ours are
> Branded with foul and horrid names t' affright us.
> Ambition in us, in him is honour;
> And our irregular appetites in him
> Pass for the noble passions of his love;
> Not only to be excus'd, but commended.
>   Who made these laws and customs? did our Sex
> Ever give up their voice, and suffrages?
> No: there's no right, or obligation then
> We should obey these orders made by men,
> So partial judges.

Antonia, the speaker of these lines, is protesting against a situation which she specifically mentions a little earlier in her speech:

> in our tender years
> Our Fathers Palaces to us are Prisons,
> Where nor our persons, nor scarce our looks are free:
> And afterward, when our maturity
> *Should change this bondage into liberty;*
> We only of all creatures are, *who buy*
> *With a vast dowry our own slavery:*
> Thus only changing a new Master, whom
> We purchase to rule o'er our souls and bodies,
> And cast us off thus when he pleases.   (pp.23-24)
>   (Italics mine)

In this case the husband has confessed to Antonia that he loves someone else, and though apologetic for this, he cannot help himself. So what should a wife do? The playwright clearly chooses a situation which contrasts with Restoration comedy: in Restoration comedy the heroes never care to apologise for their conduct. Indeed, the Restoration comic hero often 'glories to a woman's face in his villainies.' (*The Man of Mode*, V.i).

The point that all these playwrights are making is that marriage is a contract between man and woman and it is valid only as long as both fulfil the terms of the contract. If the man fails to do so, the woman is under no obligation to obey him. Indeed, as often happens in comedies of the period in such a situation, the woman has every right to rebel. Restoration comedy's protest again unsuitable marriages, therefore, should be seen as a positive merit. This comedy clearly stands for more humane relationships between husbands and wives and for a more sensible and civilized basis for these relationships. There is no doubt that many married women in this period found themselves in a situation of utter despair which could be relieved neither by law nor social custom. Mary Astell's *Some Reflections Upon Marriage* which first appeared in 1700 and which is a thoughtful attack on contemporary marriages, contains an excellent comment, from a woman's point of view, on forced marriages:

They only who have felt it, know the Misery of being forc'd to marry where they do not love; of being yok'd for Life to a disagreeable Person and Imperious Temper, where Ignorance and Folly. . .tyrannises over Wit and Sense: To be perpetually contradicted for Contradiction-sake, and bore down by Authority, not by Argument; to be denied one's most innocent Desires, for no other Reason but the absolute Power and Pleasure of a Lord and Master, whose Follies a Wife, with all her Prudence, cannot hide, and whose commands she cannot but despise at the same Time that she obeys them.[27]

V

The 'gay couple' comedies have no use for tyrannical husbands or for servile wives. Here the playwrights do present man and woman as equal. Indeed, as Katharine M. Rogers has said, the heroines in these comedies 'choose their own mates, set their own terms of courtship, hold their own in wit combats with men, and clearly do not intend after marriage to make their husbands' wishes their laws.'[28] All this is admirable, and here if anywhere, we could have a genuinely 'modern' approach to man-woman relationship. Irrespective of whether or not the comic heroines in these comedies achieve all that Katharine Rogers claims for them, the important point to notice is that even in a society where the economic and legal status of women was very low indeed, it remains their constant endeavour.

There is the view that at times the Restoration comic playwrights create the *illusion* of equality between men and women largely for artistic purposes. Dryden at least admitted as much when in his Preface to *Secret Love* (1668) he gave the following defence of 'the last scene in the play, where Celadon and Florimell are treating too lightly of their marriage:' 'This I cannot otherwise defend than by telling you I so designed it on purpose *to make the play go off more* smartly; that scene being in the opinion of the best judges the most divertising of the whole comedy.'[29] (Italics mine). The scene was bound to be most 'divertising' with Nell Gwyn playing the role of Florimell brilliantly, and with the dialogue providing some of the most delicious sexual innuendoes. Pepys was so moved by this performance that he recorded in his *Diary* (2 March 1667): 'I never hope ever to see the like again.'

In a comedy where repartee between lovers plays such an important part, it was natural that the playwrights should create women characters who possess not only an agile mind but also an exceptional mastery of the current fashionable idiom. In the wit-combats in this comedy, in its spirit of gaiety and raillery, woman cannot be shown as man's inferior. The contemporary audience would, in fact, like her to be his superior. After all it was the boast of the age, to use Vanbrugh's words in his Prologue to *The Relapse* (1697):

> This is an age where all things we improve,
> But most of all, the Art of making Love.

Vanbrugh makes a clear distinction between the Elizabethan 'Art of making Love' and the Restoration mode in the next few lines of the Prologue:

> In former days women were only won
> By merit, truth, and constant service done;
> But lovers now are much more expert grown;
> They seldom wait t' approach by tedious form;
> They're for despatch, for taking you by storm:

Quick are their sieges, furious are their fires,
Fierce their attacks, and boundless their desires.

These lines were spoken on the stage by Mrs Verbuggen who
played the role of Berinthia, the young widow in *The Relapse*,
and their main thrust is to remind the comic heroines that they
are dealing with rakes and that they must, therefore, learn how to
flirt, bandy words with men, and for sheer survival in a libertine
world, outwit them.

Shadwell described the love-game of contemporary comedy as
'that Indecent way of Writing' and said of the lovers of this
comedy — 'a Swearing, Drinking, Whoring, Ruffian for a Lover,
and an impudent ill-bred *tomrig* for a Mistress' (Preface to *The
Sullen Lovers*, 1668). But he also referred to the contemporary
'Art of making Love' when he made the hero of his liveliest
comedy, *Epsom Wells* (1673), say to the heroine: 'Take your choice; I can make love from the stiff formal way of the year '42 to the
gay brisk way of this present day and hour' (II.i). The age clearly
enjoyed this gay brisk way of making love and so it demanded
that the lovers and their mistresses in contemporary comedy be
equally witty and uninhibited. Often this total lack of inhibition
in the words and gestures of beautiful, scantily dressed actresses
like Nell Gwyn must have provided a much needed titilation of
the appetite to the old rakes and their jaded mistresses in that
period, who, as L. C. Knights has aptly said, were 'fundamentally
bored' and 'badly. . .*needed* to be entertained.'[30] (Italics Knights').

Lawrence Echard mentioned this need of contemporary
audiences in his Preface to *Terence's Comedies* (1694) when he
said that the age was 'all for Humour, Gallantry, Conversation,
and Courtship, and shou'dn't endure the Chief Lady in the Play a
Mute; or to say very little.' 'Our amorous Sparks', he added, 'love
to hear the pretty Rogues prate, snap up their Gallants, and
Repartee upon 'em on all sides.' 'We shou'dn't like to have a
Lady marry'd', he continued, contrasting the comedies of Terence with those of his contemporaries, 'without knowing
whether she gives her consent or no, (A Custom among the
Romans) but wou'd be for hearing all the Courtship, all the rare
and fine things that Lovers can say to each other.'

VI

The Restoration comedies of wit do, of course, contain 'the rare and fine things that Lovers say to each other' — as also the repartee which Dryden described as 'the very soul of conversation' and 'the greatest grace of comedy'.[31] But in modern times we are more concerned with what these comedies are really trying to *say* and how sensible their comments on human conduct are. One thing that strikes us immediately is that even the most pedestrian of these comedies asks questions about the immediate social reality which Shakespeare's comedies tended to bypass. Juliet Dusinberre, for instance, has claimed that 'the arranged marriage in the sixteenth century was only tolerable through adultery'[32] but there is no evidence that Shakespeare gave serious thought to this question. Indeed, except for some playful teasing on the part of his lovers, the question is raised in something like serious form only by his clowns and villains. Shakespeare is so committed to 'holy matrimony' that he never visualizes the possibility of either of the parties changing after marriage. Rosalind does, of course, say that 'men are April when they woo, December when they wed'. But this fate is reserved in *As You Like It* for characters like Touchstone; Rosalind and Orlando are not touched by it. Their 'true faith' (V.iv.182) guarantees that they shall live happily ever after.

It is precisely this true faith that Restoration comedy is unable to accept. It finds it false to human nature and recognizes human frailty as a fact of life. Men and women do change, it claims, and as Dorimant says, the oaths, vows and protestations of lovers 'may be a certain proof of a present passion, but to say truth, in love there is no security to be given for the future' (*The Man of Mode*, II.ii). In a state of high emotion — or 'present passion' — Dorimant makes the claim: 'I will renounce all the joys I have in friendship and in wine, sacrifice to you all the interest I have in other women' (V.ii), but Harriet has the true instinct of a Restoration comic heroine and warns him against this extravagance: 'Hold — though I wish you devout, I would not have you turn fanatic' (V.ii). This lack of faith in any moral absolutes is so strong in this comedy that when at the end of *She Would if She Could* Lady Cockwood resolves 'to give over the great business of this Town, and hereafter modestly confine [herself] to the humble affairs of [her] own family' (V.i), Courtall cannot help reminding her, though somewhat unkindly, that this 'very pious resolution' would work better if she could also 'entertain an able Chaplain'![33]

In such a general climate of scepticism, establishing stable human relationships becomes difficult. Marriage clearly seems to have lost its sanctity in this period, but there is no other institution that can replace it. The attempt of Restoration heroes and heroines is not to reject marriage — notwithstanding the scoffing attitude of most of them, particularly the men — but to make it more acceptable in terms of their real needs as men and women. Adultery may, of course, provide some temporary solace, but no one in this comedy really believes that it can be a substitute for marriage. Indeed, as Dennis Davis has said, 'inside every bawdy Restoration comedy, there is a muddled, romantic, sensual, rational plea for "wedded love" struggling to escape.'³⁴ For women especially, 'wedded love' is all important. In a society where no profession is available to her, marriage is a woman's only career. As Mary Astell puts it, marriage was the contemporary woman's 'only preferment, the sum total of her endeavours, the completion of all her hopes.'³⁵ These hopes could, however, be easily destroyed if she entered into a mercenary marriage and became the property of an unsympathetic husband.

To escape such a fate, the first thing that the woman must do is to choose her own husband and resist any interference in her life from her parents or guardians. Harriet is clear on this point, and when questioned by her woman, Busy, she tells her: 'Has thou so little wit to think I spoke what I meant when I over-joyed her [her mother] in the country with a low curtsy, and *What you please, madam, I shall ever be obedient?*' (*The Man of Mode*, III.i). She is equally vehement in her contempt for mercenary marriages: 'Shall I be paid down by a covetous parent for a purchase? I need no land; no, I'll lay myself out all in love' (III.i). Harriet, of course, does not have much of a problem with parental pressure. Hippolita in Wycherley's *The Gentleman-Dancing Master* (1673), however, has to fight a real battle against an unreasonable father, but as Peter Malekin says, in the true spirit of this comedy 'Hippolita must outwit not only her father, but also the society in which she lives.'³⁶

'I'll lay myself out all in love', says Harriet, and like other young people in Restoration comedy, she understands the nature of contemporary love. After all even love is a slave of time and its nature changes along with other changes in society. Harriet's mother has no notion of this and complains: 'Well, this is not the women's age, let 'em think what they will. Lewdness is the business now, love was the business in my time' (IV.i). Harriet and the other comic heroines waste no time on lamenting that lewdness has taken the place of love, but go about ordering their lives in a way which takes into account this aspect of male behaviour in their scheme of things. They know that the hero is a man of 'great employment' who is 'every moment rattling from the eating-houses to the play-houses, from the play-houses to the Mulberry Garden' (Etherege's *She Would if. She Could*, II.i). They also know that he is at heart a libertine, and that his chief — indeed only — 'employment' is chasing women whom he regards as mere objects of male gratification. It is a world of the idle rich and it poses special problems for women. James Sutherland has gone so far as to say that 'Comedy almost invariably saw life from a masculine standpoint, and although Congreve can rise to a Millamant, or Etherege to a Harriet in *The Man of Mode*, women in Restoration comedy are usually not much more than the physical objects of male pursuit, the necessary concomitants of sexual satisfaction.'[37] The Restoration comic heroine has got to come to terms with this disturbing fact of life and survive — even flourish — in the face of this distorted image of woman.

How distorted this image can be is seen in the remark of Dryden's Bellamy in *An Evening's Love*, when he describes women as 'our common game, like Hare and Partridge' (IV.i). At the end of the play we are told in a song, 'Passion's but an empty name / When respect is wanting' (V.i), but how does one expect a man like Bellamy to have respect for a woman whom he regards only as an object? It is not Bellamy alone who feels like this. A character in Congreve's *The Old Bachelor* describes a woman as 'a delicious melon, pure and consenting ripe, and only waits thy cutting up' (IV.ii). Such remarks lend credence to L. C. Knights' claim that this was not a representation of 'sexual relations. . .but the titillation of appetite': 'Sex is a hook baited with tempting morsels; it is a thirst quencher; it is a cordial; it is a dish to feed on; it is a bunch of grapes; it is anything but sex.'[38]

Men like Bellamy are attracted by a woman's desirability rather than by any human quality in her. A rake may sometimes demand wit in a woman in addition to beauty, as Dorimant does when he asks Medley if Harriet has 'wit' (I.i), but for him too, at this stage of his development, wit is not a quality in itself but merely an appetiser to make the woman a more exciting companion in bed.

Such rakes have lost all distinction between a wife and a whore, and they often claim that a whore is cheaper and more pleasurable. In their eyes, as we are told in a song in Congreve's *The Old Bachelor*:

> Nothing is new besides our faces,
> Every woman is the same. (II.ii)

No comic heroine would accept this kind of a situation. She is an individual with her own human dignity and man has to recognize this if any genuine relationship is to be established between the two. The question is not merely what Sir Oliver Cockwood in *She Would if She Could* thought it was when he told Courtall and Freeman: 'They [Gatty and Ariana] are for having you take a lease for life, and you are for being tenants at will' (V.i). The question is a more basic one, and essentially a moral one: it is whether one's wife is merely an instrument of sexual gratification or whether she is very much more — a companion, a friend, a sharer of one's joys and sorrows and a human being who has to be treated with respect and consideration. The question is really what Brutus' wife in Shakespeare's *Julius Ceasar* thought it was:

> Am I yourself
> But, as it were, in sort or limitation?
> To keep with you at meals, comfort your bed,
> And talk to you sometimes? Dwell I but in the suburbs
> Of your good pleasure? If it be no more,
> Portia is Brutus' harlot, not his wife. (II.i.282-287)

The hero in Restoration comedy must learn that there is a basic difference between a wife and a harlot. Unless he does that, there is no possibility of a mutually satisfying marriage. Wycherley's Alithea is saying no more than this when she tells Harcourt that 'Love proceeds from esteem' (*The Country-Wife*, II.i) or when she enunciates the 'doctrine for all Husbands': 'Women and Fortune are truest still to those that trust 'em' (V). If correctly understood, the demand made by all witty heroines in Restoration comedy is basically the same, namely, that the man should learn to recognize the difference between other women and the woman he decides to marry.

VII

The difficulty of the heroines, however, is that the men they are dealing with have not learnt that a woman is not just a sex-object but a human being with a personality of her own. These men are not wholly to blame. They have been brought up in a culture which prescribes 'conversation with ladies and *intrigues* with them' (Italics mine) as 'the best possible training in the "Rules" whereby a gentleman might become more agreeable.'[39] This is the culture of a leisure-class society and it seems to assume that 'a little gaming and a bastard or two were nothing which could not be expected of a high-spirited young gentleman.'[40] What it does to a woman's psychology is not the concern of men like Lord Chesterfield who recommended that his son should not only frequent the company of women of fashion but also have 'arrangements' with them.[41]

It need not surprise us that Restoration heroines feel so attracted towards these 'gentlemen'. Even when very badly hurt, Mrs Loveit can say about Dorimant: 'I know he is a devil, but he has something of the angel yet undefaced in him, which makes him so charming and agreeable that I must love him, be he never so wicked.' (II.ii). Mrs Loveit is not, of course, a good judge, nor is she a comic heroine. But almost all Restoration heroines fall in love with men who, in the words of Nicholas Rowe, are 'Witty, Wild, Inconstant, free Gallant[s].'[42] Perhaps Dryden provides the best explanation for this phenomenon in *Secret Love*. In Act III, Scene 1, Flavia tells Florimell that Celadon has gone with Melissa's two daughters with whom he has been flirting for some time and asks her to 'resolve to break with him'. Florimell rejects this advice: 'No, no, 'tis not come to that, yet; I'll *correct* him first and then hope the best from time.' (Italics mine). Flavia does not like Florimell's indifference to Celadon's sexual escapades and reminds her that 'Celadon loves others'. Florimell's reply to this is perhaps the most memorable in the whole of Restoration comedy:

There's the more hope he may love me among the rest: hang't, I would not marry one of these solemn Fops: they are good for nothing but to make Cuckolds: Give me a servant that is an high Flier at all games, that is bounteous of himself to many women; and yet whenever I pleas'd to throw out the lure of Matrimony, should come down with a swing and fly the better at his own quarry.

That a woman should love a man simply because he is 'bounteous of himself to many women' has been described by the California editors of Dryden's *The Wild Gallant* as 'a psychological quirk, whether it be universally true to female nature or not.'[43]

Interestingly enough, a plausible explanation of this psychological quirk is provided by Etherege's Courtall in *She Would if She Could* — 'Whatsoever women say, I am sure they seldom think the worse of a man for running at all — 'tis a sign of youth and high mettle, and makes them rather *pique* who shall tame him' (II.i). Ariana in the same play seems to agree with this view when she tells Gatty: 'The truth is they [men] run and ramble here, and there, and everywhere, and we poor fools rather think the better of 'em' (I.ii). The crux of the matter is that such a man attracts them simply because he is a challenge to them and 'makes them rather *pique* who shall tame him'.

VIII

The woman's problem in Restoration comedy, then, is to tame the rake so that he can become an ideal husband. She knows that he is 'not so foppishly in love' as to forget his intrigues since he is 'flesh and blood'. (*The Man of Mode*, IV.i). Even the hero of a moral-sentimental comedy like *The Squire of Alsatia*, Belford Junior, recognises that often men cannot help themselves. This is how he excuses his womanizing: 'we may talk of mighty matters; of our Honesty and Morality; but a young Fellow carries that about him that will make him a Knave now and then in spite of his Teeth' (II.i). And yet the woman falls for such a man. It is, of course, not her fault. He excels all others in ease and grace of manners, polished conversation and social poise. He is the most intelligent, the most dynamic and the most attractive character in the play. Though a libertine, the playwrights present him as a 'Fine Gentleman' who is 'enrich'd with all Sense and Wit the Poet can bestow.'[44] No high spirited young woman can be blamed if she thinks that in him she has found her real mate. She can also be justifiably confident of converting him into an ideal husband. We are, however, not able to shed the suspicion that at least initially his attraction for her is largely sexual, though, of course, her desire to score over other women is an equally strong motive.

But marriage is a different matter, and even at the height of emotion the Restoration comic heroine cannot be altogether oblivious of the fact that in deciding to cast her lot with a rake she is taking a grave risk. It has been claimed that even Shakespeare, none of whose heroes is a rake, 'recognized it [marriage] as a difficult state of life requiring discipline, sexual energy, mutual respect and great forbearance.'[45] It is doubtful whether the Restoration comic heroine is conscious of all these requirements — discipline most of all—something that Restoration rakes lamentably lack. Mutual respect and great forbearance, no less, are in short supply in the period. The rake is, of course, a high flier but the woman is always anxious lest even after coming down with a swing, he should fail to 'fly the better at his own quarry.'

This anxiety is further increased by the fear that is best expressed by Berinthia in Vanbrugh's *The Relapse* (1697): 'But I tell you, no man *worth having* is true to his wife, or ever was, or ever will be so' (III.ii). (Italics mine). 'No man *worth having* is true to his wife' — that is the real predicament of the Restoration comic heroine. Somehow it is a common feeling in the period that men who are true to their wives — men who believe in the antiquated virtues of truth and constant service by which women were won in former times — are dull and lack vitality, virility, spark and wit. It is not without significance that Harriet in *The Man of Mode* starts pursuing Dorimant almost immediately after her arrival in London. She has heard that he is a notorious rake, and as her mother says, 'if he but speak to a woman, she's undone' (III.iii). Yet Harriet goes to the Exchange to watch him fooling 'with the woman at the next shop' (I.i). As the Orange-woman reports to Dorimant, Harriet told her 'twenty things you said too, and acted with head and with her body so like you' (I.i). She is clearly attracted to him and does not hesitate to take the initiative. Young Bellair in this play is a virtuous young man who is wholly free from the contemporary vice of 'wenching'. But Harriet can at best endure him, and even though she recognizes that his breeding cannot be faulted, she dismisses him with the contemptuous remark: 'Varnished with good breeding, many a blockhead makes a tolerable show' (III.i). Whether Harriet is motivated by love for Dorimant or by sheer love of conquest,[46] — the Hobbesian lust for power over others — it is difficult to say. But there is no doubt that 'almost no Restoration heroine. . .falls in love with a virtuous man.'[47] Perhaps she does not regard such men as worthy of conquest. Whatever the consequences of choosing a libertine as a husband, this being her 'psychological quirk', she cannot help doing what she does. There is nothing wrong with this quirk — perhaps it is universal — but in certain periods it is easier for a man and woman to establish a genuine relationship with each other — and to achieve a companionate marriage — than in others. After all Shakespeare's women also pursued their men in their own way, but theirs was a less complicated world in which men and women found much less to distrust in one another.

To regard arranged marriages as the only cause of this distrust between man and woman is clearly too simplistic. Arranged marriages are, of course, an important social evil in the period and they embitter many marriages. But while the 'gay couple' comedies are not concerned with this problem, yet they too fail to give us a feeling of confident optimism about the future. Indeed, they seem to propound the general principle that 'love and marriage exist in a state of conflict: love exists outside marriage, or ceases when marriage begins.'[48] In *Marriage A La Mode*, Dryden perhaps puts the question a little too sharply, but what Palamede says sums up the situation in many comedies: 'You dislike her for no other reason but because she is your wife.' (I.i)[49] The first four lines of the opening song in Dryden's play do refer to a real problem in a promiscuous society:

> Why should a foolish marriage vow,
> Which long ago was made,
> Oblige us to each other now,
> *When passion is decayed?*

(Italics mine)

How boring a mere wife can be is described in a most outrageous manner by Farquhar's Young Mirabell in *The Inconstant*: 'Ay, this night shou'd I have had a Bride in my Arms, and that I shou'd like well enough but what shou'd I have tomorrow night? The same. And what next night, the same, and what next night, the very same: Soop for breakfast, Soop for dinner, Soop for supper, and Soop for breakfast again' (V.ii). Dryden in *Marriage A La Mode* handles this question very realistically when he suggests that a wife can feel equally bored with her husband, and that if a husband does not want this situation to arise, he may as well settle down with her and make his relationship with her as satisfactory and rewarding as possible.

It may also be added that arranged marriages are at worst only a social evil, and a society can eradicate this through social change as England and the West have in fact done. But Farquhar's Mirabell raises a moral question to which almost no society has yet been able to find a satisfactory answer. Dryden's answer is no absolute answer. To say that a man should stay moral lest his wife should go astray does not tell us how to deal with the general question of promiscuity. It is also curious that societies where marriages are largely arranged have perhaps a higher standard of sexual morality than the freer societies where individuals choose each other for love and not on grounds of social and economic suitability. One may, of course, challenge this view and claim, as Bruce did in Shadwell's *The Virtuoso* while defending Restoration morals against Elizabethan morals: 'I believe there was the same wenching then; only they dissembled it. They added hypocrisy to fornication, and so made two sins of what we make but one' (II.ii). There is some substance in what Bruce says but the question still remains unresolved and we should hesitate to build a theory of sexual morality on the basis of arranged marriages *alone*. Can anyone in our times, for instance, accept the optimism of the hero of Ravenscroft's *The Careless Lovers* that 'That Marriage can hardly know Repentance, in which both parties had their choice' (V.i)? It seems clear that we are dealing with a more serious malady than a student of literature can handle. Its roots lie too deep in the culture of that small minority which determined the ethos of the Comedy of Manners. Political uncertainties, economic pressures and fears, and social attitudes formed under conditions where both family discipline and religious training had sharply declined must have contributed to the emergence of the rake as a dominant figure in contemporary upper-class society and its literature.

IX

While considering the predicament of the Restoration comic heroine, we have to examine the psychological impact of this male 'wantonness of appetite'[50] on her conduct and behaviour. The playwrights may not, of course, applaud the 'promiscuity of the libertine' and may even demonstrate that the libertine's way of living is unnatural for he 'cannot live happily by his philosophy because it fails to take into account the natural desire of human kind for a permanent emotional relationship with a number of the opposite sex based on more than mere lust.'[51] But how does it help the woman? Should she wait for him to reform himself? Robert Hume has claimed that 'nowhere in late seventeenth-century comedy is there serious protest against keeping a mis-

tress.'⁵² This surely cannot mean that women were not disturbed
by this phenomenon. Indeed the lack of serious protest itself
shows the dilemma of the woman. It may be seen in the advice
that Lord Halifax gave in his *The Lady's New Year's Gift; Or,
Advice to a Daughter* (1688): 'Do not seem to look or hear that
way: if he is a man of sense he will reclaim himself, the folly of it
is of itself sufficient to cure him; if he is not so, he will be *provoked but not reformed.*'⁵³ (Italics mine). In a situation of such
vulnerability, women had to choose their own mode of protest.
Ticking off Mrs Loveit is clearly Harriet's mode of protest: 'Mr
Dorimant has been your God almighty long enough, 'tis time to
think of another' (V.ii). Robert Hume regards this as a 'perfectly
gratitutious insult to Mrs Loveit',⁵⁴ but surely it is a calculated
move on her part. It is natural that she should remove from her
path Dorimant's 'famed mistress'.

This business of removing her rivals from her path is handled
in a most amusing manner by Aminta in Mrs Behn's *The Forc'd
Marriage*. There is a scene where Aminta starts teasing Alcander
about his affairs with other women even though he has had no
such affairs at all. Aminta in this scene is articulating fears that
are always present in the mind of a Restoration comic heroine
though they are not always expressed in the form of a serious
protest. Alcander assures Aminta that he 'never knew the joys and
sorrows / That do attend a Soul in love' before this time and he
wants her to accept him. Aminta, however, wants greater
reassurance:

AMINTA: This will not serve to convince me,
    But you have lov'd before.
ALCANDER: And will you never quit that Error, Madam,
AMINTA: 'Tis what I've reason to believe, *Alcander*,
    And you can give me none for loving me:
    I'm much unlike *Lucinda* whom you sigh'd for,
    I'm not so coy, nor so reserv'd as she;
    Nor so designing as *Florana* your next Saint,
    Who starv'd you up with hope, till you grew weary;
    And then *Ardelia* did restore that loss,
    The little soft *Ardelia*, kind and fair too.
ALCANDER: You think you're wondrous witty now, *A-minta*,
    But hang me if you be.
AMINTA: Indeed *Alcander*, no 'tis simple truth:
    Then for your bouncing Mistress, long *Brunetta*,

O that majestick Garb, 'tis strangely taking,
That scornful Look, and Eyes that strike all dead
That stand beneath them.
Alcander, I have none of all these Charms;
But well, you say you love me; *could you be*
Content to dismiss these petty sharers in your Heart,
And give it all to me; on these conditions
I may do much   (Italics mine)

We should also recognize that if the woman in contemporary
comedy had accepted with equanimity the fact that men kept
mistresses, there would have been no need for many of the scenes
of conversion in the last act. There seems no doubt that many of
the comic heroines were quite concerned about the future conduct
of the heroes. If that were not so, why should Millamant suddenly
feel nervous and confide to Mrs Fainall: 'Well, if Mirabel should
not make a good husband, I am a lost thing, — for I find I love
him violently'? (*The Way of the World*, IV.i).

X

Lydia, the heroine of Wycherley's first comedy, *Love in a Wood*,
clearly lacks the sensitivity of Millamant but even she raises the
same question. She too knows that she would be lost if Ranger
did not make a good husband. Vernon asserts that their marriage
is based on 'confident ptimism.'[55] He quotes with enthusiasm the
hero's reaction to the heroine's flippant comment on matrimony,
but it is best to quote the whole passage. This is the moment
when Lydia and Ranger at last decide to marry:

LYDIA: But if I could be desperate now and give you up my liberty,
     cou'd you find in your heart to quit all other engagements, and
     voluntarily turn yourself over to one woman, and she a Wife too?
     Coul'd you away with the insupportable bondage of Matrimony?
RANGER: You talk of Matrimony as irreverently as my *Lady Flippant*.
     The Bondage of Matrimony, no —
     The end of Marriage, now is liberty,
     And two are bound — to set each other free.   (V)

Ranger's couplet sounds magnificent but in its context we are not
sure of its full import, coming as it does from a libertine of
Ranger's unsavoury past. From what does the marriage relationship set the man and the woman free? Does it set them free from
other 'engagements' — something that Lydia has in fact asked
for? Lydia in any case has no 'engagements' of any kind outside

her single-minded pursuit of Ranger. So Ranger should speak for himself, but he evades the question asked by Lydia. Leon Oser Barron's view that 'on one level' the meaning of Ranger's couplet could be 'that their marriage shall be one of trust and fidelity: she will be set free from the slavery of jealousy and he from the slavery of intrigue' would make excellent sense. But perhaps Ranger does not really mean that at all. Barron himself offers an alternative 'suggestion that he [Ranger] will be like everyone else of his world'[56] which seems nearer the truth. What 'everyone else of his world' is like is perhaps best seen in James Sutherland's comment on the scene in Sir Charles Sedley's *The Mulberry Garden* (1668) where Olivia and Wildish come to terms with each other:

While the young men in the romantic half of Sedley's play can and do assert their undying love in extravagant protestations, *the comic hero can remain a hero only if he retains something of his freedom.* (Italics mine). Although the audience must be assured that he is genuinely in love, they must also be left with the feeling that *this* (Italics Sutherland's) marriage is not going to be the end of all liberty and laughter.[57]

Whatever Ranger may say and mean, he is clearly the type of young man who can never 'voluntarily turn [himself] to one woman, and she a Wife too.' He must retain something of his freedom and, of course, use it as he has done it hitherto.

That the couplet cited above will not bear any profounder meaning is more than established by Ranger's temperament and conduct. Let us see what kind of man he is. Vincent who is the only man of sense in the play finds him not only an inordinate libertine but also a liar. Lydia painfully notices his 'natural inconstancy' (IV). But the best evidence is provided by Ranger's own actions. He is contracted to be married to Lydia but he cheerfully tells a friend how he has cheated her: 'Intending a Ramble in *St James' Park* tonight, upon some probable hopes of some fresh Game I have in chase, I appointed her to stay at home, with a promise to come to her within this hour, that she might not spoil the scent and prevent my sport.' (I). His general comment on women shows what contempt he has for them: 'Women are poor credulous Creatures, easily deceived' (I). All this is bad enough, but worse follows. The very next morning we see him at the doors of Lucy with a pimp and a purse and we feel outraged. Then there is his design on Christina. We don't know how serious his intentions are. What he says is puzzling: 'Faith I am sorry she is an heiress, lest it should bring the scandal of interest, and the design of lucre, upon my love.' (II). It is difficult to say whether he wants to marry her or all this talk about his love being totally disinterested is meant only to make the strategy of seduction more effective. This in any case is a waste of effort on his part. Christina is already engaged to Valentine and she doesn't even look at him. In a mood of frustration, he at last announces: 'Lydia, triumph! I now am thine again. Of intrigues, honourable or dishonourable, and all sorts of rambling, I take my leave; when we are giddy, 'tis time to stand still.' (V). This reformation of the rake is utterly improbable. It is promised neither by his character nor by the action of the play. But the play has to end, and being a comedy it has to end in marriage.

We are, however, justified in asking what would happen when such a man has stood still for some time. Would he then go in search of giddy adventures once again? It is in any case a painful situation for a woman. But Lydia is helpless; she has fallen so deeply in love with Ranger that she has to attend his pleasure. She knows that she is dealing with a rake. She fears that he will ramble again. Her problem is to hold him. In a way, it is an eternal problem. But it is less cruel in some periods of history than in others and perhaps more easily capable of solution in some societies than in others. Many intelligent women resent the suggestion that in this respect a traditional society like Shakespeare's may have something to be said for it. But let us come back to Lydia's case. She is willing to give up her liberty and to accept the duties and responsibilities of a wife. But she asks whether Ranger too is willing to accept the duties and responsibilities of a husband, which would include, among other things, his giving up all other women for the sake of his wife. Ranger evades the question — in a sense most Restoration comedy evades the question. One might almost say that it is this evasion which is the chief cause of the woman's anxiety in Restoration comedy.

Anne (Righter) Barton says in an important essay on Wycherley: 'Restoration comedy in general is obsessed with the idea that passion is ephemeral, that love cannot last.' She further says: 'Basically, the true wits and their ladies are romantics cursed with an inconveniently powerful strain of rationalism; they wish to believe in the performance of something which they know to be transitory.' The men, 'despite their libertine principles', fall in love and then 'try to turn away from their customary imagery of appetite and the chase in speaking to their love, to make promises and swear a fidelity which the wiser self knows time may not let them keep.' It is not only the 'wiser self' of men that knows that love may not last, but also the woman's instinct which sees the truth. At the crucial moment of elopement, another of Wycherley's heroines, Hippolita in *The Gentleman Dancing Master*, is suddenly overcome by doubt and says this to Gerard, the hero: 'I am afraid, to know your heart, would require a great deal of time' (II). This uncertainty is always there, but to quote Anne Barton again, a temporary equilibrium is established between realism and romanticism and life goes on: 'It is an equilibrium that is temporary, no doubt: sweet, yet not necessarily lasting. But this is the way of the world.'[58] Rosalind and Beatrice would not have accepted this view though they might have talked about it to tease their lovers. It is not that they lacked the 'strain of rationalism' that the heroines in Restoration comedy possess, but that their world was differently organized and they had a different view of life.[59] In Shakespeare's comedies, the rational strain does not become too 'inconvenient' and women are able to reconcile romanticism with realism and achieve companionate marriages.

XI

The Restoration comic heroines also try to achieve companionate marriages and inspite of the difficulties already mentioned, some of the intelligent ones amongst them do succeed in achieving such marriages. We may examine the case of Harriet in *The Man of Mode* and see how she succeeds in overcoming her difficulties. In her case the difficulties are much greater than elsewhere in Restoration comedy, as the hero in this play — Dorimant — takes almost a sadistic pleasure in tormenting the women who fall prey to his charm. Here we see at its most ruthless that 'cold-blooded exploitation by the stronger party, whether man or woman', which Katharine M. Rogers regards as a special feature of the 'sophisticated relationships between men and women' in Restoration literature.[60] Mrs Loveit is correct in her understanding of Dorimant's character when she says that he has 'more pleasure in the ruin of a woman's reputation than in the indearments of her love' (V.i). Her complaint that he takes 'pride' in using her ill so that 'the town may know the *power* you have over me' (Italics

mine) is more than justified in the light of Dorimant's own statement: ' 'Tis necessary to justify my love to the world' (V.i). One
may ask, why? Surely love is a private emotion and needs no
public justification. But Dorimant is not interested in love. What
he wants is satisfaction of his 'vanity' (V.i). Dale Underwood
rightly sees his activities motivated by an expression of a 'Hobbesian aggressiveness, competitiveness, and drive for power and
"glory"; a Machiavellian dissembling and cunning; a satanic
pride, vanity, and malice; and drawing upon each of these frames
of meaning, an egoistic assertion of self through the control of
others.'[61]

In order to see whether this man can ever make a suitable
husband we need to ask whether a cold-blooded exploitation of
one human being by another — whether man or woman — can
become a basis for any kind of genuine human relationship.
Dorimant describes Mrs Loveit's love as 'diseased', 'sickly' and
'desperately ill' (II.ii), but the play shows that his own love for
women is no better. Further, the play shows the debasing effects
of this kind of love on Dorimant's own personality and his relations with others.

When the play opens, Dorimant is in the process of casting off
one mistress and taking on another, with complete indifference to
the feelings of the women concerned. His only explanation to Mrs
Loveit for his discarding her is: 'Youth has a long journey to go,
madam. Should I have set up my rest at the first inn I lodged at, I
should never have arrived at the *happiness I now enjoy*' (II.ii)
(Italics mine). 'At the happiness I now enjoy' — we wonder at this
concept of happiness. Gamini Salgado has rightly said that
Dorimant is 'imprisoned in his own reduced image of himself as a
creature of mere appetite.'[62] Bellinda sees the vicious aspect of this
pursuit of appetite on the part of Dorimant in her comment:
'Other men are wicked, but then they have some sense of shame.
He is never well but when he triumphs, nay, glories to a woman's
face in his villainies' (V.ii). 'He is never *well*' — indeed, never
happy except in the kind of situation that Bellinda describes.
Hobbes said about such men that 'principally' for 'their owne
conservation, and sometimes their delectation only', they 'endeavour to destroy or subdue one another.'[63] It is essentially for his
'delectation only' — and not 'conservation' — that Dorimant
destroys others.

How can any woman deal with him? Of course, she could fight back and destroy or subdue him. Hobbes had already predicted this 'war': 'whereas some have attributed the dominion to the man only, as being of the more excellent sex, they mis-reckon in it. For there is not always that difference of strength, or prudence between the man and the woman, as that the right can be determined without war.'[64] In the light of this it is natural to believe that we have in *The Man of Mode* a 'pitched battle of the sexes' ending in 'an uneasy truce'.[65] We cannot, of course, deny the battle or the truce. But the point is whether something has happened in between. If nothing has happened, then Paul Davies is correct in saying that at the end of the play, Dorimant is 'still the same intriguing womanizer'. If that were so, why does Davies himself describe Dorimant's 'patching up his relations with Bellinda and Loveit' as 'efforts to save face rather than intimations of domestic disaster?'[66] Surely both things cannot be correct. Either Dorimant is still a womanizer, which would certainly lead to domestic disaster — or he has changed. One may, of course, claim that here too there would be a 'relapse' and the change would not last, but that is a risk that Harriet has to take if she loves him strongly enough. Moreover, it all depends on what kind of a wife she herself is going to make. On the basis of the text it is safer to come to the conclusion that though she is fighting a battle against a formidable enemy, in the process she is acquiring self-knowledge and also 'educating' Dorimant. This is the kind of thing that often happens in Shakespeare's comedies, and in this Etherege seems to be Shakespeare's heir.

It is, of course, not easy to 'educate' Dorimant, and the woman who undertakes such a task is taking a grave risk. The only way in which she can succeed is to make him fall in love with her and yet stay uninvolved herself — or at least give the impression of being so. This is precisely what Harriet does, but she needs some exceptional qualities as a woman to play this game without becoming its victim. She is endowed by nature with exceptional beauty — Medley describes her as 'the beautifullest creature I ever saw' (I.i) — but beauty is the least of her graces. She is a young woman with a highly cultivated mind and it is her intellectual maturity which makes her not only the equal of all men in the play but indeed their superior. She clearly surpasses them in self-possession, poise and judgment.

Etherege does not make her a 'learned' lady in the conventional sense of the term, as such ladies were still the object of ridicule. But he clearly makes her wholly different from those 'painted idols. . .vain, light gewgaw creatures'[67] that most contemporary women had become owing largely to their defective education. It is difficult to know how Harriet acquired such varied knowledge in the country-side, but she is very conversant with poetry and history and can easily out-quote Dorimant who professes to be a great lover of Waller. She can also quote from Cowley's heroic poem, *Davideis*. In her raillery with Young Bellair, she makes a clever reference to Jonson's *Bartholomew Fair*. She never flaunts her knowledge, but can easily trip Sir Fopling by alluding to the Comte de Bussy, a seventeenth century author of a history of love. She has clearly invaded male territory and conquered it without effort. She need not, therefore, be afraid of taking the initiative in tracking down Dorimant, the most polished, cultivated and successful rake in London.

To succeed in this encounter what Harriet needs most is skill in dissimulation — or what she herself calls 'the dear pleasure of dissembling' (III.i). After all, this is also Dorimant's main quality. As Harriet Hawkins has pointed out, it is 'the sang-froid and the talent for dissembling which make it possible for him to evoke emotion in others while remaining detached himself.'[68] Harriet uses Dorimant's own technique against him and it is this which makes her impervious to all his blandishments. When reminded by Young Bellair that conversations with men in the Mall 'have been fatal in some of your sex', she makes the important point that she cannot be treated by the audience — and by Dorimant — just like Mrs Loveit and Bellinda: 'It may be so. Because some who want *temper* have been undone by gaming, must others who have it wholly deny themselves the pleasure of the play.' (III.iii). (Italics mine). Dorimant overhears it and joins the conversation, but when he tries cleverly to insinuate that he is willing to change 'to gain *your* favour', she snubs him by telling Young Bellair: 'Mr Bellair let us walk, 'tis time to leave him. Men grow dull when they begin to be *particular*' (III.iii) (Italics mine). Dorimant is naturally offended at this treatment — something wholly new in his experience — and so he retorts that he will not flatter her 'though I know y're greedy of the praises of the whole Mall' (III.iii). 'You do me wrong', replies Harriet somewhat angrily, and then controls herself and offers a comment on Dorimant's whole 'Art of making Love' which more than deflates him: 'I do not go begging the men's as you do the ladies' good liking, with a sly softness in your looks and a gentle slowness in your bows as you pass by 'em — thus, sir (*acts him*). Is not this like you?' (III.iii). In this very first encounter, then, Harriet is telling Dorimant that he must first take a measure of the woman he is dealing with before he starts exercising his famous charm of 'wit and person' on her. She, as we know, had already taken a measure of him earlier in the scene when she told Young Bellair: 'He's agreeable and pleasant I must own, but he does so much affect being so, he displeases me' (III.iii). Dorimant, of course, cannot easily learn the difference between one woman and another. When Young Bellair's footman tells him that he is invited to Lady Townley's where he should 'own' himself as Mr Courtage for the benefit of Harriet's mother, who, along with Harriet, will also be there, he is delighted and exclaims: 'This is Harriet's contrivance — wild, witty, lovesome, beautiful and young. Come along Medley' (III.iii). Medley knows Dorimant best and reflects his friend's state of mind in his statement: 'This new woman would well supply the loss of Loveit' (III.iii). If Dorimant thinks so too, as he presumably does, one can only marvel at his lack of intelligence. He arrogantly claims: 'I fathom all the depths of womankind' (III.iii). But he has known only one kind of woman — the kind that cannot resist his sexual appeal and becomes his victim — but surely that is not fathoming *all* the depths of woman-kind. It is clear that the sooner the bubble of his male ego is pricked the better — both for him and for others. This is what Harriet does in her second encounter with him.

This time again he starts teasing her in his usual way. Finding that she is not responding, he asks: 'Where had you all that scorn and coldness in your look?' 'From nature sir', replies Harriet and then adds: 'pardon my want of art. I have not learnt those softnesses and languishings which now in faces are so much in fashion' (IV.i). Dorimant should now see the difference between Harriet and other women but he is still obsessed with his fatal charm. So Harriet has to tell him frankly that his charm has been fatal for 'some easy women, but we are not all born to one destiny'. Perhaps this has gone home and Dorimant does want to make a serious confession of his love for Harriet. But he does not want to do so in public lest people should laugh at him. Harriet wants no private conference with him and bluntly says: 'When your love's grown strong enough to make you bear being laughed at, I'll give you leave to trouble me with it. Till when, pray forbear, sir' (IV.i).

When a little later, Dorimant finds that he cannot help himself and tells her: 'But I will open my heart and receive you, where none yet did ever enter — you have filled it with a secret, might I but let you know it —', she stops him from proceeding further and turns away after telling him: 'Do not speak it, if you would have me believe it; your tongue is so famed for falsehood 'twill do the truth an injury' (V.ii). When he still persists, she frankly admits: 'In men who have been long hardened in sin, we have reason to mistrust the first signs of repentance' (V.ii). Even though this protracted courtship — pleading on one side and a calculated cold-shouldering on the other — has become a 'torment' (V.ii) to Harriet herself (as Busy, her woman, says), she has no choice but to behave like this. She is naturally sceptical of male professions and she knows that Dorimant is 'the common sanctuary for all young women who run from their relations' (V.ii). She cannot, therefore, behave as spontaneously as Shakespeare's heroines do. Indeed, she has to be vigilant all the while as there is none in her world whom she can trust.

Clifford Leech has described Harriet as a 'creature of delight' but Montague Summers finds her 'a perfectly callous little baggage with a vile tongue'. It is this dichotomy of approach which has made Robert Hume claim that there is a 'confusion' in our response to Harriet. He says: 'Dorimant is scarcely redeemed by the love of a good woman; rather, the great lady-killer here meets his match in a woman cold and tough enough to get him where she wants him. To make Harriet out as a spotless romantic heroine is either to insist on a staggeringly improbable reformation in Dorimant, or to see her caught in a degrading and potentially disastrous association. Neither seems to be the case.'[69] This confusion, however, seems quite unnecessary. Harriet is spotless. She is also a 'good woman'. But she has got to be cold and tough precisely to prevent being 'caught in a degrading and potentially disastrous association.' This toughness does at times give us a somewhat unpleasant impression, but it does so because we have come to form a certain preconception regarding the qualities of a 'good woman' which we largely derive from romantic literature. We assume that a woman should be soft and gentle, and of course, very affectionate and loving. But such women are not safe in Dorimant's world, and so Etherege creates the kind of woman who can face Dorimant on equal terms without being a libertine herself. Indeed Harriet is the only major female character in Restoration comedy who establishes genuine equality with the man whom she loves and yet of whom she is not yet sure.

There is no doubt that Harriet recognizes the risks involved in dealing with Dorimant. Dorimant's fatal charm has really worked on her, and as James Sutherland says, her 'courage and self-possession occasionally tremble on the verge of defeat.'[70] Defeat, of course, would be disastrous, as in that case she would merely join the company of Mrs Loveit and Bellinda. It is somewhat surprising that in a situation like this she should think of the countryside. After reminding Dorimant that she does not fully accept the marks of his repentance which he calls 'infallible', she suddenly asks him: 'Could you neglect these awhile and make a journey into the country?' (V.ii). When he says that he would do anything to be near her and makes the declaration that 'now my passion knows no bounds, and *there's no measure to be taken of what I'll do for you from anything I ever did before*' (Italics mine), she gives the puzzling reply: '*When I hear you talk thus in Hampshire, I shall begin to think there may be some truth inlarged upon*' (Italics mine). What is so important about Hampshire and why should she believe that his protestations there would acquire the stamp of truth?

The latest interpretation of Harriet's invitation to Dorimant to visit Hampshire is that of Peter Malekin. He says: 'Her luring of him as her suitor to the boredom of the countryside at the end of the play is not, as has often been suggested, an exodus to the land of virtue; the point of it is that it will expose him to ridicule.'[71] But surely, Harriet has played this game of exposing him to ridicule long enough and even told him at one stage, as we have already seen, that she would give him leave to trouble her with his declarations of love only when his love had grown 'strong enough to make ¿him¡ bear being laugh'd at.' So why should she continue playing this game any longer? In any case it serves no purpose as Dorimant already knows her worth and has come fully to realize that 'She is no Loveit, nor even Bellinda.'[72]

Dale Underwood's claim that 'In the context of the play Harriet's "melancholy" picture of the "country" becomes in certain ways a possible and paradoxical "symbol of fertility" ' is certainly more helpful. It is surprising, however, that he can contemplate the possibility that Dorimant might 'undergo his "trial" — a temporary endurance of the country. . .more for conquest than for love' and that 'the country' might 'become the setting for a "ruin" than a romance.' To think so is to ignore the inner resources of Harriet which have been in evidence all through the play. Underwood admits that if 'Dorimant is finally drawn into the country by love, his passion will at least to some extent have transcended the element of sterility and triviality which characterizes the total "city" milieu of the play.'[73]

We should at least be clear on one point, namely, that irrespective of whether the countryside becomes a setting for romance or not, under no circumstances can it become a setting for ruin. To think so is to misunderstand Harriet's character altogether. Once this position is recognized, we may feel certain that Dorimant has no alternative except to enter into marriage on Harriet's terms. At this stage we may ask ourselves what are likely to be Harriet's terms. After giving a dismal description of the 'great rambling lone house', Harriet had asked Dorimant whether this 'does not . . . stagger [his] resolution' and Dorimant had promptly replied: 'Not at all, madam. The first time I saw you, you left me with the pangs of love upon me, and this day my soul has quite *given up her liberty*' (V.ii) (Italics mine). If Harriet's chief intention had been merely to subdue or conquer Dorimant, it has been fully achieved. But did she really want only this? Surely in the kind of world she lived, she could not have failed to see that the desire for power — or for domination — was hardly conducive to the establishment of a genuinely affectionate relationship between man and woman. That is a situation in which one becomes a tyrant and the other a victim. There is also the possibility that sometimes the same person might become both a tyrant and a victim. Harriet should be wary of this kind of a situation and the play makes it clear that she is in search of a new basis for a stable relationship with Dorimant. So she must not only make Dorimant understand the inadequacy of the Hobbesian concept of human relationships but also see it herself. In the new relationship, each must recognise the individuality — indeed 'liberty' —

of the other and on this recognition base their love and affection for each other. Then alone can the woman attain that 'inner certainty' and 'moral equilibrium'[74] which is the special need of a woman in Restoration comedy.

Harriet's invitation to Dorimant to come to Hampshire should then be looked upon as a call to him to enter another world — a boring world perhaps, but a world governed not by power but by the more basic values of a normal human life — family affection and the natural bonds that bind human beings together. That is the kind of world, after all, in which marriage survives and often flourishes. Such a marriage may not always be exciting and may indeed be boring at times, but it is always sustained by affection. Dorimant has had no notion of this and has known only sexual pleasure which has never touched his inner being. It is important that he see life lived at a different level before he enters the married state. In rural England family relationships have not yet been eroded by urbanization and the pressures of a capitalist economy, and Dorimant's 'education' cannot be complete without a brief experience of this kind of life.

It cannot, however, be asserted with any certainty that Dorimant will change by mere change of milieu, nor that Harriet will accept him without question the moment he makes his declaration of love in the countryside. In a moment of defiance, Harriet does tell her mother that she would marry Dorimant 'and never will marry any other man' though she is clever enough to add, to soften her attitude, that she 'will never marry him against [her] will' (V.ii). But this does not mean that she has at last capitulated. Indeed her state of mind is better reflected in the rebuke she administers to Dorimant whom she suspects of having secretly 'laid' a parson in the house: 'Should it appear you did, your opinion of my easiness may cost you dear' (V.ii). So they still have miles to go. Harriet in any case cannot easily shed that 'discipline of suspicion'[75] which a woman in her society needs while dealing with a libertine. By his conduct Dorimant has to remove this suspicion so that she can be sure of his love and fidelity. That stage has not yet come but it must come if Dorimant has to win Harriet's love and trust. Anne (Righter) Barton's view that 'They must marry if they are to *possess* one another at all, yet they confront this solution at the end of the play with a dubiety which, in Elizabethan comedy, had been reserved only for clowns and fools[76] is clearly too pessimistic. (Italics mine). The question is not of marely 'possessing' each other but of finding in a difficult and sceptical age true happiness in their relationship. Unfortunately Shakespearean critics are often not able to see that in Restoration comedy too, there are men and women who can achieve a satisfying marriage. *The Man of Mode* cannot, of course, end on a note of finality — a finality that is the special characteristic of the fairy-tale endings of some of Shakespeare's comedies. But in the context of contemporary social reality, it prepares the way for a genuinely companionate marriage.

XII

Anne (Righter) Barton also calls the marriage of Mirabel and Millamant a 'risk'.[77] Millamant, it is true, lacks Harriet's assurance, but perhaps Congreve's aim in *The Way of the World* is to present the predicament of 'a sensitive girl in an insensitive society',[78] and consequently the main burden to achieve a genuinely stable marriage falls on Mirabel, the hero in this play. Mirabel is clearly not a typical Restoration rake. He is, in Lord Halifax's words, 'a man of sense' who has already 'reclaimed' himself. Nothing shows this side of his character better than his attitude to Lady Wishfort and Mrs Marwood. He could have perhaps made things easier for himself if he had agreed to satisfy Lady Wishfort's sexual hunger or responded to the advances made to him by Mrs Marwood. All his endeavours seem clearly to be directed towards winning Millamant. It would be wrong to believe that it is her fortune that he is after. Like most Restoration heroes, he is not indifferent to money, but in his case it is a minor consideration as he makes clear to Fainall:

FAIN. You were to blame to resent what she spoke only in compliance with her aunt.

MIR. She is more mistress of herself than to be under the necessity of such a resignation.

FAIN. What! though half her fortune depends upon her marrying with my lady's approbation?

MIR. I was then in such a humour, that I should have been better pleased if she had been less discreet

(I.i)

But it would be silly on the part of Millamant to be 'less discreet'. It is right and proper that Millamant should marry the man of her choice and that Lady Wishfort should accept this choice and release her fortune. It is at once honourable and prudent and it seems clear that Mirabel and Millamant are agreed that Lady Wishfort's consent should somehow be obtained before they marry.

What distinguishes Mirabel is not merely that he is a reformed man, but also that his general attitude to women is wholly different from that of Dorimant and other Restoration rakes. For them women are mere objects of sexual gratification: for him they are human beings who deserve to be treated with consideration. This trait of his character is evident in the very first scene of the play. Fainall clearly has a low opinion of women — including his wife and mistress — and when Mirabel tells him that it was Mrs Marwood — 'your friend, or your wife's friend' — who betrayed his plans to Lady Wishfort, this is the conversation that takes place between them:

FAIN: What should provoke her to be your enemy, unless she has made you advances which you have slighted? Women do not easily forgive omissions of that nature.

MIR She was always civil to me till of late — I confess I am not one of those coxcombs who are apt to interpret a woman's good manners to her prejudice, and think that she who does not refuse 'em everything, can refuse 'em nothing

(I.i)

His rebuke later to Petulant who intends to go to the Mall and be 'severe' to the ladies there also springs from the feeling that it is only men of ill breeding who behave like this to women:

PET: Enough, I'm in a humour to be severe.

MIR: Are you? pray then walk by yourselves: let not us be accessory to your putting the ladies out of countenance with your senseless ribaldry, which you roar out aloud as often as they pass by you; and when you have made a handsome woman blush, then you think you have been severe.

PET: What, what! then let 'em either show their innocence by not understanding what they hear, or else show their discretion by not hearing what they would not be thought to understand.

MIR: But hast not thou then sense enough to know that thou oughtest to be most ashamed thyself, when thou hast put another out of countenance?

PET: Not I, by this hand! — I always take blushing either for a sign of guilt, or ill-breeding.

MIR: I confess you ought to think so. You are in the right, that you may plead the error of your judgment in defence of your practice.

It is however, his relationship with Mrs Fainall which causes the greatest discomfort to modern readers. John Wain's comments on this question are quite typical. He first cites the defence of Mirabel offered by Fujimura:

Mrs Fainall, we gather, was an attachment of the past, before he fell in love; and since she was a widow at the time, and hence, according to the naturalistic conception of widows, highly inflammable, he could hardly be blamed for satisfying her sexual appetite as well as his own. When the play opens, Mirabell has apparently broken off all relations with her, and he is pursuing matrimony with a serious purpose.[79]

He then offers his own comments:

Not a word about the fact that he has pushed Mrs Fainfall into a marriage of hell, to suit his own convenience; indeed he tells her in so many words that it was in case she became pregnant: when she rounds on him with, 'Why did you make me marry this Man?' he answers airily, 'Why do we daily commit disagreeable and dangerous Actions? To save that Idol Reputation. If the Familiarities of our Loves had produc'd that Consequence, of which you were apprehensive, where cou'd you have fix'd a Father's Name with Credit, but on a Husband?' Admirable realism, no doubt, but this man is the *hero*; we are supposed to care whether he is happy or not; no wonder Lamb could only defend these plays by saying that they were simply aesthetic patterns with no humanity involved at all.[80]

Wain's anger seems quite unjustified. 'Admirable realism' it, of course, is. But it is very much more than that. The seventeenth century would have regarded Mirabel's conduct in this matter as altogether honourable. It is not as if Mirabel has seduced an innocent girl and then thrown her overboard. Mrs Fainall's complaint is only about the *kind* of man that Mirabel chose for her — something about which we will have something to say later — and not about his deserting her. There was no question of marriage between them — not because Mrs Fainall is necessarily unworthy of him — but simply because their affair is on an altogether different footing. Mrs Fainall never expected it and she nowhere blames him for ending the affair. It is clearly the case of two young people slipping into a relationship which both recognize as temporary. We may even suggest, though it is somewhat unkind to do so, that for all we know, Mrs Fainall may have forced herself on Mirabel. This view sounds plausible not only because Mrs Fainall is a widow and hence 'highly inflammable' but because of her very defective upbringing. It is obviously a misfortune for any girl to be Lady Wishfort's daughter and to be subjected to the kind of education which never permitted her 'to play with a male child, though but in coats' and impressed 'upon her tender years a young odium and aversion to the very sight of men' (V.ii). Such a girl could have easily become another Mrs Pinchwife or Prue. That she has not become so is a compliment to her. Indeed she has grown into a sensible, amiable and even cheerful person. One wonders whether her relationship with Mirabel has not really contributed to her growth as a human being.

It may be noticed that the new relationship between Mrs Fainall and Mirabel is something quite exceptional. She is, of course, not his mistress any more, but she is that rare thing in Restoration comedy, a friend. The mere concept of a man and a woman being friends is foreign to Restoration comedy. In this comedy, a woman is either a mistress or a wife. To accept a woman as a friend is to lend her a new dignity, and it throws considerable light on Mirabel's character that he has won Mrs Fainall's affection and trust in this new relationship. Peter Malekin has even claimed that 'The best case for the *quality* of Mirabel's emotional relationships is precisely Mrs Fainall.'[81] (Italics mine). She is his confidante and ally and she is also Millamant's friend and adviser. She trusts him completely; otherwise she could never have entrusted her fortune to his care. There is no doubt that he is worthy of that trust. His remark to her, which has often puzzled critics, that she knows her 'remedy' (II.ii) when she is 'weary' of her husband, means no more than this — that she can always secure her independence from her husband owing to her financial security.

And now we come to the kind of man that Mirabel has provided for her as a husband. Mirabel's statement that 'A better man ought not to have been sacrificed to the occasion: a worse had not answered to the purpose' (II.ii) does sound callous to a modern reader, and yet here too there is 'admirable realism'. A widow who is suspected to be pregnant could hardly hope to get a really suitable husband. Restoration comedy invariably treated such women with contempt and the only husbands it found for them were country bumpkins or old fops. But Mirabel makes sure that Mrs Fainall does not suffer in public estimation ('that idol, reputation') and so he selects a man for her 'whose wit and outward fair behaviour have gained a reputation with the town enough to make that woman stand excused who has suffered herself to be won by his addresses' (II.ii). Indeed, for all practical purposes, the person selected is treated by the town as a 'fine gentleman' — almost like Mirabel himself. After all, the town sees only the externals — the 'wit and outward fair behaviour' — and marrying such a man does no discredit to a woman amongst the *beau monde.* Mirabel thus has not only found a suitable man on whom could be 'fixed a father's name with *credit*' (Italics mine) but has also preserved Mrs Fainall's status in her circle. Mirabel does know that Fainall is a gentleman only in appearance and that at heart he is rotten — 'a man lavish of his morals, an interested and professing friend, a false and a designing lover' (II.ii). And yet in a hurry he is the best man available for the purpose. Mrs Fainall needs a husband and Fainall needs money and so the bargain is struck. There is no question of love here. It is a purely mercenary marriage and even when Fainall finds that Mrs Fainall has had an affair with Mirabel, all that he plans to do is to utilise this information to squeeze more money from the family. Mrs Marwood's cynicism is refreshing: 'You married her to keep you; and if you can contrive to have her keep you better than you expected, why should you not keep her longer than you intended?' (III.iii).

Mirabel understands this man well enough and so he takes precautions to protect Mrs Fainall's interests. Fainall tells Mrs Marwood: 'I have already a deed of settlement of the best part of her estate; which I wheedled out of her; and that you shall partake at least' (III.iii). He is, however, forgetting that Mirabel has already taken steps to prevent it. Even the 'deed of settlement' is of no use as Mrs Fainall had already entrusted her whole estate to Mirabel through a previous deed. So ultimately Fainall is defeated — though, of course, he would still be 'kept', a condition that Mirabel is sure he would accept as 'his circumstances are such he must of force comply' (V.iii).

It is no doubt true that Mirabel is a manipulator, but there is a *basic* difference between him and Fainall. As Peter Malekin has said, 'they both manipulate others unscrupulously, but Mirabel has respect for the nature and interest of those he is manipulating.' Fainall is just the opposite. As against Mirabel, who 'continues to remain affectionate towards, and keep the affection and trust of, people who might easily have hated him', his 'relationships involve strain and suffering.'[82] Indeed he seems utterly incapable of establishing any genuine relationship with any one. He hates his wife and distrusts his mistress. His judgment has become so perverted on account of frustration and cynicism that his claim that he understands 'the way of the world' loses all validity. His view of life is so vitiated that very many aspects of human nature are completely beyond his comprehension. He cannot, for instance, understand that an affectionate relationship can still exist between a woman and her former lover. But as Mirabel reminds him, that too is 'the way of the world' — 'of the widows of the world' (V.iii). Indeed Barron sums up Fainall's status in the play admirably: 'Fainall, despite his wit, his gallantry, his obvious superiority in many respects to the other members of the cast, with the exception of Mirabel, is only a Witwoud.'[83]

It is Mirabel who is the Truewit of the play. It is not that he does not understand the base side of human nature, but he also knows that despite the folly and the evil around man, he can still retain his integrity. Like his creator, Mirabel is no believer in 'the Golden Age'. He would have fully accepted the 'moral' contained in the lines that Congreve wrote in 1728, just before his death, in his *Letter to Lord Cobham*:

> For Virtue now is neither more nor less,
> And Vice is only varied in the Dress;
> Believe it, Men have ever been the same,
> And all the Golden Age, is but a Dream.

The message of these lines is not that we despair of human nature or of human civilization but that we make the best of the circumstances in which God has chosen to throw us. That is precisely what Mirabel does. As has rightly been said by Paul T. Nolan, 'he is *clever* enough to succeed in the way of the world and *moral* enough to make that success meaningful.[84] (Italics mine).

His success can become meaningful, however, only if he is able to win the love and affection of Millamant. There is no doubt that Millamant loves him. It is also true that she would like to marry him. But like all Restoration comic heroines, she has her doubts and fears. She lives in a world where disillusionment in marriage is common and where the normal gossip is about wrecked marriages and affairs. Marriage as an institution has been so contaminated by adultery, jealousy and suspicion that any sensitive girl would hesitate to marry. Mrs Fainall's case, which Millamant knows at first hand, should itself be frightening enough. Mirabel may be a good man but how does Millamant know that he would make a good husband?

The main reason for this anxiety seems to be the general view in Restoration comedy that love and marriage are incompatible, that familiarity breeds contempt, that, in the words of Mrs Behn, 'Marriage is as certain a Bane to Love, as lending Money is to Friendship' (*The Rover*, V.i). Shakespeare's Rosalind gave classic expression to this feeling when she said: 'Men are April when they woo, December when they wed.' Kenneth Muir has said that 'what in Rosalind is just a jest, in Millamant becomes almost her dominant mood'. He suggests that 'the most subtle way in which Millamant conveys her anxiety 'on the very Verge of Matrimony' is by her quotations from Waller and Suckling.' The poems from which Millamant quotes — and others in the same vein quoted by Muir — have only one theme: 'that desire dies with its satisfaction.' This, says Muir, 'accounts for the ambivalent feelings about marriage the heroes of many Restoration comedies have and also the reluctance of the more sensitive heroines to risk disillusionment.'[85]

There is no doubt that Millamant suffers from anxiety and nervousness. Harriet Hawkins regards 'the nervousness behind her bravura and arrogance' as 'fully justified' in view of Congreve's main 'dramatic concern' in this play being the problem 'of experiencing genuine emotion and still behaving with due decorum in a world of artificiality.'[86] To come to terms with such a world, Millamant has to hide her real feelings behind a mask. This is evident in her very first meeting with Mirabel. She arrogantly tells him that she loves to give pain. When Mirabel reminds her that this cruelty is not in her nature, she flares up: 'Oh I ask your pardon for that — one's cruelty is one's power, and when one parts with one's cruelty, one parts with one's power; and when one has parted with that, I fancy one's old and ugly' (II.ii). But surely Millamant cannot stay young for ever. She knows this and hence is subtly pleading with Mirabel to make her feel that she will always be lovely in his eyes and that his love will be undying. She says the same thing to him later on:

MIR. Do you lock yourself up from me, to make my search more curious? or is this pretty artifice contrived to signify that here the chase must end, and my pursuits be crowned? For you can fly no further.

MRS MIL. Vanity! no — I'll fly, and be followed to the last moment. Though I am upon the very verge of matrimony, I expect you should solicit me as much as if I were wavering at the grate of a

monastery, with one foot over the threshold. I'll be solicited to the
very last, nay, and afterwards.

MIR. What, after the last?

MRS MIL. Oh, I should think I was poor and had nothing to bestow,
if I were reduced to an inglorious ease, and freed from the agreeable
fatigues of solicitation.

(IV.i)

To believe, as L. C. Knights does, that Millamant 'expects to
draw vitality from the excitement of incessant solicitation', and
hence her attitude to life is not 'enlivened by the play of genuine
intelligence'[87] is clearly to misunderstand her real nature (Italics
mine). Millamant realizes that marriage is not a matter of 'incessant solicitation' but she talks like this precisely because she is in
search of that inner certainty and moral equilibrium without
which no one can feel relaxed in one's relationship with another
human being — particularly a member of the other sex.

There is no doubt that Millamant is rarely relaxed. To cover
this up — for in her society a woman must always show self-
possession and complete control over her emotions — she starts
showing off. We see this at her very first entrance. When reminded
by Mrs Fainall that she has delayed coming, she looks surprised
and turns towards her woman and asks why she was late; then
follows the delicious passage about letters: 'O ay, letters — I had
letters — I am persecuted with letters — I hate letters — Nobody
knows how to write letters, and yet one has 'em, one does not
know why. They serve one to pin up one's hair' — and then to
crush Witwoud, the added information that she pins up her hair
'only with those in verse' (II.ii). Witwoud's literary accomplishments have not yet soared that high!

Then there is her attempt to put Mirabel down. When
reminded that women are beautiful because of men's commenda-
tion, she mocks at this male vanity: 'Lord, what is a lover, that it
can give? Why, one makes lovers as fast as one pleases, and they
live as long as one pleases, and they die as soon as one pleases; and
then, if one pleases, one makes more' (II.i). Mirabel regards all
this as frivolous. But what can he do? He is in love with her 'with
all her faults; nay. . .*for* her faults' (I.i). He himself, however, is so
serious-minded that he cannot help pointing out one of these
faults, this being that she always has 'the leisure to entertain a
herd of fools', like Witwoud and Petulant. He asks her with some
asperity: 'How can you find delight in such society? It is impossi-

ble they should admire you, they are not capable: or if they were, it should be to you as a mortification; for sure to please a fool is some degree of folly.' (II.ii). After giving a flippant reply, Millamant at last comes to the real point: 'I shan't endure to be reprimanded nor instructed: ' 'tis so dull to act always by advice, and so tedious to be told one's faults — I can't bear it. Well, I won't have you, Mirabel — I am resolv'd — I think — you may go' (II.ii). And then she adds, to show her power over him: 'Ha! ha! ha! what would you give, that you could help loving me?' (II.ii). Mirabel cannot yet grasp the real meaning of this behaviour, and complains that 'a man may as soon make a friend by his wit, or a fortune by his honesty, as win a woman by plain-dealing and sincerity' (II.ii). Millamant can, of course, be won by 'plain-dealing and sincerity' — indeed finally through them alone — but the man must not commit 'the cardinal sin of responding seriously to her raillery.'[88] This is precisely what Mirabel has done and earned the epithet of 'Sententious' from Millamant.

Mirabel, however, is not altogether wrong in demanding some seriousness from Millamant. But when he pleads, 'You are merry, madam, but I would persuade you for one moment to be serious', pat comes the reply: 'What, with that face?. . .Well, Mirabel, if ever you will win me, woo me now. Nay, if you are so tedious, fare you well' (II.ii). Even when she finally accepts him, she cannot adopt a serious tone: 'Well, you ridiculous thing you, I'll have you — I won't be kissed, nor I won't be thanked' (IV.i). Novak has said that 'Mirabel will have to win her on the level of witty love play, of "enigma" and game, that is the key to her affections.'[89] But surely there is an affectionate and serious-minded woman behind this mask of 'witty love play' and Mirabel must reach her if a stable relationship is to be established between him and Millamant. On her part, Millamant too must recognize that there is a basic difference between the role of a coquette and that of a wife.

This recognition comes to Millamant in the Proviso scene, and even though she still maintains the facade of witty love play — 'Well — I think — I'll endure you' (IV.i) — she admits, though somewhat haltingly, that this scene has brought her nearer to an understanding with Mirabel: 'In the mean time I suppose you have said something to please me' (IV.i). But Mirabel has said something not only to please her but also to educate her in the new role that she is going to play as a wife. Indeed, the purpose of the scene is to reclaim Millamant and to provide her that assurance and equilibrium which she has lacked throughout.

She, of course, begins in the usual way: 'My dear liberty, shall I leave thee? My faithful solitude, my darling contemplation, must I then bid you adieu?' (IV.i). But what does this 'liberty' really mean for her? She does talk of 'liberty to pay and receive visits to and from whom I please, to write and receive letters. . .To have my closet inviolate', etc. (IV.i). But without waiting for an assurance from him she expresses her willingness to accept him and to '*dwindle* into a wife' (IV.i) (Italics mine). Why does Millamant think that marriage means loss of dignity for a woman? Surely staying unmarried was the worst possible fate for a woman in that age and such women in any case had no dignity, at least in the eyes of others. Perhaps Millamant uses this expression merely to articulate the general fear shared by most heroines in Restoration comedy that a woman is always at a disadvantage in marriage, and that, as Mary Astell says 'whether it be Wit or Beauty that a Man's in Love with, there are no great Hopes of a lasting Happiness.' Mary Astell correctly describes the situation of the contemporary woman: 'Let the Business be carried as prudently as it can on the Woman's Side, a reasonable Man can't deny that she has by much the harder Bargain: because she puts herself entirely into her Husband's Power, and if the Matrimonial Yoke be grievous, neither Law nor Custom afford her that Redress which a Man obtains.' Among other things, this feeling could also be caused by the low esteem in which women were generally held in that period. Mary Astell was making an important point when she said: 'But how can a Man respect his Wife when he has a contemptible Opinion of her and her Sex?'[90]

Mirabel does not have a low opinion either of Millamant or of her sex. His chief concern is to convince her of this fact and to show her that he is different from other men, and that his love for her is really based on esteem. To do so, he utilizes a strategy which at once shows not only his confidence in himself but also in Millamant's good sense. The first thing that he does is to dispel Millamant's fears about 'dwindling' into a wife by saying that he too should have 'liberty to offer conditions, that when you are *dwindled* into a wife, I may not be beyond measure *enlarged* into a husband' (IV.i) (Italics mine). His 'conditions' would, therefore, be such as to ensure a reasonable equality between them as husband and wife. After rejecting the silly notion of 'dwindling' and 'enlarging', he moves on to Millamant's 'liberty'. Here he takes a firm stand and reminds Millamant that both man and woman have to modify their life-styles after marriage and that this does involve losing some of their liberty. The sole purpose of Mirabel's 'conditions' is to make their marriage viable in the corrupt society in which they live. Hence the stipulations: her 'acquaintance' must be general; she should 'restrain [herself] to naive and simple tea-table drinks'; but most important of all, she should not behave like a lady-fop, but 'continue to like [her] own face as long as [he] shall' and, when 'breeding', avoid 'strait-lacing, squeezing, for a shape, till you mould my boy's head like a sugar-loaf' (IV.i). All this is indeed a lesson in wifely duties, and however loudly Millamant may pretend to protest ('O horrid provisos!. . .I hate your odious provisos!'), there is no doubt that she is pleased with Mirabels conditions. Mirabel sees this and confidently announces: 'Then we're agreed' (IV.i).

Here, then, we see the emergence of a genuinely affectionate and companionate relationship, and neither the husband nor the wife need be self-conscious about their position in the domestic hierarchy. It is true that in this play the responsibility of maintaining harmonious relationship falls largely on the husband. We may even say that the initiative here has passed into the hands of the man, which was not the case in *The Man of Mode*. Philip Roberts has claimed that 'Mirabel holds the key in the play to the plot, to the reputation of the other characters, and to the outcome.' Mirabel's conditions to Millamant more than convince us that in this play 'The world of Dorimant, of Horner, of Fainall, is exchanged for the world of the new fine gentleman.'[91] This new world does not demand from women the fighting spirit of Harriet. Indeed in this world there is no place for the usual sex-war of the earlier Restoration comedy. The emphasis here is clearly on the preservation of the nuclear family. In this family, the husband may theoretically be the senior partner, but how does it matter if the wife is assured of his love and affection? Even Mary Astell concedes that in such a case a 'peaceable Woman' need not 'question her Husband's Right, nor his Fitness to govern.'[92]

But Mary Astell is a militant and she is so obsessed with the low position of women in contemporary society that she gives a rather depressing picture of marriage in the early eighteenth century:

He [the man] wants one to manage his Family, an House-Keeper whose Interest it will be not to wrong him, and in whom therefore he can put greater Confidence than in any he can hire for Money. One who may breed his Children, taking all the Care and Trouble of their Education, to preserve his Name and Family. One whose Beauty, Wit, or good Humour and agreeable Conversation, will entertain him at Home when he has been contradicted and disappointed Abroad; who will do him that Justice the ill-natur'd World denies him; that is, in any one's Language but his own, sooth his Pride and flatter his Vanity, but having always so much good Sense as to be on his Side, to conclude him in the Right, when others are so ignorant, or so rude, as to deny it. Who will not be blind to his Merit nor contradict his Will and Pleasure, but make it her Business, her very Ambition to content him; whose Softness and gentle Compliance will calm his Passions, to whom he may safely disclose his troublesome Thoughts, and in her Breast discharge his Cares; whose Duty, Submission and Observance, will heal those Wounds other Peoples Opposition or Neglect have given him. In a word, one whom he can intirely Govern, and consequently may form her to his Will and Liking, who must be his for Life, and therefore cannot quit his Service, let him treat her how he will.[93]

But surely not all that she says, and specially the spirit in which she says it — need apply to the marriage of Mirabel and Millamant. There is no question of Mirabel treating Millamant ill. He is intelligent enough to see that to subdue a woman's personality hurts not only the woman but also the man who is in search of a companionate marriage. Such a marriage does assume that the woman would not hesitate to accept many of the responsibilities that Mary Astell mentions. But to think that these responsibilities would hurt her self-respect is to completely misunderstand the nature of this marriage. It may also be noted that the self-respect of the woman can finally be secured only by the man she marries. The man has to treat her as an equal partner in the game of life as she is his best friend and companion. If he fails to do so, he not only damages her but also himself. Mary Astell made an important statement when she said that the man 'who does not make Friendship the chief Inducement to his Choice, and prefers it before any other Consideration, does not deserve a good Wife, and therefore should not complain if he does without one.'[94] Mirabel clearly treats Millamant not only as his friend but as that special kind of friend who satisfies both the needs of the body and those of the spirit. The *quality* of this relationship is best seen in the last repartee between them:

MILLAMANT: Why does not the man take me? Would you have me
   give myself to you over again?
MIRABEL: Ay, and over and over again, for (*kisses her hand*) I would
   have you as often as possibly I can. Well, heaven grant I love you
   not too well, that's all my fear.

                                                          (V.i)

It is a very touching scene indeed and not even Anne (Righter)
Barton should convince us that all this is merely in aid of their
'possessing' one another. Surely 'possessing' is too limited a
concept of marriage and both Mirabel and Millamant recognize it
more than any other lovers in Restoration Comedy.

Historically speaking, we may say that after 1700 we are
entering the phase of male dominance in English society and
literature, and that the protest of the Restoration woman against
this dominance is now over. But we should recognize that Congreve is *not* recommending male dominance in this play. The
initiative has passed into the hands of man, but that is merely to
underscore the damage that the Restoration ethos has done to the
woman's psychology. Mirabel proposes an opting out of that
ethos and recommends adjustment of man-woman relationship
in the interest of a stable marriage. In this play Congreve achieves
that balance between 'Man's Prerogative' and 'Woman's Privi-
leges'[95] which Mary Astell herself approved. This is a balance
devoutly to be wished for and it is perhaps this which is upset in
the eighteenth century.

APPENDIX
A NOTE ON THE 'MOTHERS' IN SHAKESPEARE

I

Most critics have felt disappointed with Shakespeare's treatment of mothers in his plays, but perhaps no one has expressed this disappointment so sharply as Sri Aurobindo. 'The greatest minds have their limitations', he says in his discussion of Kalidas —

and Shakespeare's over-abounding wit shuts him out from two Paradises, the mind of a child and the heart of a mother. . . .Indeed, throughout the meagre and mostly unsympathetic list of mothers in Shakespeare's otherwise various and splendid gallery, there is not even one in whose speech there is the throbbing of a mother's heart; the sacred beauty of maternity is touched upon in a phrase or two; but from Shakespeare we expect something more, some perfect and passionate enshrining of the most engrossing and selfless of human affections. In this one respect, the Indian poet [Kalidas], perhaps from the superior depth and keenness of the domestic feelings peculiar to his nation, out-stripped his greater English compeer.[1]

Bernard Shaw may not have shared Sri Aurobindo's general approach to 'motherhood' but he would certainly have agreed with the view that the list of mothers in Shakespeare is 'meagre and mostly unsympathetic'. After saying in his usual whimsical manner that 'filial sentimentality is not an English convention, but a French one' and that 'Englishmen mostly quarrel with their families, especially with their mothers', he declares that he finds 'just two sympathetic mothers in the whole range of [Shakespeare's] plays', these being the Countess of Rousillon and Hermione. He qualifies his praise of the Countess by saying that she 'shews all her maternal tenderness and wisdom for an orphan who is no kin to her, whilst to her son she is shrewd, critical, and without illusion.' His conclusion is that nowhere do we get from Shakespeare 'as between son and mother, that unmistakable tenderness, that touches us as between Lear and Cordelia and between Prospero and Miranda.'[2]

In our own day we find Maynard Mack complaining that —

there is amazingly little interest in either mothers or mothering in most
of Shakespeare, and the comparatively few mothers who are brought to
our attention as mothers, though they include such examplary figures as
the Countess of Rousillon, Lady Macduff, Virgilia, and Hermione,
include also Tamora, cruel Queen of the Goths in *Titus Andronicus*,
Gertrude in *Hamlet*, Lady Macbeth (a mother at least by her own testim-
ony), Volumnia in *Coriolanus*, and the poisoning Queen in *Cymbeline*,
mother of the clod Cloten. Not — one may perhaps reasonably conclude
— a puff for radiant Elizabethan motherhood. The fathers in these plays
come off better.[3]

It is difficult to explain why, by and large, the portraits of
mothers in Shakespeare's plays should be not only much less
prominent but also much less sympathetic than those of fathers.
One reason may be, as Maynard Mack points out, that Shakespeare reflects in his plays the position that mothers occupy in
Elizabethan society. As he says:

Fathers dominate Shakespeare's stage for the same reason and in the
same ways that they dominate his society. The almost total authority
granted them by law and custom meant that they inevitably became the
initiators and prohibitors of action, the dispensers and withholders of
wealth and privilege (including the privilege of marriage), and the
meters-out of unappealable decrees both wise and unwise — all perqui-
sites of power that in the real world, as in fable, precipitate drama.
Mothers, lacking final authority altogether unless they were widows or
queens, the playwright quite understandably shears away, either in the
interest of dramatic clarity or possibly to convenience the boy-actors,
who must always have found it less taxing to play Rosalind than
Volumnia.[4]

Convenience of the boy-actors would at best have played only a
minor part in determining Shakespeare's general approach to
mothers, but 'dramatic clarity' is a different matter — and it is
perhaps this which explains the secondary roles that Shakespeare
assigns to mothers. V. Y. Kantak has rightly said: 'One imagines
they [mothers] would be rather a nuisance in the comedies; the
heroines would be inhibited by their presence. In the major tragedies 'motherhood' would almost certainly set up a rival force to
the male heroism and interfere with the tragic effect based on the
Western 'scape-goat' archetype'.[5] Mothers are to be introduced by
Shakespeare, therefore, only when they can serve a definite dramatic purpose without interfering with the main effect of the
play. Such a purpose is clearly served by Lady Capulet in *Romeo
and Juliet*. She may not exactly remember her daughter's age —

something quite common in a society where children are left to
the care of servants — but she considerably softens the father's
harsh treatment of his daughter. She is quite concerned about the
future of her daughter and wants to talk about it to her. She asks
Juliet:

> Tell me, daughter Juliet,
> How stands your dispositions to be married?
>
> (I.iii.65-6)

Finding that Juliet has not yet thought of this 'honour' (I.iii.67),
she reminds her that girls of her age in Verona have already
become mothers, and then mentions that Paris 'seeks [her] for his
love' (I.iii.75). She does not, however, rush Juliet. Instead, she
merely asks, 'What say you? Can you love the gentleman?'
(I.iii.79-80). As we have already seen, she also tries to intervene
when her husband starts threatening Juliet. She is, of course, convinced all the while that her husband's decision to marry Juliet to
Paris is a sensible one. In any case, she has no reason to suspect
that her daughter is already married. Throughout the play there
is no evidence that she does not have 'a mother's heart'. There is
no occasion for Shakespeare to show the 'throbbing' which might
have pleased Sri Aurobindo, though there is all the needed throbbing in the last scene when husband and wife see the dead body of
their daughter.

There is also the mother of Romeo whom no one seems to
notice. When, along with her husband, she comes to the scene of
the fight between the servants of the two families and learns that
the 'fiery Tybalt' had also participated in it, she asks Benvolio:
'O, where is Romeo? Saw you him today? / Right glad I am he
was not at this fray' (I.ii.114-115). In the last scene of the play, we
learn from Montague:

> my wife is dead to-night,
> Grief of my son's exile hath stopp'd her breath.
>
> (V.iii.209-10)

She cannot be accused of not having a throbbing heart and might
have pleased even Sri Aurobindo if given a greater part in the
action.

It is best, therefore, to keep in mind the kind of role that the
mother is required to play. Indeed, her role as a mother may
sometimes be quite secondary to some other role that the playw-

right may assign to her. Lady Macbeth, for instance, is not introduced as a mother at all but only as an ambitious wife. This ambition is so overriding in her case that she is willing to reject all human bonds to achieve her purpose. Hence her statement, which sounds quite horrifying from a mother:

> I have given suck, and know
> How tender 'tis to love the babe that milks me;
> I would while it was smiling in my face
> Have plucked my nipples from his boneless gums
> And dashed the brains out, had I so sworn as you
> Have done to this. (*Macbeth*, I.vii.54-59)

But surely this was *dramatically* necessary, to compel Macbeth to perform the deed that he had sworn to do. But however ruthless, would she really have sacrificed the interest of her children, if she had any? It is not a heartless woman who says about Duncan:

> Had he not resembled
> My father as he slept, I had done it. (II.ii.12-13)

Nor does a real 'fiend' — whatever Malcolm may say — break down under the heavy burden of guilt and take her life 'by self and violent hands.' (V.iii.70). If differently placed, Lady Macbeth might not have been a bad mother. Lady Macduff is, of course, an 'exemplary' mother but that is precisely because that is the role that Macduff's wife must play to convince us that Macbeth has really turned into a 'butcher' (V.viii.69). Lady Macbeth, if placed in Lady Macduff's situation, may not have been less solicitous for her children's safety, and no less feminine.

II

The mothers in Shakespeare should not, therefore, be approached in terms of their being a 'radiant' image of Elizabethan motherhood or otherwise. They are invariably treated with the normal respect due to them and they do have for their children the normal affection that we associate with mothers in all cultures and societies. There are, of course, some sons in Shakespeare who for ignoble reasons of their own, degrade this relationship. There is Robert Faulconbridge in *King John* who wants to get his younger brother disinherited and publicly declares that he is not his father's son. The younger brother is no better in this regard as he is more interested in being the bastard son of King Richard Coeur-de-lion than the legitimate son of Sir Robert Faulconbridge. Lady Faulconbridge's pathetic appeal to him falls on deaf ears:

> Hast thou conspired with thy brother too,
> That for thine own gain shouldst defend mine honour?
>
> (I.ii.241-2)

Another young man who has no respect for his mother — or indeed any human being — is Richard III. It does not surprise us when this 'hell-hound' spreads the rumour through Buckingham that his elder brother King Edward IV is a bastard. He, of course, does it to establish his claim to the English throne. It is painful to hear him advising Buckingham to go after the Lord Mayor and —

> Tell them, when that my mother went with child
> Of that insatiate Edward, noble York
> My princely father then had wars in France
> And, by true compunction of the time,
> Found that the issue was not his begot;
> Which well appeared in his lineaments,
> Being nothing like the noble Duke my father.
>
> (*Richard III*, III.v.86-92)

The only consideration that he is willing to show his mother is this:

> Yet touch this sparingly, as 'twere far off;
> Because, my lord, you know my mother lives.   (III.v.93-4)

What more could he have done if she were dead? But all this is not a reflection on the mother — it is condemnation of an ambitious son. The mother says in sorrow: 'He is my son; ay, and therein my shame' (II.ii.29). Her anguish is greater still when she says:

> O my accursed womb, the bed of death!
> A cockatrice has thou hatch'd to the world,
> Whose unavoided eye is murderous.
>
> (IV.i.54-6)

Bernard Shaw clubs Hamlet with Richard III and Faulconbridge, and finds the scene between him and his mother 'almost unbearably shameful'.[6] The sex-nausea in that scene is, of course, utterly distasteful, but surely it is only an expression of Hamlet's outraged sense of shame at his mother's conduct. He has a sacred image of a mother and that sacred image has been shattered by his mother's hasty and incestuous marriage. If a mother, who is a symbol of purity, can within a month of her beloved husband's death commit such an outrageous act then surely the world is—

> an unweeded garden,
> That grows to seed; things rank and gross in nature
> Possess it merely.   (*Hamlet*, I.ii.135-37)

Hamlet's mother, it must be conceded, is not fully aware of the enormity of her action in the eyes of her son. So she is amazed at the way her son is behaving to her. 'What have I done', she asks, 'that thou darest wag thy tongue / In noise so rude against me?' (III.iv.39-40). Hamlet's reply shows what a central place a mother occupies in the psyche of a sensitive son, as also the irreparable damage that a lapse on her part can cause to his moral sense:

> Such an act
> That blurs the grace and blush of modesty;
> Calls virtue hyporite, takes off the rose
> From the fair forehead of an innocent love,
> And sets a blister there; makes marriage-vows
> As false as dicers' oaths. O, such a deed
> As from the body of contraction plucks
> The very soul, and sweet religion makes
> A rhapsody of words. Heaven's face does glow
> O'er this solidity and compound mass
> With heated visage, as against the doom —
> Is thought-sick at the act   (III.iv.40-51)

We may regard Hamlet's reaction to his mother's conduct as somewhat excessive, but it is surely not abnormal. Another young man in Shakespeare, Troilus, would perhaps have almost wholly shared Hamlet's views. For him, too, a mother is a symbol of purity who alone can provide her son with a solid basis for a moral view of the universe. It may seem strange to us that his mind should go to his mother at the sight of Cressida's betrayal. At the moment of parting Cressida had said:

> Time, force, and death,
> Do to this body what extremes you can,
> But the strong base and building of my love
> Is as the very centre of the earth,
> Drawing all things to it   (*Troilus and Cressida*, IV.ii.100-104)

But soon enough — indeed within a few hours — Troilus sees Cressida flirting with Diomedes and 'the very centre of the earth' crumbles before him. It is significant that in this moment of crisis he is able to say only this:

> Let it not be believ'd for womanhood.
> Think, we had mothers.   (V.ii.127-8)

Even the hard-boiled Ulysses is aghast at the thought that Cressida should have done something 'that can soil our mothers' (V.ii.132). But Cressida has soiled all mothers, indeed all womankind for Troilus. She has destroyed the faith in female purity which he had imbibed from his mother, who was for him the ultimate symbol of purity. Once his faith in that purity is destroyed, nothing remains sacred in his eyes:

> If beauty have a soul, this is not she;
> If souls guide vows, if vows be sanctimonies,
> If sanctimony be the gods' delight,
> If there be rule in unity itself,
> This was not she. (V.ii.135-40)

And yet this *was* she. With this realization the play ends on a note of defeat, as does *Hamlet*. It is notable, however, that both plays establish the intimate relationship that exists between a son's faith in his mother's purity and his view of other women, and indeed of the universe.

III

Gertrude damaged Hamlet by her conduct, though she became conscious of it only at a very late stage in the play. But Volumnia in *Coriolanus* can never realize that she has done anything of the kind. Indeed she is all the while conscious only of the good that she has done him. She is proud of the fact that she produced a real 'man-child' (I.i.15) and proclaims:

> The valiantness was mine, thou suck'st it from me. (III.ii.128)

Elsewhere she says:

> Thou art my warrior;
> I holp to frame thee. (V.iii.62-63)

Her only regret is that he has not inherited her

> brain that leads my use of anger
> To better vantage (III.ii.30-31)

He could have perhaps inherited that too, and improved on it if she had let him grow properly as a child and had not stunted his mental growth. What she says about her grandson shows the kind of education that her son must have received from her: 'He had rather see swords and hear a drum than look upon his schoolmaster' (I.iii.53-4). She is delighted to learn from Valeria that while running after a butterfly the child had torn it to pieces. She calls it 'One on's father's moods' (I.iii.63). Such upbringing is hardly conducive to normal mental growth.

It is not that Volumnia does not love Coriolanus, but she is so obsessed with 'honour' — which is another name for ambition — that this is how she enunciates her conception of love to Virgilia, the gentle and affectionate wife of Coriolanus: 'If my son were my husband, I should freelier rejoice in that absence wherein he won honour than in the embracements of his bed where he would show most love' (I.iii.2-5). Some may treat this as an expression of the heroic ideal but surely this woman can easily destroy the normal relationship between a husband and a wife. The tension between her and her daughter-in-law is clearly present in the scene where Menenius asks the women if Coriolanus returned wounded from the war. Virgilia's natural reaction is: 'O no, no, no', but Volumnia says: 'O, he is wounded; I thank the gods for't' (II.ii.112). As John Ingledew has said, she 'must be the only mother in life or literature to thank the gods that her son is wounded.'⁷ All this is often attributed to her patriotism, but it must be admitted that as a mother she does emerge as quite heartless. This is best seen when she rebukes Virgilia — 'Away, you fool' (I.iii.37) — and declares:

> The breasts of Hecuba,
> When she did suckle Hector, looked not lovelier
> Than Hector's forehead when it spit forth blood
> At Grecian sword, contemning.   (I.iii.38-41)

She would indeed become insufferable if Shakespeare had not introduced Virgilia. This is best seen when Coriolanus returns from the war and kneels before his mother. The mother proudly picks him up — 'my good soldier. . .My gentle Martius, worthy Caius' (II.i.160-1) — and completely forgets that his wife is also waiting to receive him. She then looks behind and sees the wife in tears of joy at his safe return: 'But, O, thy wife!' Coriolanus' words have a peculiar depth and flavour:

> My gracious silence, hail!   (II.i.164)

With a mother-in-law like Volumnia, silence is perhaps the only defence for a tender wife.

At the end of the play Volumnia exacts the price of motherhood from her unwilling but helpless son. She reminds him that his

attack on Rome will mean an assault on his 'mother's womb /
That brought thee to this world' (V.iii.123-4). She also taunts him
by saying that 'there's no man in the world / More bound to's
mother, yet here he lets me prate / Like one i' th' stocks'
(V.iii.158-160) Coriolanus cannot resist this appeal and though
he is dimly conscious of its consequences, he changes his mind
and invites his death. If Volumnia had left a wholly pleasant
impression on our minds, we could have found Coriolanus' final
act a wholly redemptive one. But as things are, the play leaves us
somewhat cold.

IV

It is worth noting that neither of the two sympathetic mothers in
Shakespeare — the Countess of Rousillon and Hermione — is
either possessive or dominating. They do, of course, love their
children, but there is something soothingly affectionate about
their love — something that we miss altogether in a play like
Coriolanus or even in *Hamlet*, though we cannot doubt Gertrude's capacity for affection. The reason seems to be that the
Countess and Hermione are both eminently reasonable and
enlightened in their attitude to their children. The Countess is a
widow and her general attitude to people — at once kind and
understanding — shows that she has lived a happy married life.
After her husband's death, her love has been concentrated on her
son and now the son is going to the King of France to whom he is
'in ward'. (*All's Well That Ends Well*, I.i.5.). The first sentence in
the play is spoken by her and it immediately shows her deep
attachment both to her husband and to her son: 'In delivering my
son from me, I bury a second husband.' Her advice to her son has
a flavour of its own, altogether different from the kind of advice
that Polonius gives his son:

> Be thou blessed, Bertram, and succeed thy father
> In manners as in shape! Thy blood and virtue
> Contend for empire in thee, and thy goodness
> Share with thy birthright! Love all, trust a few,
> Do wrong to none.   (I.i.54-58)

Her son, however, is a disappointment to her. When he informs
her through a letter that he has been undone by Helena whom he
has married, and that he has decided to leave the court of France,
her reaction is as understanding as it can be in the circumstances:

This is not well, rash and unbridled boy,
To fly the favours of so good a King,
To pluck his indignation on thy head
By the misprizing of a maid too virtuous
For the contempt of empire. (III.ii.26-30)

She regards him as an 'unworthy husband of his wife' (III.iv.30)
but hopes that he will outgrow his folly. Her other regret is that
Helena has left for an unknown destination. She is confident that
she 'could have well diverted her intents' (III.iv.21) if she had had
a chance to speak to her. She loves her as a daughter and indeed —

Which of them both
Is dearest to me I have no skill in sense
To make distinction. (III.iv.38-40)

She tells Lafew: 'If she had partaken of my flesh and cost me the
dearest groans of a mother, I could not have owed her a more
rooted love.' (IV.v.9-11).

The most remarkable aspect of her character is her fairmindedness and sense of justice. Her love for her son is, of course, the one
sustaining factor in her life. When she learns that he is returning
home, she says: 'It rejoices me that I hope I shall see him ere I die'
(IV.v.82). She also pleads with the King of France to take a more
lenient view of his folly:

And I beseech your majesty to make it
Natural rebellion done i' th' blade of youth
When oil and fire, too strong for reason's force,
O'erbears it and burns on. (V.iii.6-9)

But when Diana tells her story and presents the ring, she clearly
sees that her son is telling a lie. So without hesitation she says:

This is his wife:
That ring's a thousand proofs. (V.iii.198-9).

When at one stage the King expresses his suspicion that Helena
may have been murdered by her son, the Countess does not waver
and demands 'justice on the doers' (V.iii.155). This sense of justice and fairmindedness is so ingrained in her character that when
she is told that Helena is in love with her son, she puts herself in
Helena's place and says: 'Even so it was with me when I was
young' (I.iii.123). No other aged character in Shakespeare shows
this understanding of youth.

However much we may admire the Countess of Rousillon, we

are not able to shake off the feeling that perhaps she should have taken greater interest in Bertram's upbringing. To believe that a son is bound to inherit a father's 'manners' along with his 'shape' (I.i.55) is clearly too naive. The age emphasized a fairly elaborate scheme of education for the sons of noblemen and it seems that somewhere there has been a lapse with Bertram. He has an inflated conception of his 'honour' and social status but he lacks most of the qualities of a gentleman. It would be wrong to blame his mother for his lapses of conduct — after all his company, too, has corrupted him — but her total lack of understanding of his deficiencies does not cast an altogether favourable light on her judgment.

Hermione in *The Winter's Tale* is clearly a more understanding mother. She combines in an excellent measure maternal tenderness and lack of excessive possessiveness. This latter trait of her character which Shakespeare's age regarded as the surest way to discipline children is evident in the very beginning of Act II:

> Take the boy to you; he so troubles me,
> 'Tis past enduring
>
> (II.i.1-2)

But she does not overdo this strictness and calls him back after some time, and this conversation takes place between mother and son:

HERMIONE: Come, sir, now
  I am for you again. Pray you sit by us,
  And tell's a tale.
MAMILLIUS: Merry or sad shall't be?
HERMIONE: As merry as you will.
MAMILLIUS: A sad tale's best for winter. I have one
  Of sprites and goblins.
HERMIONE: Let's have that, good sir.
  Come on, sit down; come on, and do your best
  To fright me with your sprites; you're powerful at it.
MAMILLIUS: There was a man —
HERMIONE: Nay, come, sit down; then on.
MAMILLIUS: Dwelt by a churchyard — I will tell it softly;
  Yond crickets shall not hear it.
HERMIONE: Come on then,
  And give't me in mine ear.

(II.i.21-32)

The scene is so affectionate, tender and intimate that we are not surprised that the boy feels completely shattered and lost when he is forcibly taken away from his mother and she is publicly disgraced by his father. The father has no idea of the damage that he has done to the boy and he wholly misunderstands the cause of his grief and sickness:

> Conceiving the dishonour of his mother,
> He straight declin'd, droop'd, took it deeply,
> Fasten'd and fix'd the shame on't in himself,
> Threw off his spirit, his appetite, his sleep,
> And downright languish'd. (II.iii.13-17)

Carol Thomas Neely has admirably contrasted Hermione's attitude to her son, at once affectionate and sensible, with that of the two fathers, Leontes and Polixenes, to their sons. 'The fathers', she says, 'see their sons as copies of themselves, extensions of their own egos. . .Polixenes' description, in which Leontes concurs, of the self-justifying use he makes of his son sums up the attitude of both toward their children:

> He's all my exercise, my mirth, my matter:
> Now my sworn friend, and then mine enemy:
> My parasite, my soldier, statesman, all.
> He makes a July's day short as December,
> And with his varying childishness, cures in me
> Thoughts that would thick my blood' (I.ii.166-171)[8]

Hermione could have looked upon Perdita — the daughter for whom she 'preserv'd' (V.iii.123) herself — as a natural extension of her own ego but she does nothing of the kind. The first words that she speaks are a prayer for her happiness and they are totally without any touch of selfpity:

> You gods, look down.
> And from your sacred vials pour your graces
> Upon my daughter's head. (V.iii.121-123)

She does, of course, call her 'mine own' (V.iii.123) but her sole concern is to find out how her daughter has fared:

> Tell me, mine own,
> Where hast thou been preserv'd? Where liv'd? (V.iii.123-4)

In Hermione we find that 'perfect and passionate enshrining of the most engrossing and selfless of human affections' that Sri Aurobindo regarded as the chief characteristic of a mother.

NOTES AND REFERENCES

CHAPTER I

1. Cotton Mather, *Family Religion Urged* (1709), cited by Edmund S. Morgan, *The Puritan Family* (Revised edition, New York, 1966), p. 133
2. Thomas Cobbett, *Fruitfull and Useful Discourse* (1656), also cited by Morgan, pp. 133-4.
3. W. Reich, *Mass Psychology of Fascism* (1971), p. 53. Cited by Lawrence Stone, 'The Rise of the Nuclear Family in Early Modern England: The Patriarchal Stage', in *Family in History*, ed. Charles E. Roserberg (Philadelphia, 1975), p. 25.
4. Gordon J. Schochet, *Patriarchalism in Political Thought* (New York, 1975), p. 7.
5. Cited by Schochet, pp. 79-80.
6. Cited by Schochet, p. 80.
7. Cited by Schochet, p. 80.
8. Cited by Schochet, p. 87.
9. Cited by Schochet, p. 89.
10. Cited by Schochet, pp. 91-92.
11. *Some Reflections upon Marriage.* This book first appeared in 1700. The present citation is taken from the appendix to the fourth edition, 1730, pp. 106-7.
12. Thomas Hobbes, *Leviathan* (1651), ed. Michael Oakshott, pp. 112-113.
13. John Locke, *Two Treatises of Government* (1690), ed. Peter Laslett (Cambridge, 1960), II, p. 286.
14. *Shakespeare and the Nature of Women* (London, 1975), p. 79.
15. All quotations from Shakespeare are taken from the Tudor Edition of Shakespeare's complete works edited by Peter Alexander (The English Language Book Society, 1964).
16. See Edmund Morgan, p. 140.
17. Benjamin Wadsworth, *Well-Ordered Family* (1712), cited by Morgan, p. 139.
18. John Cotton, *Christ the Fountaine of Life* (1651), cited by Morgan, p. 7.
19. *The Revolution of the Saints: A Study in the Origins of Radical Politics* (London, 1965), p. 47.
20. Christopher Hill, *Society and Puritanism in Pre-Revolutionary England* (London, 1967), p. 446.
21. *The Family, Sex and Marriage in England 1500-1800* (London, 1977), p. 169. Quotations are from the abridged edition (Harmondsworth, 1977), unless otherwise stated.
22. Morgan, p. 17.
23. Cited by Morgan, p. 18.
24. 'The Changing Family', *TLS*, October 21, 1977.

25. Louis B. Wright, *Middle-Class Culture in Elizabethan England* (Ithaca, 1935), p. 201.

26. Cited by Juliet Dusinberre, p. 31.

27. William Perkins, *Christian Oeconomie* (1609), cited by Dusinberre, p. 24.

28. Op. cit., p. 227.

29. Ibid., p. 222.

30. Ibid., p. 204.

31. *The Revels History of Drama in English* (London, 1977), III, p. 263.

32. *The Female Eunuch* (London, 1971), p. 208.

33. Ibid., p. 209. How wrong the assessment of a mere male can be is perhaps best seen in the remarks of Quiller-Couch in his Introduction to the New Cambridge edition of the play (1928), page xvi. He thought that to any 'modern civilized man, reading *A Shrew* or *The Shrew* in his library, the whole Petruchio business . . . may seem . . . tiresome – and to any modern woman, not an antiquary, *offensive* as well.' (Italics mine).

34. Op. cit., p. 320.

35. Hobbes, *Leviathan*, p. 83.

36. Ibid., p. 81.

37. Cited by Thomas H. Fujimura, *The Restoration Comedy of Wit* (Princeton, 1952), p. 41.

38. G. M. Trevelyan, *English Social History* (Harmondsworth, 1974), p. 142.

39. Ibid., p. 275.

40. *The World We Have Lost* (London, Second ed., 1976), p. 142.

41. Trevelyan, p. 276.

42. See Christopher Hill, *Puritanism and Revolution* (London, 1968), p. 207.

43. Cited by L. C. Knights, *Drama and Society in the Age of Jonson* (New York, 1968), p. 37.

44. J. P. Kenyon, *Stuart England* (London, 1978), pp. 19–20.

45. *The Worth of a Penny, or a Caution to keep Money (1647)*, cited by L. C. Knights, p. 123.

46. Ibid., p. 121.

47. The great moral damage that this 'economy of plenty' had done to England by 1778 is to be seen in the following statement of Dr Johnson in *Life of Samuel Johnson* by James Boswell (Everyman edn.), II, p. 189: 'Subordination is sadly broken down in this age. No man now has the same authority which his father had – except a gaoler. No man has it over his servants; it is diminished in our colleges, nay in our grammar schools. . . . There are many causes the chief of which is, I think, the great increase of money. . . . Gold and silver destroy feudal subordination. But besides there is a general relaxation of reverence. No son now depends upon his father as in former times. Paternity used to be considered as of itself a great thing which had a right to many claims. That is, in general, reduced to very small bonds.' It is clear, however, that not all Englishmen would have agreed with Dr Johnson. England had become the leader of the world in this period and it is only conservatives like Dr Johnson who bewailed the consequences of this 'progress'.

48. 'The Position of Women', *The Legacy of the Middle Ages*, ed. C. G. Crump and E. F. Jacob (Oxford, 1926), p. 417.

49. Ibid., p. 417.
50. Cited by Violet A. Wilson, *Society Women of Shakespeare's Time* (London, 1924), p. 9.
51. Cited by Carrol Camden, *The Elizabethan Woman* (Washington, 1952), p. 44.
52. See Ruth Kelso, *Doctrine for the Lady of the Renaissance* (Urbana, 1956), p. 46.
53. *Romeo and Juliet*, IV.iv. Robert Brustein in 'The Monstrous Regiment of Women', *Renaissance and Modern Essays*, ed. G. R. Hibbard, (London, 1966) p. 35, fails to appreciate the distinctly superior treatment of upper-class women in Shakespeare's plays when he lumps Shakespeare with other Elizabethan and Jacobean playwrights. The latter almost invariably depicted 'upper-class female character . . . as a sink of evils, a stew, a loathsome pit of rottenness, a painted image, a gilded pill, a decked idol of May-tide, a skin full of lust, a school of uncleanness'. Shakespeare, however, never sneers at women simply because they are upper-class or lower-class. In fact, the only characters in Shakespeare who have a low opinion of women are villains. When heroes start attacking them, they are clearly expressing their personal agony rather than offering a cool judgment on the female sex.
54. See Ruth Kelso, op. cit., p. 46.
55. Alice Clark, *Working Life of Women in the Seventeenth Century* (1919; reprinted London, 1968), p. 41.
56. See L. C. Knights, p. 115.
57. *The Wealth of Nations* (World's Classics), I, p. 369.
58. J. Boswell, *Life of Johnson*, I, p. 422.
59. See L. C. Knights, p. 20.
60. Ibid., p. 112.
61. Op. cit., p. 127.
62. *Love and Liberty*, (London, 1981), p. 169.
63. Ibid., p. 169.
64. Stone, *The Family* (unabridged), p. 660.
65. See Stone, *The Family*, p. 142.
66. cf. Martin Luther's view: 'Women should remain at home, sit still, keep house, and bear and bring up children'. See Stone, *The Family* (unabridged), pp. 203–4.
67. Taken from Margaret George, 'From "Goodwife" to "Mistress": The Transformation of the Female in Bourgeois Culture', *Science and Society* (1973), p. 171.
68. Op. cit., p. 122.
69. Cited by Douglas Bush, *English Literature in the Earlier Seventeenth Century* (Oxford, 1945), p. 22.
70. See M. Phillips and W. S. Tomkinson, *English Women in Life and Letters* (Oxford, 1927), pp. 184–186.
71. *Occasional Thoughts in reference to a Vertuous or Christian Life* (1694). The reference here is to the 1705 ed., pp. 195–97.
72. *The Comedy of Manners* (London, 1970), p. 34.
73. Lawrence Stone, *The Family*, p. 166.
74. Cited by Stone, p. 167.

75. Ibid., p. 167.
76. John Wain, *Preliminary Essays* (London, 1957), p. 4.
77. *The World Turned Upside Down* (London, 1972), p. 332.
78. 'Restoration Comedy: The Reality and the Myth' (1937), *Restoration Drama*, ed. John Loftis, (New York, 1966), pp. 16–17.
79. Op. cit., p. 2.
80. Harold Love, *Congreve* (Oxford, 1974), p. 60.
81. *A Christian Directory* (1673), cited by Mary Lyndon Shanley in 'Marriage Contract and Social Contract in Seventeenth Century Political Thought', *Western Political Quarterly*, March, 1979, p. 79.
82. *A Family Well-Ordered* (1699), cited by Morgan, p. 143.
83. *An Explanation of the Solemn Advice* (1683), cited by Morgan, p. 143.
84. *Two Treatises of Government*, II, p. 322.
85. *The Educational Writings of John Locke*, ed. James L. Axtell (Cambridge, 1968), p. 145.
86. Ibid., p. 145.
87. Ibid., p. 202.
88. *The Family*, pp. 122, 118.
89. James L. Axtell, pp. 155, 176, 186, 202. Italics Locke's.
90. *Two Treatises of Government*, II, pp. 337.
91. Ibid., p. 340.
92. Ibid., p. 337.
93. Ibid., p. 339.
94. Op. cit., p. 89.
95. Cited by Mary Lyndon Shanley, p. 89.
96. W. Whately, *The Bride Bush* (1617), p. 36.

CHAPTER II

1. *A Fruitful and Useful Discourse touching the Honour due from Children to Parents and the Duty of Parents towards their Children* (1656), p. 94, cited by Morgan, p. 78.
2. John Norton, *Abel being Dead* (1658), cited by Morgan, p. 103.
3. William Ames, *Conscience with the Power and Cases thereof* (1643), cited by Morgan, p. 106.
4. Cited by Morgan, p. 107.
5. *English Domestic Relations 1487–1654* (New York, 1917), p. 124.
6. Cited by Powell, p. 131.
7. Ibid., p. 156.
8. Thomas Becon, *Book of Matrimony* (1564), cited by William and Malleville Haller, 'The Puritan Art of Love', *Huntington Library Quarterly*, 1942, p. 245.
9. See G. B. Harrison, *An Elizabethan Journal, being a record of those things most talked of during the years 1591–94* (London, 1928), pp. 92–93.
10. Ibid., p. 361.
11. Cited by Catherine M. Dunn, 'The Changing Image of Woman in Renaissance Society and Literature', in *What Manner of Woman*, ed. Marlene Springer (New York, 1977), pp. 16-17.

12. Cited by C. L. Powell, p. 15.
13. Louis Wright, op. cit., p. 210.
14. Cited by L. C. Knights, p. 126.
15. Lawrence Stone, *The Crisis of the Aristocracy, 1558–1641* (Abridged edition, Oxford, 1967), pp. 271, 273.
16. Ibid., p. 273: There were various other methods which could be used to subdue a stubborn girl who refused to marry a person of her parents' choice, however abominable the proposal. As Dekker said in *The Seven Deadly Sinnes of London*: 'if she refuse this living death (for lesse than a death it cannot be vento her), She is threatened to be left an out-cast, cursd for disobedience, raild at daily, and reuylde howerlye'.
17. Ibid., p. 273.
18. Ibid., p. 279. That children did sometimes defy all restrictions is seen in the following case mentioned by Lawrence Stone in *The Family, Sex and Marriage* (unabridged), pp. 104–5:

> In 1598 the rising young shipwright Phineas Pett married Anne Niccols. Both his parents were dead, but he had two powerful and influential brothers to contend with, upon whom he depended for patronage in his career. He records that 'I did not neglect my wooing, having taken such a liking of the maiden that I determined resolutely (by God's help) either to match with her or never to marry any: the which I with much difficulty ... at length achieved, all my own kindred being much against my matching with her.'

Other examples of young men successfully defying the wishes of their kin would not be hard to find, even if they were the exception to the rule.

19. Cited by Stone in *The Crisis of the Aristocracy*, p. 279.
20. *Elizabethan Love Stories*, ed. T.J.B. Spencer (Harmondsworth, 1968), p. 205.
21. Arthur Brooke's long poem which is Shakespeare's main source for the play, mentions the powers that Roman fathers had over their children 'by lawe':

> Whom they not onely might pledge, alienate, and sell,
> (When so they stoode in need) but more, if children did rebell,
> The parentes had the power, of lyfe and sodayn death.

Narrative and Dramatic Sources of Shakespeare, ed. Geoffrey Bullough (London, 1957), I, p. 336.

22. "Thou that beget'st him that did thee beget': Transformation in "Pericles" and "The Winter's Tale" ', *Shakespeare Survey*, 22, 1969, p. 61.
23. See Coppelia Kahn, 'Coming of Age in Verona', *Modern Language Studies*, 8, 1977–8, pp. 5–22.
24. cf. his rebuke to Tybalt when Tybalt tells him that he will not 'endure' Romeo at Capulet's party:

> He shall be endur'd.
> What, goodman boy! I say he shall. Go to;
> Am I master here or you? Go to!					(I.v.76–78)

cf. his praise for Romeo:

> A bears him like a portly gentleman;

And, to say truth, Verona brags of him
To be a virtuous and well-govern'd youth.
I would not for the wealth of all this town
Here in my house do him disparagement.   (I.v.64–68)

25. Lawrence Stone, *The Family* (unabridged), p. 7.
26. Maynard Mack, *Rescuing Shakespeare*, International Shakespeare Association Occasional Paper No. 1 (Oxford, 1979), p. 15.
27. Ibid., p. 14.
28. Op. cit., I, p. 461.
29. Stone claims that arranged marriage in the period worked out 'not too badly' partly because 'the expectations of happiness from it' were not set 'unrealistically high' and partly because 'it is a fact that sentiment can fairly easily adapt to social command.' The condition for the success of such a marriage, according to him, is 'not too great a discrepancy in age, physical attractiveness or temperament.' (*Family*, p. 104).
30. Cited by John Halkett, *Milton and the Idea of Matrimony* (New Haven, 1970), p. 10.
31. Also cited by John Halkett, p. 12.
32. D. W. Harding, 'Shakespeare's Final View of Women', *TLS*, November 30, 1979, p. 59.
33. M. C. Bradbrook calls him a 'pedant' in *Shakespeare: The Poet in his World* (London, 1978), p. 11.
34. Keith Thomas, 'The Double Standard', *Journal of the History of Ideas*, XX, 1959, p. 202.
35. Van Meteren, a Dutchman, while comparing the greater freedom enjoyed by English women than by German or Dutch women in 1575, described England as 'the Paradise of married women'. But he added: 'The girls who are not yet married are kept much more vigorously and strictly than in the Low Countries.' Cited by Dover Wilson in *Life in Shakespeare's England* (London, 1915), p. 9.
36. Peter Laslett, *Family Life and Illicit Love in Earlier Generations* (Cambridge, 1977), p. 104.
37. *Shakespeare's Comedies* (Oxford, 1960), p. 220.
38. See Nicholas Knight, 'Patrimony and Shakespeare's Daughters', *University of Hartford Studies in Literature*, 1977, pp. 175–186.
39. 'Love, Marriage, and Money in Shakespeare's Theatre and Shakespeare's England', *The Elizabethan Theatre VI*, ed. G. R. Hibbard, (London, 1978) p. 154.
40. *Liberty and Love* (1981), p. 167.
41. Op. cit., p. 61.
42. See G. S. Alleman, *Matrimonial Law and the Materials of Restoration Comedy* (Washington, Pa., 1942), pp. 84–92.
43. *The Family*, p. 280.
44. *The Children's Petition* (1669), cited by Stone, *The Family*, p. 279.
45. *The Family*, p. 273.
46. James L. Axtell, p. 171.
47. *The English Humorists* (Everymans Library), pp. 58-9.

48. Cited by P.F. Vernon, 'The Treatment of Marriage in the Drama 1660-1700', (London University M.A. Dissertation, 1960), p. 26.
49. Ibid., p. 26.

CHAPTER III

1. Op. cit., p. 61.
2. 'Age and Authority in Early Modern England', *Proceedings of the British Academy*, I. xii, 1976, p. 207.
3. cf. *King Lear*, I.v.41-42: 'Thou shouldst not have been old / till thou hadst been wise.'
4. cf. The Statute of Artificers of 1563 which argued that 'until a man is grown into twenty-three years, he, for the most part but not always, is wild, without judgment and not of sufficient experience to govern himself'. Cited by Eric Midwinter, *Nineteenth Century Education* (1970, rpt. London, 1979), p. 6.
5. 'Age and Authority', p. 247.
6. Cited by Keith Thomas, p. 238.
7. Ibid., p. 239.
8. Samuel Shaw, *The True Christian Test* (1682), p. 123.
9. C. H. Hobday, 'The Social Background of "King Lear"', *Modern Quarterly Miscellany*, 1960, p. 47.
10. How unnatural it is for parents to kneel before children is perhaps best seen in Coriolanus' reaction to his mother's kneeling before him:

> What's this?
> Your knees to me? To your corrected son?
> Then let the pebbles on the hungry beach
> Fillip the stars. Then let the mutinous winds,
> Strike the proud cedars 'gainst the fiery sun,
> Murd'ring impossibility, to make
> What cannot be, slight work.   (*Coriolanus*, V.iii.57-63)

11. 'The Theme of Honour in *All's Well that Ends Well*', *Shakespeare's Later Comedies*, ed. D. J. Palmer (London, 1971), p. 15.
12. Cited by Bradbrook, pp. 17-18.
13. Ibid., pp. 23-4.
14. For an excellent analysis of Hamlet's motives, see Mythili Kaul's article, 'Hamlet and Polonius', *Hamlet Studies*, Delhi, Vol. 2, Summer 1980, pp. 13-24.
15. See the New Arden edition of Shakespeare's *Poems*, ed. F. T. Prince, (London, 1961), p. xxiii.
16. *Crabbed Age and Youth: The Old Men and Women in the Restoration Comedy of Manners* (Durham, N.C., 1947), p. 11.
17. R. W. Desai, *Johnson on Shakespeare* (Delhi, 1979), p. 133.
18. *Shakespeare's Happy Comedies* (London, 1962), p. 84.
19. See R. C. Sharma, *Themes and Conventions in Comedy of Manners* (Bombay, 1965), p. 126.
20. H. B. Charlton, *Shakespeare Comedy* (London, 1938), p. 60.
21. 'Age and Authority in Early Modern England', pp. 245, 247.

22. Elisabeth Mignon in *Crabbed Age and Youth: The Old Men and Women in the Restoration Comedy of Manners*, p. 21, has rightly said that 'There seems to be no middle or transition age in Restoration comedy: they are young; then suddenly they are old.'

23. Cited by Elisabeth Mignon, p. 121.

24. Harold Love's assessment of Lady Wishfort, though perhaps too generous, is refreshing: 'And she is tougher than Falstaff in that she is able to survive the shattering of her deepest illusion. With Mirabell lost for good, she is back in the dance . . . One would hardly wish to share her predicament in *that* world, her vulgarity, her stupidity, her blindness, but these things are redeemed for us by others, by her immense powers of resilience, her unquenchable optimism, and the sheer voracity of her hunger for life. It is certainly better to be a Lady Wishfort than to be a Marwood, or a Petulant, or a Witwoud, or a Fainall.' *Congreve*, p. 104.

25. Cited by R. C. Sharma, op. cit., p. 150.

26. *The First Modern Comedies*, (Cambridge, Mass., 1967), p. 215.

CHAPTER IV

1. Laurence Lerner, *Love and Marriage : Literature and its Social Context* (London, 1979), p. 1.

2. See what Dryden's Cleopatra says to Octavia in *All for Love*, Act III:

> If you have suffered, I have suffered more.
> You bear the specious title of a wife,
> To gild your cause, and draw the pitying world
> To favour it: The world condemns poor me,
> For I have lost my honour, lost my fame,
> And stained the glory of my royal house,
> And all to bear the branded name of mistress.

3. Op cit., p. 7.

4. Ibid., pp. 15–16.

5. Ruth Kelso in *Doctrine for the Lady of the Renaissance* (1956), p. 20, cites Firanzuolo in whose *Dialogo delle Bellezze* (1548) woman says to man: 'We are one and the same thing, of the same perfection; you have to seek us and love us, and we have to seek you and love you; you without us are nothing, and we without you are nothing; *in you is our perfection, in us is yours.*' (Italics mine).

6. Katharine M. Rogers, *The Troublesome Helpmate* (Seattle, Wa., 1966), p. 160.

7. Coppelia Kahn, '*The Taming of the Shrew*: Shakespeare's Mirror of Marriage', *The Authority of Experience*, edited by Arlyn Diamond and Lee R. Edwards, (Amherst, Mass., 1977), p. 85.

8. 'The Basis of Shakespearian Comedy', *Essays and Studies*, III, 1950, p. 12.

9. Op. cit., p. 100.

10. Ibid., p. 100.

11. Op. cit., pp. 209, 207.

12. See also Geoffrey Bullough, 'Polygamy among the Reformers', *Renaissance and Modern Essays*, ed. G. R. Hibbard, pp. 5–23.

13. Bullough cites Martin Luther's view on the question of Henry VIII's divorce of Katharine: 'Rather let him take another queen, following the example of the patriarchs, who had many wives even before the law of Moses sanctioned the practice, but let him not thrust his present wife from her royal position.' Bullough adds: 'It is said that the Pope also urged Henry to commit bigamy rather than divorce his Queen', (pp. 8–9).

14. *The Crisis of the Aristocracy 1558–1641*, p. 298.

15. Cf. Alfred Harbage, *Shakespeare and the Royal Traditions* (Bloomington, 1971), p. 207: 'in thirty two of his thirty eight plays no act of fornication or adultery occurs in the course of action'.

16. Ibid., pp. 192–194.

17. Op. cit., p. 25.

18. Cited by W. Lee Ustick, 'Advice to a Son: A type of Seventeenth Century Conduct Book', *Studies in Philology* 1932, p. 411.

19. *Huntington Library Quarterly* (1942) p. 245. Bullinger's quotation comes from *The Christian State of Matrimony* (1541), and Henry Smith's from *Preparative to Marriage* (1591).

20. Cited by the Hallers, p. 259.

21. Ibid., p. 261.

22. Ibid., p. 269.

23. Ibid., pp. 244–5.

24. Op. cit., p. 209.

25. Carol Thomas Neely, 'Women and Issue in *The Winter's Tale*', *Philological Quarterly*, Vol. 57, Spring 1978, Number, 2, p. 181.

26. Even Benedick is conscious of the difficulties involved in achieving a successful marriage with Beatrice: 'Thou and I are too wise to woo peaceably' (*Much Ado*, V.II. 63). What Richard Brathwait said in *The English Gentlewoman* (1631) is quite typical of contemporary thinkers: 'wit in a woman is like Oyle in the flame, which either kindleth to great virtue, or extreme vanity', cited by Carol Camden, *The Elizabethan Woman*, p. 63. Most early writers on the woman's question saw greater possibility of vanity – and hence of vice – than of virtue in a witty woman. It is not surprising that most men in the seventeenth and eighteenth centuries distrusted women with cultivated minds. Damaris Lady Masham expressed 'an apprehension that should daughters be perceived to understand any learned language or be conversant in books, they might be in danger of not finding husbands, so few men, as do, relishing these accomplishments in a lady.' *Occasional Thoughts*, (1705 ed.) p. 197. Jane Austen would have agreed with Lady Masham. She knew the risks that a talented woman took in her society. This is what she says in Chapter XIV of *Northanger Abbey*: 'A woman, especially, if she have the misfortune of knowing anything, should conceal it as she can . . . a good-looking girl, with an affectionate heart and a very ignorant mind, cannot fail of attracting a clever young man.'

27. Another description – somewhat more concrete than Benedick's though equally conventional – of a woman's qualities occurs in *King John* II. i. 426 ff.:

If lusty love should go in quest of beauty,
Where should he find it fairer than in Blanch?
If zealous love should go in search of virtue,
Where should he find it purer than in Blanch?
If love ambitions sought a match of birth,
Whose veins bound richer blood than Lady Blanch?

28. Pandarus in *Troilus and Cressida* is not a reliable witness. Moreover, he has to impress Cressida. But his enumeration of the qualities of a man whom a woman may admire is much more comprehensive: 'Is not birth, beauty, good shape, discourse, manhood, learning, gentleness, virtue, youth, liberality, and such like, the spice and salt that season a man?' (I.ii.244 ff.).

29. *The Bodley Head Bernard Shaw: Complete Plays with their Prefaces* (3rd ed. London, 1971), Vol. III, pp. 572–3.

30. Stone, *The Family*, p. 81.

31. Cited by Dusinberre, p. 117.

32. Martha Andersen-Thom, 'Thinking About Women in their Prosperous Act: A Reply to Juliet Dusinberre's *Shakespeare and the Nature of Women'*, *Shakespeare Studies*, 11, 1978, p. 263: 'in the hierarchical and patriarchal culture of England, a popular ideology held that speech is a gift much abused by women. The Temptress talks to seduce men, the Shrew talks to emasculate men, the Gossip talks to annoy men, and the talk of the Prophetess is often equivocal and baffling.'

33. Carol Thomas Neely, 'Women and Men in *Othello:* "What should such a fool / Do with so good a woman?" ', *Shakespeare Studies*, 10, 1978, p. 140.

34. Op. cit., p. 73.

35. Cited by Dusinberre, p. 72.

36. Also cited by Dusinberre, p. 72.

37. Op. cit., pp. 207–8.

38. See Carol Neely's excellent article on 'Women and Men in *Othello'*, op. cit.

39. Ibid., p. 136.

40. Cited by Juliet Dusinberre, p. 112.

41. Ibid., p. 115.

42. *Rescuing Shakespeare*, International Shakespeare Association Occasional Paper No. I, 1979, p. 8.

43. Wright, op. cit., p. 204.

44. Op. cit., p. 44.

45. Martha Andersen-Thom, op. cit., p. 273.

46. Op. cit., p. 228.

47. Cited by William and Maleville Haller, op. cit., pp. 251–252.

48. See Ruth Kelso, pp. 93–94.

49. Mary Astell, op. cit., p. 7.

50. The Restoration woman had clearly more avenues of self-expression available to her.

51. *A Room of One's Own* (15th impression, London, 1974), pp. 70–73.

52. Op. cit., p. 274.

53. Op. cit., p. 308.

54. How far some feminists can go to 'rewrite' Shakespeare is clear from a report

that appeared in *London Times* on July 27, 1978: 'The Avon Touring Company at Bristol is changing the sex of Shakespeare's characters in order to discriminate in favour of women. It believes women have too few parts. So in its production of *Measure for Measure*, Claudio becomes Claudia and Pompey becomes Poppea. Carol Braithwaite, their administrator, said the Company felt there was no longer any excuse for doing Shakespeare or any playwright with the sex roles written by the author.' Martin Huckerby, 'Arts Diary', *Times*, July 27, 1978.

55. Op. cit., pp. 148–149.
56. Cited by Juliet Dusinberre, p. 83.
57. *Society and Puritanism in Pre-Revolutionary England* (London, 1964), p. 351.
58. 'The Rape of Shakespeare's Lucrece', *Shakespeare Studies*, 9, 1976, p. 53.
59. Interestingly enough, the idea is not absent even from the mind of a twentieth century male as is seen in an interesting book entitled *Gender Advertisements* by Erving Goffman (1979) where we find the following revealing sentence: 'A male pictured with a female sometimes appears to employ an extending arm, in effect marking the boundary of his social property and guarding it against encroachment.' It is useful to remember that advertisements reflect almost accurately, though somewhat disturbingly, contemporary attitudes.
60. 'The Double Standard', *Journal of the History of Ideas*, XX, 1959, pp. 199–200.
61. *The World Turned Upside Down*, p. 249.
62. This savagery can sometimes occur even when the woman concerned is a mother or a daughter as in *Hamlet* or *King Lear*.
63. See Carol Thomas Neely's illuminating article on this subject, 'Women and Issue in *The Winter's Tale*', *Philological Quarterly*, 1978, p. 185.
64. *Complete Works*, ed. J. P. Kenyon (London, 1969), p. 279.
65. Luciana in *The Comedy of Errors* would perhaps agree with Dr Johnson that if a man conducts his extra-marital affairs discreetly, he does not do much harm to his wife:

> If you did wed my sister for her wealth,
> Then for her wealth's sake use her with more kindness;
> *Of, if you like elsewhere, do it by stealth*:
> Muffle your false love with some show of blindness;
> Let not my sister read it in your eyes;
> Be not thy tongue thy own shame's orator;
> Look sweet, speak fair, become disloyalty;
> Apparel vice like virtue's harbinger;
> Be secret-false. What need she be acquainted?

(III.iii.5 ff.)
(Italics mine)

66. Cited by Keith Thomas, 'The Double Standard,' p. 209.
67. Op. cit. p. 52.
68. See Rodney Poisson, 'Death for Adultery: A note on *Othello*', *Shakespeare Quarterly*, Vol. 28, November 1977, p. 90.

69. Ibid., p. 90.
70. Eva Figes, *Tragedy and Social Evolution* (London, 1976), p. 108.
71. 'Women and Men in *Othello'*, op. cit., pp. 141-2.
72. How easily — and without any special provocation — men pass such a judgment on women can be seen in *King John* where the king tells Robert Faulconbridge, the elder brother of Philip the bastard:

> Sirrah, your brother is legitimate:
> Your father's wife did after wedlock bear him,
> And if she did play false, the fault was hers;
> Which fault lies on the hazards of all husbands
> That marry wives. (I.i.116–120)

73. *The Bride Woman's Counsellor* (1700), p. 4.

CHAPTER V

1. D. H. Lawrence, *Women in Love*, Chapter 16, cited by Brian Morris, *Congreve*, p. ix.
2. 'The Challenge of Restoration Comedy', *Restoration Drama*, ed. John Loftis, p. 39.
3. *Seventeenth Century English Literature* (London, 1950), p. 153.
4. Ian Watt, *The Rise of the Novel (Harmondsworth, 1976), p. 157.*
5. The seemingly 'positive advances' in the position of women in the Restoration period had 'the effect of stripping away from marriage one by one many of those external economic, social and psychological supports which normally serve as powerful reinforcing agencies to hold together the nuclear family'. Stone, *The Family*, p. 246.
6. Ian Watt, p. 157.
7. Angelo in *Measure for Measure*, who was betrothed to Mariana but who broke the betrothel because between the 'time of the contract and limit of the solemnity her brother Frederick was wreck'd at sea, having in that perished vessel the dowry of his sister' (III.i.217 ff.) is still quite a familiar type in some developing societies.
8. P. F. Vernon, 'Marriage of Convenience and the Moral Code of Restoration Comedy', *Essays in Criticism*, 1962, p. 373.
9. Cited by J. B. Botsford, *English Society in the Eighteenth Century* (London, 1924), p. 151.
10. Op. cit., p. 20.
11. Cited by Ian Watt, p. 161.
12. Op. cit., p. 375.
13. *Some Passages of the Life and Death of . . . John Earl of Rochester* (1680), pp. 100–1.
14. *A Short View* (1698), p. 24.
15. So does J. W. Dodds who conjectures whether 'Mrs Friendall's citadel of virtue remained intact beyond the fifth act', *Thomas Southerne, Dramatist* (New Haven, 1933), p. 87.
16. Surely Dorimant holds such an honourable opinion of the female sex, 'I have

known many women make a difficulty of losing a maidenhead, who have afterwards made none of making a cuckold:', *The Man of Mode*, I.i.

17. See Eric Rothstein, *'The Beaux' Strategem'*, in *The Recruiting Officer and the Beaux' Stratagem*, ed. Raymond A. Auselment (London, Casebook Series), p. 147.

18. See Robert D. Hume, 'Marital Discord in English Comedy from Dryden to Fielding', *Modern Philology*, 74 Feb. 1977, p. 265.

19. See Peter Malekin, *Liberty and Love*, pp. 188–9. The book contains a thought-provoking chapter on marriage in Restoration comedy.

20. Cited by Michael Cordner in his note on p. 70 in New Mermaids edition of the play (1976).

21. 'Women and the Civil War Sects', *Past and Present*, No. 13, April 1958, p. 55.

22. Cited by Keith Thomas, ibid, p. 57.

23. *The Vertuous Wife is the Glory of her Husband* (1667), p. 9.

24. *The Ladies Calling, Part I* (1673), p. 40.

25. *The Bride-Womans Counsellor* (1700), p. 4.

26. Ibid., p. 7.

27. Op. cit., p. 7.

28. *The Troublesome Helpmate*, p. 160.

29. *Of Dramatic Poesy*, ed. George Watson (London, 1962), I, p. 107.

30. 'The Restoration Comedy: The Reality and the Myth', in *Restoration Drama*, ed. John Loftis, pp. 13, 16–17.

31. George Watson, I, p. 149.

32. Op. cit., p. 3.

33. See Peter Malekin, p. 182.

34. Introduction to *Restoration Comedies* (Oxford, 1970), ed. Dennis Davison, p.xv.

35. Op. cit., pp. 57–8.

36. Op. cit., p. 162.

37. *Restoration Tragedies* (Oxford, 1977), ed. James Sutherland, p. vii.

38. *Restoration Drama*, ed. John Loftis, p. 13.

39. See Jean Gagen, 'Congreve's Mirabel and the Ideal of the Gentleman', *PMLA*, Vol. 79, 1964, p. 424.

40. See Robert D. Hume, 'The Myth of the Rake in "Restoration" Comedy', *Studies in the Literary Imagination*, 10, Spring 1977, p. 40.

41. See Jean Gagen, p. 424.

42. Epilogue to Farquhar's *The Inconstant* (1702).

43. *The Works of John Dryden*, Vol. VIII, (California, 1967) p. 238.

44. See Sir Richard Blackmore's Preface to *Prince Arthur* (1695).

45. Germaine Greer, Op. cit., p. 209.

46. Virginia Ogden Birdsall in *Wild Civilty* (Indiana, 1970), p. 28, says that 'in Restoration comedy, the power instinct and the sex instinct are, in fact, really working in the same direction and indeed cannot be legitimately separated.'

47. Margaret Lamb McDonald, *The Independent Woman in the Restoration Comedy of Manners* (Salzburg, 1976), p. 17.

48. Laurence Lerner, op. cit., p. 1.

49. See what Sir John Brute in Vanbrugh's *The Provok'd Wife* says: 'The woman's well enough; she has no vice that I know of, but she's a wife, and – damn a wife!' (III.iii).

50. A phrase of Dr Johnson cited by Keith Thomas, 'The Double Standard', p. 209.
51. Vernon, pp. 377-78.
52. 'The Myth of the Rake', p. 34.
53. *Halifax: Complete Works*, ed. J. P. Kenyon (Harmondsworth, 1969), p. 279.
54. *The Development of English Drama in the late Seventeenth Century* (Oxford, 1976) p. 89.
55. Op. cit., p. 379.
56. 'The Quest for Good Society: Friends and Families in Restoration Comedy' (Ph.D. Dissertation, Harvard, 1960), pp. 102-3.
57. *English Literature of the Late Seventeenth Century* (Oxford, 1969), p. 113.
58. 'William Wycherley', *Restoration Drama*, ed. J.R. Brown and Bernard Harris (London, 1965), pp. 76–77.
59. See Margaret Lamb McDonald, op. cit., p. 16: 'In Beatrice's Renaissance world we find no sense of wariness over a problematic future. Her milieu blesses and upholds the glory of marriage, and she herself reflects the security of life in Leonato's honest household. We experience no sense of conflict or apprehension over the stability of marriage that will characterise the Restoration comedies a century later.'
60. Op. cit., p. 160.
61. *Etherege and the Seventeenth Century Comedy* (New Haven, 1957), p. 73.
62. *Three Restoration Comedies* (Harmondsworth, 1968), p. 21.
63. Hobbes, *Leviathan*, p. 81.
64. Ibid., p. 131.
65. Virginia Ogden Birdsall, *Wild Civility*, p. 25.
66. 'The State of Nature and the State of War: A Reconsideration of *The Man of Mode*', *University of Toronto Quarterly*, XXXIX, 1959, p. 62.
67. *A Serious Call to Devout and Holy Life* (1728; reprinted London, 1955), pp. 247–8.
68. *Likenesses of Truth in Elizabethan and Restoration Drama* (Oxford, 1972), p. 89.
69. *The Development of English Drama*, (Oxford, 1976), p. 89.
70. *English Literature of the Late Seventeenth Century*, p. 111.
71. Op. cit., p. 179.
72. Ibid., p. 179.
73. Op. cit., p. 91.
74. See Brian Morris' Introduction to *Congreve*, pp. viii-ix.
75. See D. R. M. Wilkinson, *The Comedy of Habit* (1964), p. 33, cited by Harold Love, *Congreve*, p. 110.
76. 'Heroic Tragedy', in *Restoration Drama*, ed. J.R. Brown and Bernard Harris, p. 154.
77. Ibid., p. 154.
78. Kenneth Muir, *The Comedy of Manners* (London, 1970), p. 115.
79. Thomas H. Fujimura, *The Restoration Comedy of Wit*, p. 187. 187.
80. *Preliminary Essays* (London, 1957), p. 21.
81. Op. cit., p. 189.
82. Ibid., p. 189.

83. Op. cit., p. 275. See also A.N. Kaul's important though somewhat neglected discussion of Restoration comedy in *The Action of English Comedy* (Yale, 1970) for a different point of view. He finds *The Way of the World* 'an insufferably dull play' precisely because the 'villain' Fainall and the 'hero' Mirabel — 'speak, think, and act alike' (p. 101).

84. '*The Way of the World*: Congreve's Moment of Truth', *The Southern Speech Journal*, Vol. XXV, Winter 1959, Number 2, p. 89.

85. Op. cit., pp. 116–118.

86. Op. cit., pp. 135–6.

87. Op. cit., p. 16.

88. Maximillian E. Novak, *William Congreve* (New York, 1971), p. 145.

89. Ibid., pp. 145–6.

90. –Op; cit., pp. 27, 34, 52.

91. 'Mirabel and Restoration Comedy', *William Congreve*, ed. Brian Morris, p. 42.

92. Op. cit., p. 91.

93. Ibid., pp. 41–2.

94. Ibid., p. 18.

95. Ibid., p. 91.

APPENDIX

1. *Kalidas*, Second Series (Pondicherry, 1954), p. 76. Also in *Sri Aurobindo Birth Centenary Library* (De Luxe Edition, Pondicherry, 1972), Vol. III, p. 285. I owe this reference to V. Y. Kantak.

2. *Shaw on Shakespeare*, ed. Edwin Wilson (New York, 1961), p. 201.

3. *Rescuing Shakespeare*, p. 7.

4. Ibid., p. 8.

5. V. Y. Kantak in a private communication to the author.

6. Op. cit., p. 201.

7. See his edition of *Coriolanus* in the New Swan Shakespeare Advanced Series (London, 1975), p. xxxvii.

8. 'Women and Issue in *The Winter's Tale*', op. cit., p. 183.

SELECT BIBLIOGRAPHY

Alleman, G. S., *Matrimonial Law and the Materials of Restoration Comedy*, (Wallingford, Pa. 1942.)

Anderson-Thom, Martha, 'Thinking About Women and Their Prosperous Art: A Reply to Juliet Dusinberre's *Shakespeare and the Nature of* Women', *Shakespeare Studies*, 11 (1978).

Astell, Mary, *Some Reflections Upon Marriage* (4th ed., London, 1730; New York, 1970).

Axtell, J. (ed.), *Educational Writings of John Locke* (Cambridge, 1968).

Barber, C. L., ' "Thou that beget'st him that did thee beget": Transformation in "Pericles" and "The Winter's Tale" ', *Shakespeare Survey*, 22 (1969).

Barron, Leon Oser, 'The Quest for the Good Society: Friends and Families in Restoration Comedy' (Harvard University Ph.D. Dissertation, 1960).

Barton, Anne Righter, 'William Wycherley', in *Restoration Drama*, ed. J. R. Brown and Bernard Harris.

—— 'Heroic Tragedy', in *Restoration Drama*, ed. J. R. Brown and Bernard Harris.

Camden, Carol, *The Elizabethan Woman* (London, 1952).

Clark, Alice, *Working Life of Women in the Seventeenth Century* (London, 1919).

Davies, Paul, 'The State of Nature and the State of War: A Reconsideration of *The Man of Mode*', *University of Toronto Quarterly*, XXXIX, 1959.

Diamond, Arlyn & Edwards, Lee R. (eds.), *The Authority of Experience* (Amherst, 1977).

Dusinberre, Juliet, *Shakespeare and the Nature of Women* (London, 1975).

Gagen, Jean, 'Congreve's Mirabel and the Ideal of the Gentleman', *PMLA*, Vol. 79, 1964.

George, Margaret, 'From "Goodwife" to "Mistress": The Transformation of the Female in Bourgeois Culture', *Science and Society* (1973).

Greer, Germaine, *The Female Eunuch* (London, 1971).

Halkett, John, *Milton and the Idea of Matrimony* (New Haven, 1970).

Haller, William and Malleville, 'The Puritan Art of Love', *Huntington Library Quarterly*, 1942.

Harbage, Alfred, *Shakespeare and the Rival Traditions* (Bloomington, 1952).

Harding, D. W., 'Shakespeare's Final view of Women', *TLS*, Nov. 30, 1979.

225

Hawkins, Harriet, *Likenesses of Truth in Elizabethan and Restoration Drama* (Oxford, 1972).

Hibbard, G. R., 'Love, Marriage and Money in Shakespeare's Theatre and Shakespeare's England', *The Elizabethan Theatre*, VI, 1978.

Hill, Christopher, *Society and Puritanism in Pre-Revolutionary England* (London, 1967).

—— *Puritanism and Revolution* (London, 1968).

—— *The World Turned Upside Down* (London, 1972).

Hobday, C. H., 'The Social Background of "King Lear "', *Modern Quarterly Miscellany*, 1960.

Holland, Norman, *The First Modern Comedies* (Cambridge, Mass., 1959).

Hume, Robert D., 'Marital Discord in English Comedy from Dryden to Fielding', *Modern Philology*, 74, 1977.

—— 'The Myth of the Rake in "Restoration Comedy" ', *Studies in the Literary Imagination*, 10, 1977.

—— *The Development of English Drama in the late Seventeenth Century* (Oxford, 1976).

Kahn, Coppelia, '*The Taming of the Shrew*: Shakespeare's Mirror of Marriage', *The Authority of Experience*, ed. Arlyn Diamond & Lee R. Edwards (Amherst, Mass., 1977).

'Coming of Age in Verona', *Modern Language Studies*, 8, 1977–8.

Kaul, A. N., *The Action of English Comedy* (New Haven, 1970).

Kaul, Mythili, 'Hamlet and Polonius', *Hamlet Studies*, Vol. 2, Summer 1980.

Kelso, Ruth, *Doctrine for the Lady of the Renaissance* (Urbana, 1956).

Kenyon, J. P., *Stuart England* (Harmondsworth, 1978).

Knights, L. C., *Drama and Society in the Age of Jonson* (New York, 1968).

—— 'The Challenge of Restoration Comedy', *Restoration Drama*, ed. John Loftis (New York, 1966).

Knight, Nicholas, 'Patrimony and Shakespeare's Daughters', *University of Hartford Studies in Literature*, 1977.

Laslett, Peter, *The World We Have Lost* (1965; second edition, London, 1971).

—— *Family Life and Illicit Love in Earlier Generations* (Cambridge, 1977).

Lenz, Carolyn Ruth Swift, et al. (ed.), *The Woman's Part: Feminist Criticism of Shakespeare* (Urbana, 1980).

Lerner, Laurence, *Love and Marriage: Literature and its Social Context* (London, 1979).

Love, Harold, *Congreve* (Oxford, 1974).

Mack, Maynard, *Rescuing Shakespeare*, International Shakespeare Association Occasional Paper No. I, 1979.

Malekin, Peter, *Love and Liberty: English Literature and Society, 1640–88* (London, 1981).

Mignon, Elisabeth, *Crabbed Age and Youth: The Old Men and Women in Restoration Comedy of Manners* (Durham, N.C., 1947).

Morgan, Edmund S., *The Puritan Family: Religious and Domestic Relations in Seventeenth-Century New England* (New York, 1966).

Muir, Kenneth, *The Comedy of Manners* (London, 1970).

Select Bibliography 227

Neely, Carol Thomas, 'Women and Issue in *The Winter's Tale*', *Philological Quarterly*, Vol. 57, 1978.

—— 'Men and Women in *Othello*: "What should such a fool / Do with so good a woman" ', *Shakespeare Studies*, 10, 1978.

Nolan, Paul T., 'The Way of the World: Congreve's Moment of Truth', *The Southern Speech Journal*, Vol. XXV, 1959.

Notestein, Wallace, 'The English Woman, 1580–1650', *Studies in Social History*, ed. J. H. Plumb (London, 1955).

Novak, Maxmillian E., *William Congreve* (New York, 1971).

Phillips, M. and Tomkinson, W. S., *English Women in Life and Letters* (Oxford, 1927).

Powell, Chilton, *English Domestic Relations 1487–1654* (New York, 1917).

Roberts, Philip, 'Mirabel and Restoration Comedy', *William Congreve*, ed. Brian Morris.

Rogers, Katharine M., *The Troublesome Helpmate* (Seattle, 1966).

Schochet, Gordon J., *Patriarchalism in Political Thought* (New York, 1975).

Shanley, Mary Lyndon, 'Marriage Contract and Social Contract in Seventeenth Century Political Thought', *Western Political Quarterly*, 1979.

Springer, Marlene (ed.), *What Manner of Women: Essays on English and American Life and Literature*, (New York, 1977).

Staves, Susan, *Players' Scepters* (Lincoln, Nebraska, 1979).

Stone, Lawrence, *The Family, Sex and Marriage 1500–1800* (London, 1977).

—— *The Crisis of the Aristocracy 1558–1641* (Oxford, 1967).

—— 'The Rise of the Nuclear Family in Early Modern England: The Patriarchal Stage', *The Family in History*, ed. Charles E. Rosenberg (Philadelphia, 1975).

Sutherland, James, *English Literature of the Late Seventeenth Century* (Oxford, 1969).

Thomas, Keith, 'The Changing Family', *TLS*, Oct. 21, 1977.

—— 'The Double Standard', *Journal of the History of Ideas*, XX, 1959.

—— 'Age and Authority in Early Modern England', *Proceedings of the British Academy*, I.xii, 1976.

—— 'Women and the Civil War Sects', *Past and Present*, No. 13, 1958.

Trevelyan, G. M., *English Social History* (London, 1974).

Underwood, Dale, *Etherege and the Seventeenth Century Comedy* (New Haven, 1957).

Vernon, P. F., 'Marriage of Convenience and the Moral Code of Restoration Comedy', *Essays in Criticism*, 1962.

—— 'The Treatment of Marriage in the Drama 1660–1700' (London University M.A. Dissertation, 1960).

Watt, Ian, *The Rise of the Novel* (London, 1975).

Wilson, Violet A., *Society Women of Shakespeare's Time* (Washington, 1924).

Wright, Louis B., *Middle-Class Culture in Elizabethan England* (Ithaca, 1965).

Index

229

43,327

Date Due